"No one likes to think about death, de
is unavoidable. That has meant that,
our professional lives, psychoanalysts h..... .... ..
erature anywhere near as much as would be helpful. *What Happens When the Analyst Dies* is an important step forward in providing thoughtful reflection and tools enabling analysts to engage in a far more practical way with the various effects of the death of analysts. I strongly recommend this book."

Brent Willock, Founding President, Toronto Institute for Contemporary Psychoanalysis; Board Member, Canadian Institute for Child and Adolescent Psychoanalytic Psychotherapy; Faculty, Institute for the Advancement of Self Psychology; Advisory Board, International Association for Relational Psychoanalysis and Psychotherapy

What Happens When the Analyst Dies

What Happens When the Analyst Dies explores the stories of patients who have experienced the death of their analyst. The book prioritizes the voices of patients, letting them articulate for themselves the challenges and heartache that occur when grappling with such a devastating loss. It also addresses the challenges faced by analysts who work with grieving patients and/or experience serious illness while treating patients.

Claudia Heilbrunn brings together contributors who discuss their personal experiences with bereavement and/or serious illness within the psychoanalytic encounter. Chapters include memoirs written by patients who describe not only the aftermath of an analyst's death, but also how the analyst's ability or inability to deal with his or her own illness and impending death within the treatment setting impacted the patient's own capacity to cope with their loss. Other chapters broach the challenges that arise (1) in "second analyses," (2) for the ill analyst, and (3) for those who face the death of an analyst or mentor while in training.

Aiming to give prominence to the often neglected and unmediated voices of patients, as well as of analysts who have dealt with grieving patients and serious illness, *What Happens When the Analyst Dies* strives to highlight and encourage discussion about the impact of an analyst's death on patients and the ways in which institutes and therapists could do more to protect those in their care. It will be of interest to psychoanalysts, psychotherapists, counselors, gerontologists, trainees, and patients who are currently in treatment or whose therapist has passed away.

Claudia Heilbrunn, LP, is a psychoanalyst in New York City, USA. She received her training at the Institute for Psychoanalytic Training and Research.

Psychoanalysis in a New Key Book Series
Series Editor
Donnel Stern

When music is played in a new key, the melody does not change, but the notes that make up the composition do: change in the context of continuity, continuity that perseveres through change. *Psychoanalysis in a New Key* publishes books that share the aims psychoanalysts have always had, but that approach them differently. The books in the series are not expected to advance any particular theoretical agenda, although to this date most have been written by analysts from the Interpersonal and Relational orientations.

The most important contribution of a psychoanalytic book is the communication of something that nudges the reader's grasp of clinical theory and practice in an unexpected direction. *Psychoanalysis in a New Key* creates a deliberate focus on innovative and unsettling clinical thinking. Because that kind of thinking is encouraged by exploration of the sometimes surprising contributions to psychoanalysis of ideas and findings from other fields, Psychoanalysis in a New Key particularly encourages interdisciplinary studies. Books in the series have married psychoanalysis with dissociation, trauma theory, sociology, and criminology. The series is open to the consideration of studies examining the relationship between psychoanalysis and any other field—for instance, biology, literary and art criticism, philosophy, systems theory, anthropology, and political theory.

But innovation also takes place within the boundaries of psychoanalysis, and *Psychoanalysis in a New Key* therefore also presents work that reformulates thought and practice without leaving the precincts of the field. Books in the series focus, for example, on the significance of personal values in psychoanalytic practice, on the complex interrelationship between the analyst's clinical work and personal life, on the consequences for the clinical situation when patient and analyst are from different cultures, and on the need for psychoanalysts to accept the degree to which they knowingly satisfy their own wishes during treatment hours, often to the patient's detriment. A full list of all titles in this series is available at: www.routledge.com/series/LEAPNKBS

What Happens When the Analyst Dies

Analyst Dies

Unexpected Terminations in Psychoanalysis

Edited by Claudia Heilbrunn

Routledge
Taylor & Francis Group

LONDON AND NEW YORK

First published 2020
by Routledge
2 Park Square, Milton Park, Abingdon, Oxon OX14 4RN

and by Routledge
52 Vanderbilt Avenue, New York, NY 10017

Routledge is an imprint of the Taylor & Francis Group, an informa business

British Library Cataloguing-in-Publication Data
A catalogue record for this book is available from the British Library

Library of Congress Cataloging-in-Publication Data
A catalog record has been requested for this book

ISBN: 978-0-367-26106-1 (hbk)
ISBN: 978-0-367-26108-5 (pbk)
ISBN: 978-0-429-29149-4 (ebk)

Typeset in Times New Roman
by Swales & Willis, Exeter, Devon, UK

MIX
Paper from
responsible sources
FSC
www.fsc.org   FSC® C013985

Printed in the United Kingdom
by Henry Ling Limited

For C.S., F.C., and A.F. — you are missed.

For C.S., P.C., and A.H. — you are missed

Contents

List of contributors   xii
Preface: introductory reflections   xvi
CLAUDIA HEILBRUNN

Acknowledgement   xix

Introduction   1
CLAUDIA HEILBRUNN

PART I
Patients   9

SUB-PART I.I
Illness and death within the context of long-term
treatments   11

1 Disappearing shrinks   13
   CLAUDIA HEILBRUNN

2 Unfinished business: the impact of denial on the grieving
   process   34
   JENNIFER GRANT

SUB-PART I.II
Sudden death   47

3 The art of grief   49
   RACHEL BRANDOFF

4 Monumental losses, monumental gifts: analysand
and analyst mourn the death of an analyst
and friend   61
VANESSA HANNAH BRIGHT AND MERLE MOLOFSKY

SUB-PART I.III
Inconsolable grief and recovery following the death of
a young analyst   **79**

5 Birth interrupted   81
LYNNE JACOBS

6 Re-finding a way   99
LYNNE JACOBS

SUB-PART I.IV
Making room for death within the treatment
setting   **123**

7 After the first death, there is no other   125
MARIA K. WALKER

8 The gift of goodbye and the invisible mourner   136
IRIS HELLNER

PART II
Practitioners   **157**

SUB-PART II.I
The post-death analyst   **159**

9 Defenses, transferences, and symbolism after an
analyst's death   161
JEROME S. BLACKMAN

10 A patient's and analyst's self-experiences with
shared loss   182
DAVID BRAUCHER

SUB-PART II.II
**The ill analyst: coping with illness and picking up
pieces** **211**

11 The analyst's illness from the perspectives of analyst and
   patient 213
   THERESE ROSENBLATT

12 Experiences of a bereaved and suffering second therapist:
   replacing a beloved student therapist and a gay
   psychoanalyst 235
   HENDRIKA VANDE KEMP

SUB-PART II.III
Psychoanalytic institutes and training **259**

13 Death begets growth 261
   CATHERINE LOWRY

14 Hidden illness 272
   NANCY EINBINDER

Epilogue 286
   CLAUDIA HEILBRUNN

Index 290

Contributors

Jerome S. Blackman is Professor of Psychiatry at Eastern Virginia Medical School, Distinguished Professor of Mental Health at Shanxi Medical University in China, Training Analyst with the Washington, D.C. Freudian Society, and past President of the American College of Psychoanalysts. His books on diagnosis, defenses, and technique have been translated into Chinese, the best known being *101 Defenses: How the Mind Shields Itself* (New York: Routledge, 2003).

Rachel Brandoff, ATR-BC, ATCS, BCPC, LCAT, is a board-certified, New York State-licensed and credentialed supervisor with a clinical practice. She was one of the founders of the Expressive Therapies Summit (www.expressivetherapiessummit.com), a professional conference in New York City. Rachel is an assistant professor and coordinator of the Art Therapy Specialization at Philadelphia University (www.philau.edu/ArtTherapy).

David Braucher is a psychotherapy supervisor and member of the faculty at The William Alanson White Institute. He is an Editorial Board Member of the journal *Contemporary Psychoanalysis* and Co-editor of the upcoming special issue "The Unconscious." He is the executive editor of and a contributor to the blog "Contemporary Psychoanalysis in Action" on PsychologyToday.com. He is a psychoanalyst and psychotherapist in private practice in the West Village/Chelsea neighborhood of Manhattan.

Vanessa Hannah Bright is a licensed psychoanalyst and graduate of the Institute for Expressive Analysis. She also has a master's degree in acupuncture from the Pacific College of Oriental Medicine (New York) and is a licensed acupuncturist. She is a writer and publishes an independent blog called "Loving Psychoanalysis," in which she explores the psychoanalysis of everyday experiences, as well as her process of becoming (and being) a psychoanalyst. She has a private practice in New York, and she integrates her knowledge of Chinese Medicine, Buddhism, and somatic awareness with psychoanalytic work.

Nancy Einbinder is a licensed and certified clinical social worker and a training and supervising analyst and faculty member at IPTAR, where she served as President from 2016 to 2018. She is in private practice in New York City, where she works with individuals and couples.

Jennifer Grant is a psychotherapist in private practice, treating adults and couples in New York City. She holds a master's degree in addiction studies from the Hazelden Graduate School, Center City, MN and a master's degree in social work from The University of St. Thomas, St. Paul, MN. Ms. Grant is a candidate at the Contemporary Freudian Society.

Claudia Heilbrunn is a licensed psychoanalyst in private practice in New York City. She received her BA from Columbia University, her MA from the University of Pennsylvania, and her analytic training from the Institute of Psychoanalytic Training and Research. Claudia is also the owner of Claudia Ink Tutoring, a company devoted to helping students of all aptitudes improve their writing and reading comprehension skills, and their college entrance exam scores.

Iris Hellner, PhD, is a clinical psychologist and psychoanalyst in private practice in New York City. She is a faculty member and supervisor at the Metropolitan Institute for Training in Psychoanalytic Psychotherapy and a clinical supervisor in the Clinical Psychology Doctoral Program of the City College of New York. She is a graduate of the New York University Postdoctoral Program in Psychotherapy and Psychoanalysis.

Lynne Jacobs is a psychologist and a training and supervising analyst at the Institute of Contemporary Psychoanalysis, Los Angeles, California. She is also the co-founder of the Pacific Gestalt Institute and has a private practice in Los Angeles.

Catherine Lowry is a licensed clinical social worker, who lives and practices in the United States. She has been in private practice since 1998.

Merle Molofsky is a psychoanalyst, writer, and produced playwright. She serves on the faculty of the Training Institute of the National Psychological Association for Psychoanalysis (NPAP), on the faculty and Advisory Council of the Harlem Family Institute, and on the editorial board of *The Psychoanalytic Review*. She has published articles and chapters in psychoanalytic journals and books. Her novel, *Streets 1970*, and her collection of short fiction, *Necessary Voices*, were published by International Psychoanalytic Books.

Therese Rosenblatt, PhD, is a psychologist and psychoanalyst in private practice in New York City and Westchester Country, NY. She treats adults, adolescents, couples, and families. She leads parenting groups privately and at the Early Childhood Development Center in New York City. She is on the faculty of the Metropolitan Institute for Training in Psychoanalytic Psychotherapy. She is Adjunct Clinical Supervisor at Yeshiva University and Pace University, and an active member of the New York University Postdoctoral Program in Psychoanalysis and Psychotherapy. Dr. Rosenblatt is co-editor and co-author with Linda Hillman of *The Voice of the Analyst: Narratives on Developing a Psychoanalytic Identity* (Routledge, 2017).

Hendrika Vande Kemp, a Fellow in the American Psychological Association, was on the faculty of the Graduate School of Psychology at Fuller Theological Seminary for 25 years, and then worked in private practice for 13 years. Retired in Durham, North Carolina, she is writing a book about the twentieth-century Boston psychologist Lydiard Horton, and she has exhibited her iris folding artwork in local galleries.

Maria K. Walker is an artist and art therapist working in the Bronx, NY. She specializes in trauma therapy with adolescents and families, and has worked for seven years at a psychiatric residential treatment facility for adolescent girls.

Preface: introductory reflections

I was unprepared for just how hard working on a book about the death of an analyst would be. The pain of losing someone so integral to one's own conception of self, of a person who plays a multitude of roles in an effort to heal, and who is critical to one's own hope for a future that is different – more vital and satisfying in wholly new ways – continues for me, resurfacing unexpectedly, months, years, even decades after I thought I was done with grieving. As someone who has lost three analysts, and who has still not fully recovered from those losses, I have suspected in moments that I may not be the person best equipped to write in this format and forum about how one moves forward after the death of an analyst, and about what the analytic community can do to help patients whose analysts have died. I still suffer, sometimes intensely, from the pain of my losses, from the dashed hopes, the unfulfilled dreams, the obliterated connections to people I loved so much. I still crave aspects of each of my analysts: the black-and-white answers my first therapist offered; the laughter and acceptance I received from my second; and the feeling of security provided by my third. None died as merely analysts: they died as mothers, fathers, siblings, friends, tormentors, traitors, victims, and damaged ghosts, who shall live on eternally unless I can manage somehow to put to rest all the people they became to and for me. They died when I still believed in the psychoanalytic mythology that so many patients hold dear while in treatment: that we will, with the help of this *one particular person*, be cured of what ails us, and thereby embrace a life as our best possible selves.

I've repeatedly asked myself: How does someone finish treatment in the face of three analysts' deaths? After old wounds, and traumas, and conflicts, and pain from a lifetime of experiences have come alive again and again, only to be obliterated in the face of the ana-lyst-savior's demise? How does one venture forth knowing that everything can be swept away not only once, but then again, and yet again? What kind of bravery does psychoanalysis take?

Flashback to 2012: I sit in my new therapist's office and am star-tled by how smart she is. I feel envious of, and yet grateful for, her ability to see things that I and my other analysts couldn't see. How lucky that I ended up here, and – a real bonus! – she isn't much older than fifty. But how am I to know that the world won't wipe her away? Years ago, when I was a teenager lying wrapped up in the arms of my first love, he posed the question: "Is it better to love and risk loss or never to love at all?" In the face of my three ana-lysts' deaths, my firm answer is: "Not to love at all!" But in the face of living this thing called life, I have been and continue to be unable to abide by my belief: I still love, I still connect, I still depend, I still need. At times, I cannot help but ponder the terror I once brought into every new relationship, and how in moments it rose up and threatened to decimate me. To slice me up and reduce me to smith-ereens. It shouldn't have had to be so very hard. Hence the urgency with which I pose my questions and offer my call to action: What can an analytic community do to protect patients? What can the analysts themselves do? How can the people who come to us, those who are vulnerable and disturbed already, be protected from more of what already incapacitates them?

I think of the #METOO movement, of the #NEVERAGAIN movement, of the adults whose renewed pain has motivated them to act, and of the youths upon whom the responsibility to change the world inevitably falls. And I wonder if a similar sense of movement and initiative must happen in our field: Awareness of just how ter-rible it can be to lose an analyst must strike at the deepest level, so that practitioners *have* to recognize that it falls squarely upon them to protect their patients in ways they never realized before. Child analysts, in particular, recognize the vulnerability of the youngsters they treat, children who may lack adequate parenting and support-ive care. Training is modified so as to include coverage of how to deal with analysts' illnesses and deaths (both one's own and others'); such coverage is integrated within mandatory curriculums not only in analytic training programs, but also in social work, psychology, psychiatry, and counseling programs. Analytic wills become required, another item of paperwork essential to retaining one's licensure. Ill analysts routinely seek supervision so that someone outside the analytic dyad is looking in on the analytic hour with an eye focused on the patient in order to ascertain what the ill analyst might perhaps be missing or overlooking in the face of his or her own illness or impending death. Within this supervision (and with the utmost sensitivity and care), the closed room which only the ill analyst and patient inhabit will be opened up so that degrees of denial can be ascertained, the patient's need to protect the analyst – to become caretaker of the caretaker, and to help push away reality – can be monitored, and the analyst is no longer alone when facing what may be beyond his or her current ability to face. Through such initiatives patients will gain a safety net that was created just in case this devastating loss happened, and they will be provided with names for further help and – if the patient is a candidate (or perhaps even if he or she is not) – with a community in which he or she can feel held.

Acknowledgement

I thank Sam Semper for her close reading of this volume and her helpful insights, guidance, and advice; Julian Webb, Charles Bath, and Kate Hawes for managing the production process so well; Nicholas Fox for his expert copy-editing; and Donnel Stern for his belief in this project's merit. I am grateful to Susan Lepselter not just for her friendship, but also for reading my then journal entry (now my chapter) several years ago and for encouraging me to pursue its publication; and I am grateful to Gil Katz, Rhonda Ward, and Sharone Bergner for their consistent support and practical help. I am especially thankful for and indebted to Gareth Williams, whose sharp editorial eye, extensive expertise, and ever-present support made this volume possible. I finally thank Bryley Williams, who makes everything worthwhile.

Introduction

Claudia Heilbrunn

The genesis of this book

The idea of, and even the urgent need for, putting together a book that focuses on what happens to patients after their analysts die struck me well over a decade ago, when I was grappling with the illness and then the death of my second analyst, after a twelve-year analysis. At that time, I tried to find literature – journal articles or, even better, personal essays – that would inform me about others who had gone through similar losses. I wanted to know how they dealt with their isolation and unfathomable grief, and how they eventually moved on. During this period I wrote Part I and Part II of the essay entitled "Disappearing Shrinks" as presented in this volume. I chose not to alter my original essay because, in all its rawness, it reflects what it was like to be solely a patient – not an analytic candidate or analyst – who felt utterly alone, with no other individual in my world who knew the person I had lost, and with no one who could even vaguely understand just how much my analyst meant to me. After my second analyst's death, I searched for people who would contribute to the volume I wanted to write, putting an advertisement or two in Craigslist, and asking for contributions. When I received no replies, I put the idea to rest. Two years later, however, I began training at the Institute for Psychoanalytic Training and Research (IPTAR), and – in my sixth year of treatment – I said goodbye to my training analyst, who died of cancer. Losing an analyst while part of an institute dramatically changed the experience of loss: I was no longer the only person in my world

who knew the person who had died, people understood the significance of my loss, and I was not an outsider at the memorial service,
which I was able to attend as a candidate-analysand. And yet my
grief in response to the illness and death of my third analyst
impelled me to move forward with the book project that I had put
aside; for despite the integrity and strength with which my third
analyst handled his illness and impending death, I believe that still
more can and should be done by both analysts and institutes to
protect and support patients who experience the loss of an analyst
during an ongoing treatment.

While the existing bibliography does not of course entirely exclude
articles that focus on the illness and death of analysts, the condition
and trauma of loss as experienced by patients has yet to receive,
I believe, the attention it deserves in psychoanalytical discussion
forums. Volumes including *Illness in the Analyst: Implications for the
Treatment Relationship* (eds. Schwartz & Silver, 1990), *The Empty
Couch: The Taboo of Ageing and Retirement in Psychoanalysis* (ed.
Junkers, 2013), and *Traumatic Ruptures: Abandonment and Betrayal
in the Psychoanalytic Relationship* (ed. Deutsch, 2014) deal with
issues relating to analysts' ageing, retirement, illness, and death, as do
papers that focus on illness and death within the analytic encounter
(see, e.g., Pizer, 1997; Feinsilver, 1998); but the voices most often
heard in these works are those of the analysts (Dimen, 2014): the
experiences and perspectives of the patients who are left, so often
alone, to grapple with the aftermath of their analyst's death frequently remain out of sight, as invisible as the patient mourning an
analyst's death routinely feels.

I seek in this volume to give prominence to patients' voices, and so
the book is replete with very personal, first-hand accounts: narratives
are at times intimate and undisguised, transmitting the intensity of
patients' experiences in order to convey to the psychoanalytic and
other communities what's at stake for patients who lose their therapists to death. Likewise, first-person narratives by "second" analysts
and once-ill analysts focus on the very personal challenges that arise
both for the grieving patient and for the clinician entrusted with that
patient's care.

I am awed by the degree of honesty that the authors have brought
to bear in each and every chapter. Facing again what it feels like to

lose an analyst is no easy feat, and it is also hard to admit to the ways in which we've failed to be perfect when treating patients while ill ourselves or while treating a given patient whose analyst has died. I am grateful that the contributors to this volume had the courage to speak out, and so to contribute to our vital communal effort: only by voicing our experiences will the analytic community come to know the realities of facing up to the death of an analyst, and thereby recognize the need for change in the face of the ultimate termination.

My overall aim for this book is to offer insights into how different individuals with distinct aptitudes, backgrounds, psychic vulnerabilities, and sensibilities have responded to this enormous psychological challenge. And it is my hope that the essays in this book convey the vital experiences of patients – the idiosyncrasy of experience in grappling with the loss of one's analyst, the many different kinds of highly individual trauma and disorientation, the difficulty of knowing how best to anticipate and/or to respond to such a loss, and the frequent lack of any outlet for intensely felt feelings, especially when one's relationship with a therapist is invisible to the external world.

A further concern that motivates many of the contributors is that far more could be done in contemporary institutional practice (1) to safeguard participants in therapeutic relationships that show an obvious risk of rupture through serious illness and/or death; (2) to alleviate the plight of those who confront such a death; and (3) to publicize what, in our ageing society (and an ageing psychoanalytic community), is surely a burgeoning problem that will affect many more members of our communities in the years and decades to come.

The scope of the book

The essays in this volume are arranged in two parts: the first, entitled "Patients," consists of first-hand accounts of each author's experience as a patient confronting the death of a current analyst, with one chapter (Vanessa Hannah Bright and Merle Molofsky's) co-written by a patient and her second analyst. The second part, "Practitioners," consists of chapters written by analysts who (1) worked with patients whose previous analyst had died; (2) were seriously ill themselves while treating patients; (3) tragically lost a beloved mentor/teacher;

and (4) worked to improve institutional policy pertaining to the deaths of member analysts.

The two main parts are divided into sub-parts, each of which presents a dyad of essays, and thereby attempts to reproduce through their dialogical relation something of the back-and-forth and give-and-take of therapeutic relationships. The variety of contributors offers multiple viewpoints on the relationship between the patient and analyst in circumstances where the death and/or serious illness of an analyst complicates, disrupts, or ends treatment. In sum, the combination of the essays presented in "Patients" and "Practitioners" seeks to provide a helpful collection of perspectives on how so many in the psychoanalytical community deal with the actuality of the analyst's serious illness or death, whether on the side of the patient or on the side of the practicing analyst.

Part I: patients

Sub-part I.I, "Illness and death within the context of long-term treatments," describes patients' experiences both while in treatment with a seriously ill analyst and after the analyst dies. Chapter 1, "Disappearing shrinks," describes my experiences during and after two very different twelve-year treatments, each of which was marked by the analyst's incurable illness and eventual death. I address how both the nature of the treatments themselves and my therapists' varying degrees of ability to deal with his or her impending death dramatically impacted my own ability to cope with my traumatic losses. In Chapter 2, "Unfinished business: the impact of denial on the grieving process," Jennifer Grant reflects on how her total denial of her analyst's impending death, and the analyst's *own* denial, complicated Grant's grieving process, which was characterized by feelings of betrayal, loneliness, guilt, and, eventually, anger and compassion. Grant highlights the pressures felt by an analysand who is invested in being a "good patient," especially when being "good" replicates issues already at play in the transference.

The two chapters in sub-part I.II, "Sudden death," focus on the perception and actuality of unexpected death, and on how each impacts the shocked and bereaved patient. Chapter 3, Rachel Brandoff's "The art of grief," tells of the feelings of despair, isolation, and discomfort that arise when a patient's analyst suffers a fatal accident. Brandoff explicates not only the difficulties she faced when pursuing a new treatment, but also how she employed art to explore, experience, and understand her grief. Brandoff also raises questions about the responsibility carried by both analysts and analytical organizations in relation to bereaved patients who seek treatment through psychoanalytic institutes.

A different perspective is offered in Chapter 4, "Monumental losses, monumental gifts: analysand and analyst mourn the death of an analyst and friend," written jointly by Vanessa Hannah Bright, a patient who lost her analyst, and Merle Molofsky, Bright's second analyst and a close friend of the first analyst. This chapter raises important issues, including how an analyst's failure to discuss her illness can affect patients, and the myriad challenges that arise in a second analysis when the second analyst replaces a beloved and still desired first analyst.

Two chapters by the same author, Lynne Jacobs, are set out in sub-part I.III, "Inconsolable grief and recovery following the death of a young analyst." The swift illness and sudden death of Jacobs's analyst at the age of only thirty-three left her world "shattered." In Chapter 5, "Birth interrupted," Jacobs describes not only the acute grief that she felt when her analyst died, but also the complex emotional reactions she experienced in response to the discrepancy between (i) her analyst's and others' optimistic reassurances about the former's prognosis and (ii) her own perceptions of imminent calamity. In Chapter 6, "Re-finding a way," Jacobs describes the difficulty she faced in her second analysis, when what she believed she needed most of all was a *de facto* duplication of her first analysis.

Sub-part I.IV, "Making room for death within the treatment setting," consists of papers by patients whose analysts engaged in discussions about their illness and impending death within the analytic setting. Chapter 7, Maria Walker's "After the first death, there is no other," and Chapter 8, Iris Hellner's "The gift of goodbye and the invisible mourner," reflect upon what it means to terminate long-term psychoanalytic treatments in the face of death; and what it means to engage with an analyst who is able to discuss to a particular degree her current illness, her eventual and then imminent demise, and her patient's wishes pertaining to post-treatment planning (including notifications about worsening health and the analyst's death) and to funeral arrangements. Both Walker and Hellner describe the difficulties that they faced when their analyst ultimately died – difficulties that centered on the sense of isolation resulting from losing not just someone who was known to no one else in their world, but also a relationship to which no one apart from the deceased had borne witness.

Part II: practitioners

Part II opens with "The post-death analyst," a sub-part compiled by "second analysts" who worked with patients just after their first analysts had died. In Chapter 9, "Defenses, transferences, and symbolism after an analyst's death," Jerome Blackman describes his work with a patient whose analyst died suddenly. He articulates both the complexities of her loss and the challenges that he faced in treating a patient whose deceased analyst was also his own mentor and friend. Blackman suggests how a patient's unresolved conflicts, trauma, and other pressing current-day issues, along with the analyst's own countertransference and unconscious conflicts, may impact analyses that take place after the first analyst has died. Then, in Chapter 10, "A patient's and analyst's self-experiences with shared loss," David Braucher offers an account of his work with a traumatized young woman whose unfailingly available and maternal analyst died in a tragic accident after ten years of treatment. Braucher explicates the challenges that arise when a bereft patient cannot tolerate mourning and desires instead a replica of her lost object; he also explores how the second analyst's countertransference reactions and theoretical leanings can both complicate and inform an analyst's understanding of the given case and his ability to treat his patient successfully.

Sub-part II.II, "The ill analyst: coping with illness and picking up pieces," assembles the papers of analysts who grappled with their own health crises while treating patients: each author reflects upon how best to deal with significant health problems within the therapeutic encounter, and discusses particular issues, including the ill analyst's self-disclosure. In Chapter 11, "The analyst's illness from the perspectives of analyst and patient," Therese Rosenblatt describes her experiences on both sides of the couch: on the one hand, as a seriously ill analyst treating patients; and, on the other, as a patient of an ill analyst. Rosenblatt discusses the matters and challenges that inevitably arise when an analyst is ill, including analytic transparency in relation to the analyst's illness, and how the analyst's fear impacts the degree to which she can weather the discussion of her own illness within the treatment. Rosenblatt also offers advice on how best to work with patients when seriously ill. In Chapter 12, "Experiences of a bereaved and suffering second therapist: replacing a beloved student therapist and a gay psychoanalyst," Hendrika Vande Kemp describes her work as the second analyst of two patients whose previous analysts had died. In the one case, the first analyst was Vande Kemp's own supervisee, whom she too was mourning; the other case was complicated by the impact of severe injuries that Vande Kemp had incurred in a car accident.

Part II concludes in sub-part II.III, "Psychoanalytic institutes and training," with coverage of the experiences of candidates and other student-therapists. In Chapter 13, "Death begets growth," Catherine Lowry describes her reaction to the murder of her idealized mentor and teacher, whose death at the hands of his patient prompted in Lowry grief, horror, disbelief, and yet, eventually, personal and professional growth. In Chapter 14, "Hidden illness," Nancy Einbinder considers the responsibility carried by psychoanalytic institutes, and how the death of an analyst can impact candidates who are in treatment when the end comes. Einbinder details her experiences at IPTAR over the last twenty-eight years, first as a candidate, and then as a member; there she formed, and is still a part of, the Disabled Analyst Committee. In her essay she brings to light some of the ways in which institutes have colluded with ill analysts, maintaining a secrecy about terminal illness and thereby leaving candidate-analysands bereft and without support from their mother institute.

The contributions to this volume offer a body of experience, challenges, and suggestions to the analytic community in the hope of effecting positive change. I offer in the Epilogue a prescriptive list, which includes the recommendations I have gleaned from others (including those already listed within particular chapters of this book) and incorporates some of my own proposals. This list, and this volume as a whole, are motivated by the wish to inspire therapeutic communities to take concrete steps to protect not only their ailing members and patient-candidates, but also those patients who are left bereft when their analysts pass away, and whose suffering is too often passed over in silence.

The names of all analysts and patients featured in this book have been fully anonymized to conceal identity.

References

Deutsch, R.A. (2014) *Traumatic Ruptures: Abandonment and Betrayal in the Psychoanalytic Relationship.* New York/Hove, UK: Routledge.

Dimen, M. (2014) 'Foreword.' In R.A. Deutsch (ed.), *Traumatic Ruptures: Abandonment and Betrayal in the Psychoanalytic Relationship* (pp. xv–xvi). New York/Hove, UK: Routledge.

Feinsilver, D.B. (1998) 'The Therapist as a Person Facing Death: The Hardest of External Realities and Therapeutic Action,' *International Journal of Psychoanalysis* 79: 1131–1150.

Junkers, G. (ed.) (2013) *The Empty Couch: The Taboo of Ageing and Retirement in Psychoanalysis.* London/New York: Routledge.

Pizer, B. (1997) 'When the Analyst Is Ill: Dimensions of Self-Disclosure,' *Psychoanalytic Quarterly* 66: 450–469.

Schwartz, H.J. & Silver, A.-L. (eds.) (1990) *Illness in the Analyst: Implications for the Treatment Relationship.* Madison, CT: International University Press.

Part I

Patients

Illness and death within the context of long-term treatments

Chapter 1

Disappearing shrinks

Claudia Heilbrunn

My two therapies mirrored each other in duration and ending: both therapists died before the natural termination of my treatment. My treatments were diametrically opposed in the ways in which each doctor handled letting go not only of life, but also of the patient each treated. Their different ways of saying or of neglecting to say goodbye have greatly impacted my life; their ability or inability to face their own deaths was critical to my own capacity to cope with the greatest losses of my life.

Dr. Cecil Smit

I first met Dr. Smit when I was fourteen years old. I was a depressed and empty teenager struggling with anorexia, which was soon to become bulimia. Dr. Smit became my god and stayed my god until I was compelled, after his death, to look at the disturbingly destructive methods he used in his treatment of me. Dr. Smit laughingly told me and the rest of my family – who were also in treatment with him – to call him Dr. Shit in order to remind us that he was not a god. And yet he knew that he was and enjoyed his position. Dr. Smit was arrogant and "above." I loved and worshipped him more than anything in the world. He was the first person who told me that I was smart; he was the first person who made me feel loved and valued; he stood up to my mother, and then made fun of her "inanities" behind her back; and he obviously hated my mean older sister and favored me. He told me that I could be like him, one of the elite few. I could enjoy literature, music, and art. I could be happy and not waste my time with the neurotic mental shenanigans and behaviors that controlled the peons of the world. He told me that he could cure me, and I believed him. I wanted more than anything to be cured.

Dr. Smit gave me orders, and I followed all of his commands. When I failed to make sufficient progress, he threatened to kick me out of treatment. When I sobbed and sobbed because I couldn't stop throwing up, he laughed and told me of the unconscious pleasure I derived from my pain: "For every ounce of conscious misery, there is a pound of unconscious pleasure," he would say. He told me it was my fault that I couldn't stop throwing up. That if I really wanted to, I would be able to. I could do it at any time. When I asked him how, he was silent. And yet I knew he was right. Something was wrong with me. I had to work harder, I had to be better, so that I could be loved by – and exactly like – him. I wanted to breathe freely, to be one of the up and above.

Dr. Smit had many orders and dictums that impacted the ways in which I thought and the ways I ran my life. At various times I broke off relations with my family members because he told me I had to do so in order to be healthy. I was not allowed to discuss even a word about my treatment with anybody. In the end, I was a devotee worshipping her savior, and working towards the day when I could be good enough to join him in a life free of neurosis and pain.

His other dictums included telling me, when I was fifteen and during the height of the AIDS epidemic, that I never had to use a condom when having sex. Dr. Smit said that I could not get AIDS because AIDS was psychological, and I did not have the psychological make-up of an AIDS victim. Homosexuals and other people who got it were playing the role of scapegoats for mass anger. Their own self-perceptions caused them to be sick. "Condoms are for sissies," he would say in his usual arrogant way. At one point he told me that I was getting healthier because I was not friendly with as many gay people as I had once been.

I was utterly dependent on Dr. Smit and would do anything for him. I became for him what he wanted me to be. Dr. Smit told me what to study, which art exhibits to attend, and what was unacceptable for me to do. He also told me what I felt and why I felt it, where I was at fault and what I had done well. My mind worked like a computer ticking off all the things I did that were "healthy" or "neurotic": if I was tired, I was repressing a feeling; if I sat on my hands, I was angry; if I ate a carrot, I wanted to bite a penis; if I ate a low calorie muffin, I was identifying with my mother, a chronic dieter; if I had a headache, it was murderous rage; and when I sprained my ankle badly before a trip to France, I did it on purpose because I could not allow myself to have anything good. I remember how he laughed and laughed at the sorry spectacle of me crying because of what I had done – me, now a peon again.

I loved Dr. Smit with everything I had. Every thought that I thought and every rule that I followed was because of him. The life that I built was a life dedicated to living the image he envisioned. At the time of his death, I was a straight A student at Columbia University. As he prescribed, I studied Latin, classical literature, and ancient Greece. My future studies were to include the Renaissance, Wagner, and art. Anything less was unacceptable. Any grade below an A meant I was doing myself a disservice. Not meeting his standards meant that I would be nothing again.

And then one day, eleven years into my treatment and seven months into my college career, he announced that he was going away for six weeks. He was leaving the very next day. He also reported to me that I was ready to end therapy. I was fine. And with that statement, Dr. Smit broke the one and only promise that he ever made to me. Years earlier, after he kicked me out of treatment because I was not changing enough, I collapsed in tears outside his front door. He came out of his office, saw me, and brought me back into his treatment room. I was sobbing with anguish, begging him to take me back, pleading with him, "You're all I have. I have nothing else. I have nobody but you." He took me back, and at that moment I asked him to promise me that he would never kick me out of therapy again. He promised. And yet, he was now telling me that I was fine and had to leave treatment. I realized that he had lied, but I said nothing. What can you say to protest against God?

Dr. Smit returned six weeks later and, although we had plenty of time to discuss the termination of my treatment, nothing was said. The only comment he made when I asked him why I had to leave was, "You have everything it takes. All you lack is the conviction."

Since everything he said was true, I imagined he was right. "The conviction," I would repeat to myself after my therapy was done, "All I lack is the conviction, the conviction."

I don't remember when I realized that Dr. Smit was sick. It started with a cold and weight loss. It progressed to a white film covering his eyes, a cough which produced a lot of phlegm, and emaciation. "I have a pneumonia," he said when I asked what was wrong. Most of my questions about his sickness were met either with the answer of silence – as if it was therapeutic to let my questions hang in the air – or with a rhetorical comment that took the spotlight off him and focused it on me: "You are concerned I am sick," he would say. I had no answer. I was concerned – the truth was that he was right. So I stayed silent. I am a good student. I stopped asking and noticing as I watched him disappear.

I do not remember for how many months I watched. As I think back, I realize it started before he told me he was ending my treatment. The act of watching and remaining silent about what I saw put a fog over me, as if the white film that covered his eyes were now covering mine too. He never told me not to ask him questions, but his answers of silence made his orders clear. Three times a week, I would enter his office and follow the rules. I no longer remember what I talked about; I only remember what was not discussed: the imminent termination of my treatment, his worsening health, and my terror about what was to come.

Weeks before the date set to end my therapy, I sat in Dr. Smit's waiting room as usual. When the time of my appointment came and left, I began to panic. Not because I was worried, but because if he was not there, I knew I had somehow made a mistake: Had he told me to come at another time? Was something wrong with what I was doing – with my watch? I decided to sit there a few more minutes. Dr. Smit appeared a few moments later. He walked out of his kitchen and into the corridor in front of me. He stood there, obviously in a confused state – as if he were not quite sure of where he was. He was naked, except for a pair of white jockey underwear – the same ones I had seen my father wear when I was young. I stared, shocked at the thinness of his body, the drooping skin that no longer stuck to his muscles and bones. I sat breathless.

As his mind cleared, Dr. Smit looked around quizzically, turned his head in my direction, and suddenly realized what was going on. "Oh my goodness," he said, and then he disappeared behind the kitchen door. Minutes later he reappeared, in his regular attire, his calm and arrogant self. "You may come in," he said. I followed him into his office and sat down. The session began. Nothing was said.

During my last session with Dr. Smit, I sat on the floor. It was the second time I actually spoke about the fact that I was never coming back. The first time, I wondered what the last session would be like, and now it was here. On that final day, I told him that he broke his promise to me. He said he had not. "We made an agreement that the treatment would end." And then for the first and only time in my life I stood up to him. I said that that was a lie. I did not make any agreement: "You made an agreement and told me what it was." His answer was silence again. I told him that I did not feel ready to end therapy. He said, "If you weren't ready, you would have started to purge again." I was amazed: You mean all I had to do was throw up? If I had only thrown up, you would have kept me? I didn't say it out loud, but not returning to my bulimia became the biggest regret of my treatment. Dr. Smit then told me that I was fine, that I should never seek treatment with another therapist, and that I was never allowed to call him again. I needed no contact. I had everything – all I lacked was the conviction. I wondered for months, while sitting on my bed, not knowing what to do or how to get through the day, how I could get the conviction. And then, after twelve years of seeing him three times a week, it was suddenly done. "Well, goodbye," I said, and I walked out of his office for the very last time.

I held myself together after Dr. Smit kicked me out of treatment by following all of his rules. I knew people who were still seeing him: my parents had periodic appointments and my friend, Lynne, was still in treatment. I lived for the moments when my mother would return from one of her appointments with Dr. Smit and tell me how his eyes lit up when she mentioned my name. It meant that he still loved me – that he still cared. Dr. Smit's god-like power was strong enough to keep me on track, albeit internally insane. Outwardly I was fine: I still got my As at Columbia, I still held down my job, and I went on with my life. Inwardly I was falling apart.

I sat on my hands when I wanted to binge and purge: "All you lack is the conviction, the conviction," I repeatedly said. All of his rules ticked off in my head like an internal, pre-programmed computer that kept me on track and kept me from failing at life. I analyzed every feeling and thought that I had, as he had trained me to do. I tried to understand everything that was happening to me. Every thought, every feeling had a reason. It was my job to figure them out. When I was tired, hungry, anxious, out of my skin, or physically ill, I was failing. I was supposed to feel everything in its "authentic" form and then be done with the feeling. I was supposed to come out the other side. Fatigue was my biggest problem because it meant that I was repressing a feeling. The search for what I repressed and the analysis of what I was doing wrong were endless.

A few months after my treatment ended, my friend, Lynne, called me in hysterics. She was downstairs in Dr. Smit's building. "Claudia, something's wrong with Dr. Smit. He was taken away in an ambulance. What if he dies?" "Dies!" I responded, "He's not going to die. He's still young." And I believed it. After all, God can't die. After that, Dr. Smit disappeared. I began calling his answering machine to hear his voice and to make sure that he was okay. I found out a month later that he was in St. Vincent's hospital. Three weeks after that I called the hospital to see if he was still a patient. They said he was not. I imagined he went home. One week later, my friend, Bob, told me that Dr. Smit was dead. My parents had known for days, but did not have the courage to tell me themselves. They thought I would be "too" upset. Upset does not quite describe how I felt. In fact, nothing can describe it. I did not understand. How could a force that strong be dead? How was it possible that he was not in the world? The only force that kept me standing had vanished.

The pain I felt when Dr. Smit died was beyond any pain that I had ever felt. Even after he kicked me out of treatment, knowing that his force was still in the world, and that he was out there rooting for my wellbeing, kept me afloat. Now, there was nothing for me to hold on to, except for his rules, which were getting harder and harder to follow. After I heard of his death, I spent every minute that I was not at work in bed, listening over and over to a song that somehow reminded me of him. I listened to Dr. Smit's voice on his answering machine until the "hello" message disappeared. I held my own "goodbye" ceremony during which I read Ezra Pound's Canto #3, a poem Dr. Smit read to me one day to demonstrate the musicality of its lines. Standing, poem in hand, looking out at the ocean and at sunrise, I said goodbye and waited to feel something, anything, that would make me feel okay. Yet I was spinning out of control and coming closer and closer to bingeing and purging. So for the first time in my life, I disobeyed Dr. Smit. I went to seek help from my sister's therapist, who gave me a prescription for Prozac and told me that Dr. Smit was abusive. "Do you know how long you've suffered for no reason?" she said. "You could have been helped years ago. He was a sadist, a fraud." She sent me away with a prescription and a recommendation that I read *The Drama of the Gifted Child*.

Dr. Smit had forbidden me to take anti-depressants. He prescribed them for other people whom I knew, but I was different: I had to become healthy in the same way I became sick – naturally. Taking drugs was somehow impure. The up and above do not use drugs to feel well. Although my parents wanted me to take the medication – they thought that my grief was too intense – I did not. I ripped up the prescription, threw it in the garbage, and celebrated my feat. I could withstand my feelings. I could live my life as Dr. Smit intended me to live. And yet I knew I needed help.

After consulting with a few therapists, I finally came upon Belinda, a lovely social worker who felt safe. Although I did not think she was very smart (after all, whose intellectual ability could match Dr. Smit's?), she gave me what I needed: a place to go each week and cry. And that is what I did. I cried and cried and cried. I did not understand how the world had not stopped moving, and I needed, somehow, to make sense of how Dr. Smit could disappear. With Dr. Smit dead, the point of life seemed unclear; I was like a religious person who realized that God is dead – or that God never existed at all.

I felt like I could not live until I understood why I was here and he was not, so I went on an active search to figure it out. It was in Seattle, at Mount St. Helens, that I got my first glimmer of understanding. Seeing a little green shoot of grass sprout up amidst what seemed like absolute destruction made me think about the cycle of nature and life, of utter death and destruction and the possibility of rebirth. My next clue as to my reason for staying alive was found at a children's museum in Vancouver. I saw a short film on evolution and decided that my purpose in life was to take as big a psychological step forward as I could in order to help to give birth to a healthier next generation. I dedicated my life to living out this purpose, of becoming as psychologically healthy as I could.

The process of mourning for Dr. Smit was complicated by my recognition of all the falsehoods he told, for with his death came a harsh reality that I in no way wanted to know. Over the next several years, I slowly awakened to the truth of what had happened during my treatment. When I could finally see it all, that insight ripped to shreds all the rules and dictums on which I based my life: Dr. Smit was gay and he had died of AIDS. All of his anti-homosexual statements were feelings he had about himself. Dr. Smit was not a happy man who lived loftily above the peons of the world. In fact, I eventually realized that, for him, I was a kind of Pygmalion figure; he was trying to make me into the person he could never be. My therapy was a farce. The interpretations that I thought were biblical truths, truths on which I based my life, were all, seemingly, false. The life I created was created for him: I had become a straight A/A+ student at Columbia University who majored in Classical Studies, and who eventually married the "Smitian" ideal: a brilliant and intellectual professor at Columbia.

As I faced the truth of my relationship with Dr. Smit, the foundation of my life crumbled. I recognized, bit by bit, all the lies that he had told. And then the recognition of the harm he did made me completely lose my footing. He made my sister wear a phallus during family therapy so that she would deal with her wish to be a boy – my father's son; he ordered me to throw up on my parents after they force-fed me, since my bulimia was about my taking in, and then throwing out, their feelings. He told me everything I felt and analyzed everything I did without ever asking about or hearing thoughts and feelings that organically came from me. He dictated the "me" that I was allowed to be and pushed into me all of his own feelings and thoughts. After his death, I did not know which thoughts were mine and which were his. My own and Dr. Smit's beliefs, points of view, values, and goals were inextricably linked. Was it my brain or his? Tangled, it took years to know.

I knew I was supposed to hate Dr. Smit for all of the damage he did, but the truth was that I still loved and missed him. No longer did I feel that there was somebody in my corner cheering me on; no longer did I have a rigid set of rules by which I could live. Everything was messy and conflicted, and I had no idea of who I was. I made another attempt at finding "someone who could help" a few years after Dr. Smit had died. The person whom I met I ended up in treatment with for twelve years. She is the woman who helped me to discover my voice. She is the second therapist whose death I had to face.

Dr. Florence Cagan

Dr. Cagan was different: a thin, gray haired woman in her early sixties, who wore no make-up, but had a wedding ring, and with whom I felt comfortable from the start. I found Dr. Cagan through a New York City clinic, so I paid a reduced fee for what turned into a twelve-year psychoanalysis. Dr. Cagan helped me to do many things: to disentangle – for the most part – Dr. Smit's brain from my own; to come alive in a more vital way than I had ever known; to gain a more realistic understanding of life and of the human condition, so that I understood that conflict, ambivalence, repression, and struggle were all normal and impossible to avoid; that I was not a machine who could perfectly feel a feeling when I was "supposed" to, and then be done with it; and to increasingly come to terms with the damage done to me by Dr. Smit. She was also somebody by whom I felt accepted and eventually loved, and who worked very hard to help me to discover *from myself* who I am.

Dr. Cagan gave me many gifts, but that is not to say that she was a "perfect" therapist. And yet her imperfection – her humanity, her admission of ignorance and of mistakes – made her a much-needed antidote to the force-feeding that I had undergone with Dr. Smit. When I began therapy with Dr. Cagan, I asked her to promise to tell me if she ever became sick. Unlike Dr. Smit, she kept her one and only promise. Her telling me the truth impacted my treatment in positive, negative, and inevitably unforeseen ways.

Six years before she died, Dr. Cagan told me during a phone session that she had breast cancer. Needless to say, I was horrified and concerned. She asked me not to tell anyone because she thought I had a tendency to tell multiple people when something "bad" had happened as a way of discharging my negative feelings; although this was at least in part true, I felt that she did not want me to tell anyone because she did not want word of her illness to get around. It was the first and only secret she ever asked me to keep, but in the moment when she asked me not to tell, a shift in our dynamic took place: I now would knowingly take care of her needs as she had been taking care of mine.

I had been a caretaker, I think, since birth. With an often anxious and depressed mother and a father who suffered from Crohn's disease, I learned early to be vigilant, and I worked assiduously to master the art of keeping people well. Of course, mastery of something that was out of my control proved to be challenging, and yet I never gave up trying to keep people happy and alive. This effort extended to Dr. Cagan when she became ill, although I knew enough to understand that I wasn't supposed to try to make her well, and – even if I were supposed to – as her patient, I could do very little. Dr. Cagan's illness was, for me, a monkey wrench thrown into what was a successful treatment thus far; for her, it was clearly something much worse. Her illness, and my reaction to it, inevitably changed our therapeutic relationship. Given my history of being the caretaker for my psychologically and physically ill parents, and my history of having my utterly depended upon therapist die, Dr. Cagan's illness was covertly catastrophic. I say covertly because I don't think either Dr. Cagan or I were aware of the extent of the changes that took place between us. When there were signs that I was taking care of her rather than the other way around, we – of course – discussed it. Yet my vigilant watch over Dr. Cagan to make sure she wasn't ill, and my need to protect her from material that would be "too much" for her to handle in her now weakened state, stayed present within me and eventually went underground. Taking care of a therapist can come in many forms: I became particularly watchful, making sure she looked okay each day, and noticing when she didn't; I think I lightened my narratives when I thought she felt tired, although at the time I was not totally aware that I was doing either of these things.

Dr. Cagan took off one week to have a double mastectomy and one kidney removed. It turned out that she had had cancer in two places. Before her surgery, I gave her the novel *The Samurai's Garden* to read because the book felt so sustaining and life-giving to me. When she returned, she told me she loved the book, which made me feel good. But during that first session back, it became clear that it was too early for her to return to work. She was exhausted and in pain, and yet she was an admitted workaholic who found that working helped her to focus on something outside of herself. As so many do, she used work as an escape from her physical and, I imagine, her psychical pain. At the time I didn't question what she was doing. I just picked up the signal and helped her in her effort to feel better.

For the next five years Dr. Cagan was well, although my analysis never fully recovered from the period during which she was ill. I do not think its inability to recover was the particular fault of either of us. It was a bad mix of events and psyches, sicknesses and limitations of both the body and the mind. Agreements were unsaid, but enacted, and I – in my never ending attempt to keep those I love alive – stuck with Dr. Cagan to the end. Through the years during which Dr. Cagan's cancer was in remission, we went on knowing what had happened, and discussing it when necessary, as good analysts and patients do: she would comment when I asked if she was tired or if I would take stock of how she was doing for a moment too long. We would analyze my need to take care of her and my fear of her dying, but we never figured out a way for me to stop feeling how I felt, or behaving as I behaved. I loved her; I knew she had been sick and could get sick again; I had spent a lifetime feeling that I myself was toxic, the cause of my mother's depressions, my father's illness, and perhaps my first therapist's death. Now I was faced with yet another life to save, and with the tenacity I have had since my youngest days, I worked hard to accomplish my impossible goal.

This is not to say that I wasted six years in analysis. Things have a way of moving forward at the same time as others regress and still others stand still. But as time progressed, I noticed that Dr. Cagan and I became more muddled within what was by then *our* treatment. We couldn't see out of the box which we currently inhabited, although we both knew that we entered a box in which our perspectives were limited and our insights were scarce. Dr. Cagan shared with me more than she used to. She was never a doctor who was silent and withholding; when she felt it appropriate, she answered my questions and acknowledged that what I thought about her was right. Her ability to do this was critical for my development. After having a therapist who put feelings into me to the point that they became my feelings, and who failed to respond in helpful ways when I asked him to confirm my perceptions, I needed someone who acknowledged and confirmed what my instincts and perceptions told me. "Are you tired today, Dr. Cagan?" I would ask. "I am. I didn't get enough sleep last night," she would reply. "You seem frustrated, Dr. Cagan," I would say. "I am," she would reply. And I would feel relief because my perception aligned with reality. In the years that followed her illness, Dr. Cagan eventually acknowledged that she shouldn't have told me to keep her cancer a secret, and that she had asked for her own benefit. I had known why she had asked and felt no anger. Everything she did was so human, so understandable. Who could be mad? For the most part, I felt stuck for those five years after her cancer surgery: stuck within myself and probably stuck in a therapeutic dyad that was no longer working well. When I spoke about the treatment not helping me and about the possibility of my leaving, we discussed the reasons I wanted to go, and my reasons would be talked away. That she might get cancer again never came up. Until it actually did.

I had been an analytic patient who used the couch for many years, but after Dr. Cagan became ill, I found lying down too difficult. I was like a jumping bean, lying down, turning over, and popping up. We'd analyze why I didn't want to lie down, but all the analysis in the world didn't shift that I didn't want to. Seeing that she was still there, that she wasn't sick, was too important to me. Once she was sick, there was no way for me to feel safe and secure in her continued presence. I felt that if I lay down, she could somehow just shrivel up and disappear. On one particular day after five years of being cancer free, Dr. Cagan walked to the window to pull down the blind next to her large green plant. She did this every week at this particular hour because the sun shone too brightly on the couch. But that day, as I watched her walk by, I knew she was sick again. I asked, "What's wrong?" Her face collapsed. The cancer had spread and it was now everywhere. She would be beginning chemotherapy, alternating between six weeks of it and six weeks without it, but she would keep working. I burst into tears, unable in that moment to think solely about her. What was I going to do?

Like Dr. Smit, Dr. Cagan started to disappear. The chemotherapy made her nauseous and she could not eat. She was hospitalized repeatedly for dehydration, but she still made it to work. And I cried and cried in session after session because she was so sick and I knew I was going to lose her. I didn't know how to make her well. She still thought she could fight the cancer, while I recognized that she could not. I had researched her condition and read extensively about her odds, while she hadn't. The odds were beyond bad. I knew she had little time left, yet I felt an extreme need to protect her from my knowledge. I didn't let on what I observed in her and what I had read; her denial was serving a good purpose, and I supported her need for it, as I would for anyone who was fatally ill.

When Dr. Cagan ultimately knew she would die, she faced it with more dignity and grace than I had thought imaginable. She told me that she was really okay, even ready, because during her life she made good choices and had no regrets. Our conversations by then were quite open. I knew I was the only patient she had told about her illness and how great a strain it would be for her to begin to tell the others, and I suggested ways for her to tell them the news. She still felt she had time to tell them, but I knew she didn't. She needed to tell them right away. I recognized that she couldn't go on for long when, during a session, she forgot something I had said. This, of course, is not unusual for a therapist, but it was for Dr. Cagan. In all the years I had known her she remembered everything I said. When she had no idea of what I was referring to, I realized that the tumor was affecting her brain. I covered up her lapse, but felt crushed. The discomfort I experienced when I realized that I knew more about what was happening to her than she did was acute, but I made every possible effort to alleviate her pain by keeping away the stark reality.

The day after Dr. Cagan had finished telling all her patients about her cancer was a Friday. She was noticeably tired and terribly thin. She was no longer undergoing chemotherapy and had acknowledged to me that she was ready to die: "I lived my life well. I have no regrets." The awe and respect I felt when she made that statement were extreme. She was a pillar of strength and grace as she faced what I imagine was terrifying. I knew Dr. Cagan well enough to believe what she said. And in my awe, I also felt envy, because she was able to achieve what I still couldn't manage to create: A life in which she could breathe freely because she filled it with pursuits and people she loved, and because it was free of debilitating conflicts.

Dr. Cagan never made it to our Monday appointment. She had deteriorated over the weekend and couldn't leave her apartment. I was not surprised that she could no longer continue working, but I felt a deep sense of loss because I would never again see the room that held so many memories for me. I wished I could say goodbye to the space. So many characters lived in it; so many scenarios were played out. It was a safe place to which I was very attached. I imagine that when analyses aren't ended abruptly there is a slow withdrawal of all your selves from the analytic space. I picture it as a thousand little genies who live in the world, enacting scenes, comedies, and dramas, until they have nothing to act out anymore outside of their bottle. So the genies – when ready – say goodbye to the space and fly in their misty light back into the now functional home from which they came. I felt that my characters, my selves, were somehow still in her room living without me. I wasn't my whole self yet, and I needed to collect the fragments – the me's I was meant to be. But I couldn't get to them. They were shut up in her room where she no longer was.

I stayed in touch with Dr. Cagan for the remainder of her life. She called me one day to see how I was, and I told her that I was okay, although I was really dying inside. We spoke about her work and she said she felt good that she had helped a lot of people, but that there were a few people she felt she hadn't helped enough. I was one of those people. For years we had been trying to deal with a particular issue that never got resolved; it was an issue that jointly confused and muddled us, and now she could no longer help, despite her assurance throughout the years that she thought she could. So she apologized for not helping me enough, and as I cried on the phone I told her that what she said was untrue. That probably nobody could have helped me, and that she had helped so much. I told her how much better I was, and listed all the ways in which she had enabled me to grow, and how I owed the me who I am to her. I also told her how much I loved her and would miss her. And in that mix of lies and truths I tried as well as I could to let her off the hook before she died. And she thanked me.

I saw Dr. Cagan twice more before she died. I came to her apartment, which I had never seen. She sat as emaciated as a concentration camp victim and told me that the cancer wasn't going to kill her: she was going to starve to death – an ironic twist for someone who first went to therapy because she was struggling with anorexia. During that first conversation at her home we spoke about our mutual love of Bach, and she promised to send me a CD she had recorded of her playing his music on piano. She also said she would mail me the writing that I had given her over the years. She had a large folder filled with my poems and stories. Ultimately, both the CD and the writing were never sent because she was too ill to remember what she had said. The next time I came she was sicker and could barely stand up, but she did. She refused not to hug me goodbye. It was the first and last time I ever hugged Dr. Cagan, and it was like hugging bare bones, yet I never wanted to let go. Dr. Cagan's spirit was still with her, and she let me know that I was special to her. That I was a real gift. And that I could live a life that is good. The life I deserved. And after twelve years of analysis all I could think was, "How?" But I knew I couldn't ask her the question because clearly she didn't know either; when she disappeared my hope for answers from her went, too.

I was again stuck and alone in this little world of dead-therapist despair that nobody ever talks about. What does the patient do when their therapist – the person they depend on most – dies? Their friends and family don't know the person (or necessarily even about the person), so there is no personal support. There's no shiva to join, no mourning event in which you can partake; you don't know the family and they don't know you. They could never understand why you would feel as close to their mother, their wife, their friend, as you feel. And yet I was the one who sat in her office four times a week for twelve years, being taken care of by her and taking care of her. So when she was gone, there was yet another hole. A big one. And it grew and grew, especially after I started to see that, even though she had done such a stellar job in handling her death, there were still so many things that could have been done better or, at least, differently.

I have a very strange relationship with therapy and psycho-analysis. I keep going back for more because it's the only method that, for me, makes sense. I don't know of anything else that could help me to change in the ways that I want. Deep change. Lasting change. Change that affects the parts of me that were set up so long ago, the parts I knew were in some way faulty. I needed a form of treatment in which I could grapple with issues that prevent me from living as I consciously choose to live; and yet I am always faced with just how human the specialists are. How blind, twisted, hurt, sick, angry, fearful, non-conscious, per-verse, and destructive they can be. Many people become therapists because they have lived through tremendous difficulty, but many of the challenges they faced in their pasts, they still face today. It is a giant leap of faith to lay yourself open to someone who is only as able to help as his or her own psyche allows. A leap of faith that the person you pick will have the courage and fearless-ness to face him or herself every day, to look within him or herself to see what part of their past or present they are bringing into the room that doesn't belong there, and why they feel the need to bring it.

I have been angry at Dr. Cagan for many things, first among them that she died. At times I was angry that she didn't see that after her first episode of cancer I may have been better off going to another therapist. I don't even know if that would have been true, and I doubt I would have left her anyway. I would have fought to stay. But what my anger brought to mind was that the question was never broached between us. We never thought together about the impact her illness would have on me, and whether – with my history of taking care of people and of a therapist's death – it would have been better for me to work with someone else. Mind you, I can see the argument from the opposite viewpoint, a viewpoint that I think Dr. Cagan had: working with her was the best scenario because, in the transference, I could work through my care-taking issues and my issues relating to Dr. Smit's death. In a perfect psychoanalytic world, I guess that is what would have occurred.

Dr. Aaron Feldman

Written in Starbucks the day after Dr. Feldman was diagnosed with cancer, something I had already suspected.

My analyst said yesterday that his dying wasn't a big deal. Not really. Everyone dies. I'll get over it. It will be hard, but I'll go on. So what? And in that moment – not to say I didn't know it before – I knew he was really dying. My analyst. The one I know. The one I have seen for almost six years. The one who sits while I lie on my back four times a week, and who listens to my thoughts, my feelings, and his words, would not say such a thing. And if he did, it would not be with the particular emotion I heard yesterday. Was it a plea? A request? A belief he had within himself despite it not existing within me? No. It certainly was not within me. Because when my third analyst dies, a pin will be removed from my bubble of life. The one I inhabit in which nothing really lives anyway; so who really cares if all the air is sucked out? It's been sucked out before. Sucked out several times. So many, I can't remember. Air gets sucked out and we go on. Air gets sucked out and we bear it. Perhaps he's right. Perhaps, it's not such a big deal. A third analyst. A third hope dead. Yesterday, when my analyst said that, my analyst disappeared. The floor shook, earthquake, tremor, all stability gone. Melodramatic? Perhaps. But what happens when shrink-number-three dies? Is it the end of the line? Termination was never so concrete. Concrete Termination. Black Widow Patient. So many stories to tell.

There is no good way to handle one's own death when one is an analyst. As soon as an illness is terminal, there is no escape from just how human the analyst is: he fumbles, he pretends, he cancels, he plays it by ear. And the patient follows his lead. "I'll see you tomorrow" turns into "I'll see you next week, perhaps in two, perhaps in a month, or perhaps not at all, never again." The feel of the bones I hugged when I last saw shrink-number-two stays with me. And her final wish for me – that I feel good in the world, that I Like Life. And yet I still wonder: How do people do it? How do people like the world? Feel comfortable in it? What do they have that I lack? I've come so far. I've made so much progress, and not the fake kind, but the real kind whereby your life really improves. But feeling good in the world. At ease. Safe. Where daily life isn't a struggle. I don't know what that feels like. And with shrink-number-three on his way out, I don't think I ever will. "I hate my life" will be a refrain 'til death do I part. Until my very own concrete termination.

Written eight months later, after having just said goodbye to Dr. Feldman.
I said goodbye to my analyst today. After a ten-month battle with lung cancer, he is in too much pain and too weak to come in. I have not seen him in two months, so I was unprepared for the finality of the phone call. Although I expected him to end our treatment, I had hoped that I would at least be able to say goodbye in person, as I did with Dr. Cagan. I told him how much he helped me. That I had really changed over the past six years.

To be the doctor calling patients to tell them they will never see him again must be excruciating. To be on the other end of the line – the patient listening to the finality of a treatment that was not over, a treatment that was helping but can no longer help – is incomparable to what the analyst is going through. Yet it hurts beyond what I remember. The pain of losing someone you love is intensely life-sucking. But oddly, it is life-giving, too, because to feel so deeply connected to another person is to live. Coming through my third analyst's death, I can actually recognize the gift of analysis. I can feel deeply connected to people, to love them, and to want them to stay in the world forever so that I can enjoy them, grow with them, and just be. It's a seismic shift for me to see death as affirming life.

Perhaps despite my third analyst's death – my third concrete termination – analysis has done exactly what I wanted it to do.

Addendum: November 2018

I have felt ambivalent about writing to the analytic community about what to do when an analyst dies. In some ways, I have felt too shattered by my own experiences to rise to the task. After my first analyst died, I believe it took great courage to walk into another analyst's office, and not just because I feared my new analyst's death; by then, I had also come to recognize just how destructive my first analysis had been. How was I to trust again after having been so dependent, damaged, and then deserted?

After my second analyst died, I was heartbroken: not only did I love her, but I also thought she would enable me to become the person I sought to be. She told me that she really thought she could help me in very particular ways, and while she really did help me, she also didn't – couldn't – finish the work we began. I went through a period of depression after she died: it set in slowly, reaching its peak about eight months later, after I had lived with both her absence and the recognition that I still had so much more to do to reach my desired goal.

A few years after her death, I decided to undertake psychoanalytic training at IPTAR. The reasons I made this choice are complex and multi-determined: it was a way to stay connected to my dead analyst, who had also trained at IPTAR; it was a way to be self-sufficient – if my analysts were all to die, I would become an analyst and cure myself; it was a way to force myself to set foot in yet another analyst's office, since a four-times-a-week analysis is a training requirement; and – of course – it was a way to pursue something I believed (and still believe) in, not least because I retained within me elements of all my analysts, who also (I imagined) loved and valued their work. When my third analyst died, I decided I was finished with analysis. I had fulfilled my requirement, so there was really no need to be in treatment ever again. I didn't want to become dependent on anyone new. And, when an analyst, who saw me speak at my third analyst's memorial service, jokingly said to me, "Well, don't come to me for treatment – I don't want to die," it really wasn't very funny; I felt toxic enough already.

I now look back at my twenty-six-year-old self, an utterly dependent devotee caught up in a cult-like relationship with my sadistic-yet-savior-like analyst who was the foundation of my world. After some time in analytic training, after learning about such things as concrete thinking, symbolization, merger fantasies, splitting, enactment, and projective identification, I understood more about who I had been: sitting in Dr. Smit's office, desperate and willing to do anything he said, believing he could fix me and that I could become free of everything that made me so laden, leaden, heavy, and numb; day after day, I told myself, "Well, you can kill yourself tomorrow, but today you can try again to get better." I feel grateful that I could keep going. By the time Dr. Smit died, I was doing better in the world, but I still had no semblance of a solid sense of self. He was in me, and everything I did was for him.

I am often aghast at the degree of my own difficulties and pain. I hesitate writing about it now because it seems so startlingly "bad." And yet I write about the girl who I was because she was the one who experienced the death of her analyst, the pillar who supported her and kept her upright. It was as if I were built around an armature that was forcibly and too suddenly removed, and I went to pieces. Or that's what it felt like; the reality was that I kept going while in excruciating pain. I can still feel it and remember it, and I'm shocked and horrified by what it was like – at how utterly alone and bereft I felt after he disappeared.

When Dr. Cagan died, I was different. By that time, I had a separate self. I now understand how difficult I must have been as a patient. I was the kind of patient who felt impingements often: whenever she was out of alignment with me, I could feel it in my arms: they began to tingle, and I was terrified, knowing that something terrible could happen. She didn't "get" me, and I felt as if everything could fall apart. I have such respect for Dr. Cagan, for the patience she had, for her willingness to stick with me, to refrain from telling me what I felt or interpreting what I had no ability to hear or take in. I am forever grateful because, with her and in her, I found not only my voice, but also my self.

When she died, I did not melt, or crumble, or fall apart. I loved her, and I felt an intense loss. And yet anger as well, because she didn't do what she said she could do, and because I felt that so much of my treatment over the previous year, and even before the recurrence of her cancer, had been devoted to her. I now understand that the enactments in which we were caught left both of us blind. We did not have the luxury of indefinite time and of expanding psychic space within which we could again begin to see. At times during the last year of my treatment, I wanted to end it; at other times, as much as I wanted out, I yearned to stay in treatment because there was no way to stay connected to her if I wasn't her patient. There was no other relationship with her that I could have had. I still don't think I could have made a different choice. How could I have said goodbye to someone – the real person, not just the transferential object – whom I had been with and loved for over a decade? How could

I have said goodbye when I sensed that terminating my treatment meant never knowing how she was faring, whether she was failing, or if she had actually died? It was beyond me.

In hindsight, I believe that one of the hardest parts of losing Dr. Smit, Dr. Cagan, and Dr. Feldman was that with them went the fantasy of what I could have become with their help. I believed that, when the time would come to terminate my treatment, I would have done what I had set out to do. Dr. Cagan (or Dr. Feldman) and I would have talked, I imagine, about the process of termination, coming to the conclusion together that I was finished. In reality, however, I never had the opportunity to decide with my analyst to terminate my treatment and to go through any kind of termination process, and so I am still not sure of what either procedure entails.

When I asked my most recent therapist what being done actually means, she explained it in terms of a brownie. I had just told her about my daughter's ability to stop eating mid-brownie because she had had enough. My daughter's ability seemed miraculous to me, as someone who had struggled so greatly with how much is enough food. My therapist said that enough analysis is like enough brownie: at a certain point, you know you can keep going and going (or eating and eating) but you don't need to; you already feel satisfied. You've had enough. We had this conversation during one of our first sessions, when I went back on my decision never to return to therapy, and I walked through yet another analyst's door. Despite my trepidation, I sought actually to finish treatment, to be the one to decide that (and when) I'm done. I never had the chance to conclude the three most important endeavors of my life – the projects that were to give me *my* life, meaning the life I actually desire. Finally, I wanted to finish what I had started: to say when I had had enough to someone who was actually still alive, and to choose to say goodbye even if I didn't have to and solely because I felt done; that is, because I felt *satisfied*.

Chapter 2

Unfinished business
The impact of denial on the grieving process

Jennifer Grant

The last time I spoke with Ellen, my therapist for over 15 years, was on a Wednesday morning in August, 2014. I was getting ready to leave my apartment for our morning session when my phone rang. "Hi, Jennifer," she said. "They're taking me to the hospital again. It doesn't look good. I'm so sorry." I remember thinking at the time that she was apologizing for having to miss our appointment. Such is the power of denial. She died five days later.

Of course, Ellen's death didn't come out of the blue. In February of that year, she had been in the hospital for two weeks for what she had described as a "procedure." In May, three months before she died, she had another one-week hospital stay, after which she looked so thin and frail that it frightened me. "You look so small, Ellen," I remember saying during our first session after she returned. "I know," she said. It was then that she told me that she had cancer. She explained that she had completed two unsuccessful rounds of chemotherapy and that they would try one more.

My disbelief left me speechless. The shock couldn't have been greater had she told me she was planning a visit to the moon. Yet why should I have been shocked at all? The evidence of her illness had been visible to me for some time. As I look back, it's clear to me that I was already engulfed by denial, choosing to believe that what I was witnessing was not really what it seemed. After a long, agonizing pause, I said, "I'm so sorry." "Thanks, Jen," she replied. "Yes, it's really awful." Another long pause. "I just want to work," she said, "so let's get into it." As if responding to a command,

I began to talk, carefully dodging my feelings and confusion about Ellen's diagnosis and what it meant for both of us.

Our sessions continued on schedule for the next two months, during which time we both avoided any discussion about her illness.

I remember the exact moment I learned of Ellen's death. In a sad nod to the impersonal and intrusive nature of electronic communication, I received the news on my phone, in the process of checking my email at a coffee shop. The email was sent by her partner to what I presumed to be a list of her family members, friends, and patients. She had been sent to hospice the day after I had spoken with her, and she had died four days later. I must have read the email 100 times. Gone? Ellen? Gone?

Grieving is a lonely business, and made still more acutely so when the object of one's grief is unknown to those who might provide comfort. In the days and weeks following Ellen's death, I felt utterly alone in my sadness. At random moments, the grief would well up and I would find myself in tears – walking down the sidewalk, sitting in a cafe. I remember one day riding the subway on my way to a meeting when the tears started streaming down my face, my emotions beyond my control. The woman sitting next to me silently offered me a tissue. There was something about this non-verbal exchange that was profoundly validating.

In the days immediately following Ellen's death, I spent a great deal of time thinking about all the things that she would never experience again – as if processing the finality of her death in bite-sized pieces. I wrestled with the knowledge that I was still alive, still enjoying the things that were gone from her forever. She was gone, and gone from me, forever. The finality of her death was beyond my understanding.

Over and over again, I tried to imagine what it would be like not seeing her every Monday and Wednesday morning, being greeted by her warm smile. It seemed impossible that I would never hear the sound of her voice again and, almost obsessively, I tried to remember things she had said to me over the years, as if by preserving the memories I could preserve her. Several times a day, I would picture every detail of her office and find myself wanting to return to make sure that she was really gone.

I also found myself wondering what her final days were like: Was she in pain? How had she come to terms with her feelings about dying and saying goodbye? Was she at peace? Sometimes I was overcome with shame when I wondered if she had thought of me at the end – would she miss me? What had I meant to her? It felt surreal to be struggling with all of these complicated feelings about the person who could have helped me work through them.

My friends and family tried to understand and console me, but their words of sympathy felt hollow and meaningless. I remember one close friend offering her condolences. Although she meant well, the inadequacy of the words enraged me and made me feel incredibly lonely.

How could anyone understand the significance of this loss? The person who had sat with me twice a week, year after year, while I revealed my deepest fears, my most painful memories, my least tolerable feelings, was gone. The person who had assumed the roles of mother and father, the person who had projected parts of myself to help reveal the conflicts buried deep in my unconscious life – she was gone. The one person who knew the inner workings of my mind and still welcomed me back was gone. It was the most jarring loss I had ever experienced, and I still wasn't fully aware of all that was gone.

My sorrow was compounded by a sense of betrayal: How could my therapist be gone? How could Ellen have left me? Therapists are supposed to be forever – transcending mortality. Unconsciously, I often engaged in the fantasy that Ellen only existed in her capacity as my therapist and that she would always be around. I never wanted to consider her as a regular human being, constrained by the same limitations that all humans face. Her death punctured this notion, but it remains a resilient one: I find myself lulled into the same fantasy with my current analyst, wanting to believe that she (and I) will exist forever.

I attended the memorial service for Ellen at a temple on the Upper West Side. The room was filled with her family, friends, and patients. I sat in the back, alone. I listened to her loved ones share memories of her and of what she had meant to them. It struck me that I didn't know a single person in the room. It felt like a trespass to hear personal stories about Ellen that revealed intimate aspects of her life. I learned about her closest relationships, what she meant to those who cared the most about her, and what she valued and enjoyed about her life.

At one point, one of her patients spoke. He talked about how much Ellen had helped him, both personally and in his capacity as a candidate in psychoanalytic training. As I listened, I thought: "I should say something. I should get up in front of this room and talk about how much Ellen meant to me and about how much I would miss her." "Maybe it would be cathartic," I thought. "Maybe she would hear me." I remember feeling an almost desperate need for Ellen to know what she had meant to me.

In the end, I decided not to speak. Something told me that it was too early to try to articulate my sadness about Ellen's death and the complicated feelings I had about her being gone. I was sitting in a room full of people who loved and would miss Ellen and, although I was one of those people, I felt, once again, utterly alone.

In the week after Ellen's death, I attended my weekly analytic supervision. Supervision turned into a therapy session – the first opportunity I had to talk openly about what I was feeling with someone I knew would really understand the significance of the loss. At the end of our meeting, my supervisor generously offered to begin working with me in a new treatment. The sense of relief was immense – it was as if a safety net had caught me in free fall.

The next week, I returned to my supervisor's office. She explained to me that she had given the matter more thought and had decided that it wouldn't be a good idea for her to see me as a patient, as she was already treating a friend and colleague of mine; and so she offered to refer me to another analyst.

While I respected her decision and the rationale behind it, I experienced it emotionally as another devastating loss. I felt rejected and hurt and painfully alone. The startling reality of starting a new treatment with someone I didn't know filled me with dread.

A new treatment

During my first session with my new (and current) analyst, B, I explained in a detached way that my therapist had recently died. I remember very little else about that session, other than that she wasn't Ellen. Her office was different and more sparsely furnished. She looked different. She sounded different. She wasn't Ellen and she knew nothing about me. I felt exhausted at the prospect of starting again.

I also couldn't shake the thought that I was betraying Ellen by starting treatment with someone new. This, of course, was a way in which I kept Ellen alive in my mind and punished myself for moving on – a variation on an already familiar transference theme. It was also a way in which I avoided feelings of being betrayed and left behind; but that awareness wouldn't be clear to me for quite some time.

The first few weeks of this new treatment felt like a blur. We met once a week at the start of the process, and so I sat opposite B. After being on the couch with Ellen for many years, this felt strangely intimate. I felt exposed – like a candle-lit room suddenly illuminated by florescent light. I was face-to-face with my own sense of being unknown to another in a way that had become so important to me, and which I had taken for granted. I left those early sessions feeling held, but that feeling would give way to frustration at the thought of starting all over again. It was as if a part of me was lost, submerged. It was profoundly unsettling and, occasionally, frightening.

As weeks turned into months, I remember talking about Ellen's death with B, but in a way that was disconnected from my feelings about the loss. I believe that this feeling of distance was, in part, due to the fact that it wasn't clear to me what I was in fact feeling; but it was also a repetition of a familiar transference dynamic in which I responded to a perceived need to protect my analyst: how would she feel if our sessions were filled with my complicated feelings about the loss of Ellen? How could I burden her with my grief? What if my feelings overwhelmed her and, in turn, I was left alone once again?

This dynamic, of course, provided me with an easy way out, perpetuating a fantasy that I could leap frog over my deep sadness, disappointment, and anger. Consciously, I experienced a need to move on, to pick up where Ellen and I had left off.

Moving on proved to be difficult. I found myself rehashing old sessions with Ellen, trying to put myself back in her office and to remember the sound of her voice, the sound of her laugh. I frequently made comparisons between Ellen and my new analyst. Where Ellen had been a more active participant in our sessions, B was less so, and I sometimes experienced the silences as punishing.

I felt an intense longing for the shared understanding that had developed between Ellen and me over the years – that indescribable analytic third that emerges within the therapeutic relationship. I missed the way in which Ellen knew me and, without it, I felt disconnected from myself.

One particular session with my new analyst during this time comes to mind. I was talking about my long-distance running, something that is loaded with meaning for me, in terms of my identity and my separateness from my mother. In this session, I was describing an emotionally painful weekend and how a run had provided some relief from the intensity of the feelings. At one point, my analyst asked me, "What happens when you don't run?" A reasonable question, but one that, at the time, felt like a crushing blow. I remember thinking to myself that Ellen would never have asked me that question. Over the course of my treatment with Ellen, she had helped me to develop a sense of pride about my running and to incorporate my athleticism into my sense of femininity. She had supported my running as a way to help manage intense emotional pain. The question posed by my new analyst, then, confronted me once again with the painful reality that B was not Ellen. In that moment, I realized that I missed Ellen terribly.

After about a year of treatment with B, a new theme emerged. My analyst and I had been discussing increasing our session frequency from two to three sessions per week. My initial reaction to this idea had been one of fear. I found myself worrying about what would be uncovered and what it would mean for both of us. I remember wondering if my analyst really knew what she'd be getting into and feeling pretty sure that she would come to regret the suggestion.

At that time, a recurring image would come to mind: I pictured a "trust fall" in which I was falling backward while my analyst stood behind me, with arms outstretched. This simple image was layered with meaning. On the surface, it represented my fear of burdening my analyst with parts of myself that felt heavy and dark: would she buckle under the weight of me? On a deeper level, it represented my fear that I would crush her: would the burden of my weight destroy her? Ultimately, I was struggling with my fear that I might lose her, too, and the fantasy that I could prevent such an outcome helped me to defend against so terrifying a prospect.

Hindsight on denial

It has taken me several years after Ellen's death, well into my current treatment, to realize that it was the power of denial – mine and hers – that helped us both to create an emotional separation from the reality of her deterioration. In not speaking about her progressive illness, we were colluding in an enactment that served to protect the treatment from painful feelings of loss. The result was a missed opportunity to address the transference and countertransference dynamics that may have deepened the treatment and helped us both to say goodbye.

By not giving voice to my own feelings about Ellen's illness, I became the "good" patient, much in the way I had felt I had to be the "good" daughter with a mother who had suffered from severe depression and bouts of rage. As a child, it was enormously helpful for me to believe that I could "do" something to help my mother feel better. In this way, I had fantasized about having the power to help her and, therefore, to keep myself safe.

In staying silent about my own painful and complicated feelings concerning the potential loss of Ellen, I again became lost in a seductive fantasy in which I imagined I could protect her from her own painful feelings and, in the process, protect myself from the loss of her. So powerful was this fantasy that her death, when it came, was experienced as a shock.

Of course, there's a flip side to this perceived omnipotence. If I had the power to protect, I also had the power to destroy. Denial, then, also helped me to defend against my aggression and perceived fears of its destructive power. It is important to note that during the final two years of my treatment with Ellen, I had begun a psychoanalytic psychotherapy training program. I had spent many sessions talking about what it meant to me to do the same work that Ellen did – my wish to be like her, or to be even better than her, and the fears that arose from such wishes. I had unconsciously created various compromise formulations (including downplaying my own abilities and idealizing Ellen) in order to distance myself from my fear of destroying her in the process of becoming a psychotherapist.

This dynamic was made more complicated by the fact that there was a powerful similarity between what I was experiencing with Ellen and what I was experiencing with my mother. As I watched Ellen become smaller, I had at the same time watched my own mother become smaller during her recovery from her second major spinal surgery. I remember feeling like I was suddenly towering over both of them, as if my progress was making me bigger and stronger and, in turn, making them smaller and weaker. By not acknowledging my fear that Ellen was fading away before my eyes, I carefully dodged my fear that I was behind it – in effect, that in propelling myself forward, I was slowly destroying her.

In the months leading up to Ellen's death, our sessions felt like a carefully orchestrated dance in which we each maneuvered around the glaring reality we dared not face. I brought material into the room that, although real and alive, also kept us conveniently distracted. Looking back, I'm struck by the effort that went into maintaining this collaborative state of denial; but, of course, at the time, it felt effortless compared to what it would have been like to confront and process painful emotions about what we were both trying to ignore. In this way, the material of the treatment became fuel for a joint fantasy in which we could escape from the conscious thoughts and feelings about her death, and possibly even prevent it from happening.

Slowly, with the help of my current analyst (for whom I am immensely grateful), I have become more aware of, and able to experience, the full range of feelings related to the loss of Ellen. I have started to connect with my anger toward her for not encouraging me to process my feelings about her illness, and to understand the significance of these feelings as they played out in the transference dynamics.

My denial, as long as it went unchallenged, helped me to repeat a life-long pattern of losses that were not acknowledged and, therefore, were felt to be not painful or real. I am beginning to understand how distancing myself from others helps me to distance myself from my fear of loss. By not exploring with Ellen my feelings about her illness, I was attempting to avoid connecting with the complexity of emotions about Ellen's real importance to me and with what it would mean to lose her.

Over time, I have also come to understand the defensive role that my anger can play in masking feelings of sadness and grief. Over the past four years, I have spent many sessions detailing the various ways in which Ellen had disappointed me, and examining my indignant anger about her imperfections. I remember several sessions in which I detailed a therapeutic rupture with Ellen, after which I stayed out of treatment for six months. There was something pleasurable about connecting with my self-righteous anger toward Ellen and my unconscious wish to have my analyst join me in acknowledging Ellen's failure. Despite my best efforts, however, my analyst has not colluded with me in my attempts to make Ellen "bad." Instead, she has helped me to understand that, although my anger and disappointments are real, they also conveniently serve me as a way to disguise my profound feelings of loss.

I have had to grapple with the real anger I feel toward Ellen – not just for leaving me, but also for leaving me with the unfinished business of saying goodbye. Indignant at the loss of her, I have asked myself how someone like Ellen – a seasoned analyst – could have allowed my denial (and hers) to go unchecked. I have vowed to myself that I would never repeat this dynamic with my own patients: if presented with similar circumstances, I would do things better. These thoughts represent feeble attempts to punish Ellen posthumously, and so to distance myself from both her and my own imperfections.

The missed opportunity to say goodbye to Ellen has resulted in moments of incredible loneliness – a sense of being totally alone with grief that, at times, has felt like a living presence – a creature that could swallow me whole. The very nature of the therapeutic relationship means that there is no one in my life with whom I have shared memories or shared experiences of her. The grieving is made more complicated by the fact that, in addition to the loss of Ellen, I have been grieving the loss of the work that we did together: the loss of the treatment itself. I have also struggled with giving myself permission to keep moving forward – to go on living and striving, personally and professionally, and so to enjoy the benefits of my treatment with Ellen and thereby allow myself to want even more.

I realize now that the denial that served to guard against painful feelings about the loss of Ellen also helped me to distance myself from feelings about my own mortality and that of others in my life. If Ellen wasn't dying – wouldn't die – I was spared from the reality of death. I'm reminded of the denial that I experienced when my mother was diagnosed with breast cancer – twice. To this day, I have to ask her how it was treated. The power of the denial interferes with memory and, most importantly, with my knowledge that even my mother won't be here forever.

It's not easy to think about death, let alone to come to terms with your own end. Immediately after Ellen's death, so many elements of daily life felt almost silly to me – I found myself questioning the importance of just about everything. How could anything be important when she was gone forever? I thought about the meaning I gave to my own life: how would I feel if I were facing its end?

More recently, I have been processing my mixed feelings about my progress in a deepening treatment and what that means, in terms of my treatment with Ellen and my feelings about her. I find that the comparisons I make between my analyst and Ellen vary according to my willingness to connect with my feelings of loss. For example, after five years of treatment, I experienced the therapeutic rupture with Ellen, after which I didn't see her for a period of six months. I have discussed this rupture several times with my current analyst, processing the complexity of my feelings about it, including my fear that it might happen again.

When I am connected to my sadness about the loss of Ellen, I am able to acknowledge her imperfections (and my own) with compassion, and so to appreciate the emotional complexity of that rupture. When I fall back into an unconscious wish to avoid these painful feelings, my memory of and feelings about that time become overly simplistic: she failed me and I'm angry. During these times, I become aware of a wish to idealize my current analyst and attack Ellen – once again, anger used as an attempt to defend against loss.

It has been more difficult for me to process feelings about the ways in which my current analyst has helped me – ways in which I didn't feel helped by Ellen. Of course, this feeling is due in part to the fact that I have changed in a manner that enables me to see and hear things now in ways I wasn't able to before. But there are also real and positive differences in this treatment that result from the aspects in which my analyst is different from Ellen. I can remember several times when Ellen's use of self-disclosure felt intrusive or when she reacted defensively to a critical comment. The fact that my current analyst is different from Ellen in these specific ways has helped me to feel safe expressing feelings that previously felt "dangerous," and to learn that my anger doesn't actually have quite the power to destroy that I have long imagined it had.

A few weeks after Ellen told me that she had cancer and that the treatments had not been successful, I had a dream. In that dream, we were both sitting on her analytic couch. She had a sandwich and offered me half. We sat together on the couch, eating together. I remember the warm feeling of the dream and how it washed over me. When I recalled the dream in the session that followed, I talked about how good it felt to be symbolically welcomed by her (which, of course, meant giving myself permission to be welcomed) as an equal in her world.

I'm now able to see this dream with more nuanced complexity. The warm feeling that I experienced when sharing a couch and a sandwich with Ellen masked my conflicted feelings about my aggression – the aggression that moves me forward, and which (I imagine) has the power to destroy. In the dream, the mixed feelings I had about entering Ellen's "world" by becoming a therapist were avoided. In the treatment, I avoided this conflict by not allowing myself to think and talk about the symbolic meaning of her illness and pending death. The result was a missed opportunity to expose these conflicts and to begin to work through them.

From time to time, I still find myself overwhelmed by sadness when it hits me again that Ellen will never know exactly what she meant to me and how much I still miss her. Of course, Ellen understood her importance in my life in a profound way, but I often wish I had had the opportunity to put my feelings into words. I have rehearsed this imagined dialogue with her hundreds of times – all the things that I would have liked to say to help her know how much she had helped me, how much I valued her, and how I knew that she loved me in a way that I struggled to love myself. I would like to tell her that I forgive her for her inability to process her illness with me in order to say goodbye – that it has become safer for me to see her (and myself) as imperfect.

In a recent session with my analyst, I discussed the feeling of guilt I was having about writing this chapter. "Isn't it like profiting from her death, in a way?" I asked. As soon as the words were out of my mouth, I imagined what Ellen's reaction might have been if she knew that I was writing this piece. "Good for you," I could hear her say. I could picture her smile and I could hear her laugh. My analyst offered up the idea that perhaps it is a tribute to my work with Ellen that I am writing about the loss of her – a way to honor the treatment by sharing what it has meant to me to lose her and to move on. Suddenly, I could see the guilty feeling for what it was: an attempt to punish myself for moving forward and to reduce the complexity of the situation into a simple matter of right and wrong.

Later that day, I realized that something profound had happened: I no longer felt as if I had to protect my analyst from my sadness about the loss of Ellen. I had stopped believing that missing Ellen and valuing B were opposing forces. New space had been created in which I was able to see Ellen in a more realistic, more human way, and this development had helped me to process feelings of sorrow, anger, and loss in a way that felt safe.

Slowly, I'm starting to understand that if I become more known to myself and to my analyst, neither of us will fall or fail. This insight goes hand-in-hand with my letting go of the long-cherished fantasy that it is within my power to destroy or protect. It's a fantasy that has helped me to avoid the fear of my powerlessness and, ultimately, my feelings of loss. As a child, I told myself that I could console my mother when she was depressed or in a rage because I needed to feel safe: If I couldn't help her, what would become of me? In the same way, I avoided talking with Ellen about her illness because, unconsciously, I was acting on the belief that somehow I could prevent her death from happening. To release myself from this fantasy is both to acknowledge that there was nothing I could have done to keep Ellen alive and to experience the painful feelings about her being gone.

Sub-part 1.11

Sudden death

Chapter 3

The art of grief

Rachel Brandoff

A new year

It was an unseasonably warm, early January day. I was thrilled to be outside in the sunshine with a relatively light jacket and to walk the twenty-five New York City blocks to one of my most fulfilling self-care activities. I had been seeing K, my analyst, for almost four years at this point, and it had been a difficult road. I came into therapy with a host of relational issues, deep mistrust expectations, difficulty making decisions, and a pervasive habit of devaluing myself: these behaviors had become commonplace in my life. A number of things may have contributed to these issues, including authoritarian parenting, relationships with addicts and narcissists, and social and familial pressure to couple.

I got to K's office. She saw clients in the first room of her New York City apartment, which had an unusual wooden scroll room-divider; at each session she showed me into the room, and then unrolled the screen to create a visual barrier from the hallway. I never knew what was beyond that room or the nearby bathroom that I occasionally used. She lived on a lovely tree-lined block right off Central Park.

I arrived at the door of her building and rang the bell. There was no answer. I walked around under the large awning and paced up and down the street. It was just after New Year's, and there was a feeling of getting back to the grind post-holidays. All of the unrealized tasks and projects from last year now had possibility again. I rang the doorbell again. I waited, slightly confused as to why she wasn't buzzing me in as rapidly as usual. I only hesitated for a moment; how many times, I reasoned with myself, had somebody come and rang my doorbell at the exact moment that I went to the bathroom. It happens!

I continued to pace. I waited. I called her on the telephone, thinking that perhaps her doorbell was broken again: another reality of New York City apartment living that has befallen more than one person I've known. No answer on the phone. Well, this was odd, and not at all like her. I checked my voicemail to see if I had missed a message about rescheduling, and I checked my email and my text messages. The modern age of technology sometimes requires one to check multiple applications for communication with one person.

I looked at my calendar, which confirmed what I had thought. We were scheduled for this day and time. Yet sure enough, I was not sure. I must have made a mistake, I thought. We must have scheduled for a different time, and I wrote it down wrong. She was still out of the country, which perfectly explained why she was not able to answer my phone calls let alone her door. I had made a mistake. I clearly had incorrectly logged the appointment date and maybe she wasn't back from her holiday travels yet. I should mention that these are not things I typically do. While I don't have a track record of mixing up appointments, I do have a track record of blaming myself or assuming blame when something goes wrong in a situation. "Hope you're still having a great trip," I said in the voicemail message I left her. "I'm sorry about the mix-up. Enjoy the rest of your vacation and I'll see you when you get back."

Learning the truth

That night my phone rang close to 9 p.m. I wasn't expecting anyone, and the number was unfamiliar. Or maybe it was K's number calling. I can't remember. I answered the phone. "I'm K's daughter," a young, tired voice said on the line.

A daughter? K's daughter? Why was her daughter calling me? What business would her daughter have calling a client?

"There's been an accident. She died."

I think that was what was said. There was an accident. There was a fire. She didn't make it out. Didn't survive. Died. I don't remember what was said precisely – how the news was conveyed. Somehow it feels like a cruel thing not to remember exactly how it was stated. For a while I wished that I could recall the exact words that she said and how she gave me this news, even though I know that it would not change a thing. It was an unrehearsed and unscripted phone call.

I don't remember what I said. Thank you, perhaps? Is that something to say to someone who delivers such awful and catastrophic news? Thank you for calling and telling me that the person whom I need most in my life right now is gone.

Somehow I got off the phone. I was in shock. I couldn't move. My partner, who could tell that it had been an unusually short, awkward phone conversation, looked at me with concern. What's wrong? What happened? Are you okay? And more questions. I felt numb. Tears welled up. He guided me to the couch and helped me to sit. Salty water started flowing down my face. Gone. Dead. She didn't make it out. Questions continued to fill my mind. I felt paralyzed. I was in disbelief – this couldn't be real, but at the same time I knew how real it was. It was a really long night where sleep only came out of exhaustion. And it was a really long year.

Sometimes I would walk over to her building and just meander around or pace out front. I would linger on the sidewalk hoping that she'd buzz me in. I was devastated a few months later when her name was taken off the door directory of the building. How dare the world keep turning! People went about their daily lives as if nothing had happened. I knew that everything was different. Nothing was linear anymore. Nothing was clear. Everything I had been working on and towards stopped mattering. It felt hard to laugh or smile. Usually laughter has helped me get through the tough times and difficult circumstances. It was quite a while before I felt able to use laughter to cope again.

The details

I didn't even know she had kids. Five of them it turned out, teenagers and young adults. Perhaps I should have guessed. In hindsight there was some suggestion of children, but in true psychoanalytic fashion our sessions were always about me. Aside from an obviously impossible-to-keep-quiet small barking dog, and a never-renovated bathroom adjacent to the sitting room where we conducted sessions, I didn't really know anything about her personal life until after her death. A therapeutic relationship is sometimes focused on only one member of the dyad.

She died.

I wasn't wrong about the scheduling, as it turned out. I showed up just as planned and when she did not answer the door it wasn't because she was in the shower, or because I had gotten the date wrong. It was because she was dead.

I had never spent much time caring before about her life or circumstances, but now I felt obsessed with her life and, more specifically, her death. I combed the internet looking for a news story, a police blotter, or some detail that would confirm that it was all in fact real and had happened. Maybe she went on vacation and was having such a good time that she decided to never return – haven't we all fantasized about that at one time or another? And if that's what it was, I wouldn't even take it personally. After all, it wasn't a rejection of me so much as an embracing of vacation. I would much rather believe that that was so.

If this fire had really happened, and someone had really died, it would be on the internet, right? Isn't the internet for finding out about how people died and when? If it was on the internet, I did not know where to look or how to find it. I could only assume that no one, least of all her children, would make up such a hideously ugly story.

The phone call with her daughter felt like an eternity but probably lasted under a minute. What a crappy job: combing through your mother's phone records to find her clients and call them to report her dead. It's hard enough to lose a parent and worse still to have to attend to such details.

Her mother did not have a professional will, apparently. Many of us do not have professional wills, a plan for what happens if we suddenly die. Who will contact our clients and supervisees and attend to the workings of our practice? A thorough and thoughtful professional should name an executor to carry out issues pertaining to professional life, just as one would with personal matters. Designated persons would inform and respond to clients, assess and close the business, and refer clients in need to other qualified practitioners (Pope & Vasquez, 2016).

Days later, when I was thinking somewhat more clearly and processing what had happened, I wanted to reach out to her daughter. I wanted to tell her how amazing and phenomenal and wonderful her mother was, how much she had meant to me, and how much she had helped me transform my life. It felt silly and indulgent. She probably already knew how great her mother was.

Perhaps it was more about my longing for connection with somebody who could understand how important she was on this earth. And the part of me that is a therapist (or was it the part of me that was human?) felt a great deal of compassion for her daughter and the other children who were left behind. I wanted to call her daughter and console her, to be an ear to which she could vent her pain and frustration over this loss – feelings I assumed she had, since I was having them. I didn't have her number and, of course, even if I did, it would have been enormously inappropriate.

The grief rituals

I learned through a random post on social media that there was to be a memorial for K at the hospital where she had worked in multiple units for years. Several professional colleagues commented online and sent condolences that were polite and yet seemed dry to me.

People dealing with grief frequently feel that there is no specific script to follow or to dictate what comes next in life. The process of navigating grief is sometimes made easier by the grief rituals that people have; these rituals are intended as anchors, and they give people a means of coping during pain. Frequently these grief rituals are connected to religious or cultural traditions; sometimes there is room for modernization and development, and at other times they are very strictly adhered to. Sometimes this is dictated by the person facing the grief and by the nature of the loss that they are mourning.

I have many times encountered in my personal life and in my work grieving people who have made statements such as "I didn't know what to do next" or "I wasn't sure which way was up or how to go through the normal motions of life." Grief can be so disorienting that it uproots lives, activities, and decisions. This is, in fact, part of the reason why rituals exist. A grieving person is often so overcome by feelings of bereavement that having to figure out what to wear, what to eat, or when to do something may be more than they can muster. Redefining your life after the loss of an integral loved one can take time and be an exhausting process, and so little things should sometimes be taken out of the realm of daily consideration. Rituals sometimes bring great comfort to those who otherwise do not know how to continue in life.

There were two notable things that played out in terms of rituals with the loss of K. One was the fact that customary American funeral garb – all black – seemed inadequate. The second was that my understanding of memorial services serving to connect the bereaved was challenged.

On the day of the memorial service, I got dressed as I would for a funeral. Black pants and a black blouse. Maybe a black dress; I can't remember. But of course it was funereal black. I remember leaving my apartment to go to the memorial service and passing hundreds of other New Yorkers also donned in black. For a split second I wondered if everyone had funerals that day. Of course, black is the uniform of choice for many people who live in New York. In all of the years I had lived and worked there, I had never attended a funeral, and I had never considered that the black clothes I wore daily had symbolism in a different context.

The memorial service, which was held in the large multi-purpose room at the hospital, was packed. There were hundreds of people: family, including her children, friends, professional colleagues, and those who admired her work through her multiple professional iterations. I felt invisible. I was scared to talk to anyone. Funerals, wakes, shiva, and memorials of various kinds are often designed to connect those who share the bond of grief. "How did you know K?" was a common question I overheard after the service had ended, as I saw loved ones milling about, wanting to share their stories. There didn't seem to be an appropriate way to say who I was or how I knew this woman, let alone to convey what she meant to me. I was an outsider yearning for connection, but the psychotherapeutic relationship is a deeply personal one. As when I knew her, our relationship stayed private.

Community responsibility

Aside from the daughter who contacted me to let me know that her mother was dead, I never heard from anybody else. Should I have? At various times I felt as if it would have been responsible for someone to call me or check up on me. Perhaps no clear breakdown of responsibility exists in the face of grief from the death of an analyst.

If someone should have contacted me, who would that be? When would have been the right time for contact? I had started seeing K through the analytic institute in the city, where she had been doing her training. Is it the responsibility of the managing/referring institute to follow up on the clients of the deceased practitioner? I am not sure how I would have responded had somebody contacted me from the institute. Would they call to inform me of a death I already knew about? Ask me if I was okay? I was not okay. Perhaps offering services from a new and different clinician might have been useful.

It took me a long time to be willing and able to consider seeing another therapist. And when I finally did so, I was not able to resume the work that I had been doing previously in therapy. I spent two full therapeutic relationships processing K's sudden death and trying to reorient myself in the wake of that loss. In both cases I felt that the therapists politely acknowledged my grief, though they didn't offer much in the way of commentary, suggestions, or psycho-education. They seemed to condone my process, which included making a lot of art about this loss. There were no suggestions of support groups, books to read, art directives, rituals to employ, or things to do to help move me through my grief. What could they say? I was already employing my number-one coping mechanism by indulging my grief creatively. I don't blame either therapist for not doing enough, but I feel like I got very little out of that time, save for solidifying the belief that I was truly on my own in my efforts to deal with K's death. I began to wonder more about the quality of training that therapists get to assist people who are struggling with grief.

Is there a responsibility that exists for dealing with situations of grief? Many organizations and practitioners think: yes. Some proactively address the fact that therapists can become incapacitated or die, and that contingency plans should be made on behalf of the clients. Some clinicians and theorists recommend having a professional will, and some even offer up sample templates to adopt and customize to one's own practice (DeAngelis, 2008; Holloway, 2003; Pope & Vasquez, 2016; Rutzky, 2000; Steiner, 2011, 2013). The point of these tools is to avoid both the situation whereby family members, or even children, have to call clients and report a death and the situation in which a client is unsupported in dealing with the loss of a therapist. In the event that a therapist dies, a person should be identified who can attend to their practice, help refer clients to new therapists, and close out the business. In my own practice, I examined who would make the calls to my clients should I suddenly die, and how that person would know whom to call. I thought about if there was a need to notify former clients, as in some cases old clients have returned to me. It was hard to find a one-size-fits-all answer.

Fortunately, there is no need to reinvent the wheel. There are tools out there to serve as guides for a professional will (Pope & Vasquez, 2016; Zur Institute, n.d.), which, like most wills or advanced directives, provides a contingency plan in special circumstances. I have found that it is not uncommon for people in a personal or professional realm to know that these tools exist and to feel that they are important to use: yet they still choose not to use them. Thinking about these things forces us to consider our own mortality, and that is no easy project. But not thinking about them is a disservice to the clients we work so hard to serve.

Should clinicians be pushed to have contingency plans in place for their deaths as a way of considering their clients' needs and of putting their clients first? I have my own graduate counseling and art therapy students consider a living will and advanced directives as a class project, and I think that I will begin to have them also consider a professional will. This loss has guided the trajectory of my career, including my doctoral dissertation research, for over a decade. I see no signs of this topic becoming any less relevant.

The art

After the memorial service was over, and I was left with myself, I retreated into my art. I should first say that this was a comfortable processing tool for me, one that I had been engaging in throughout my whole life. I was lucky enough to have a tiny studio within my apartment. It was actually an awkwardly shaped 4 by 5 foot porch that hung out over the building's airshaft. It was winter, so it was just myself and the loud "oh-oo-oor" cooing of the building's pigeon population; most crouched in small nests below dormant window-banger air conditioners. I had so many boxes and drawers of art supplies crammed into the small space that there were only about 2 square feet of space to move around in. I did not care. All I needed was enough room for me and for my portable electric space heater.

The art poured out of me. I filled large journals with art related to themes of death, grief, grief rituals, and memories. I built sculptures and totems. I painted and drew and made prints. I was frequently working on multiple pieces of art at a time, several of which unfolded into series. The themes were evident. The work was entirely motivated by loss. Every time I finished a piece, I started a new one, or two, and there seemed to be no end in sight.

There were no blocks. There were no pauses. There was no wondering what to create next. It just came. It just manifested. Whole works were inspired by a single thought, a single word, a picture in a magazine, a color, a feeling, a memory, and sometimes a single object could inspire many works.

As an art therapist, I am used to developing art directives to give to clients I work with and to the students I teach. I help develop art tasks that will specifically direct a client's process and help them face certain issues or work towards certain goals. In my own training I've made art many times when prompted by a certain directive that was designed to elicit particular learning, processing, or consideration. There were no official prompts that dictated my artwork at this time. I seemed to know that the overarching goal of "processing grief" was the unwritten and unspoken goal, and I heeded this call interminably.

I started first with mandalas. I had become slightly obsessed with making mandalas after teaching a human development class that included them as assignments that invited artistic exploration and renderings of each major life stage. Now I made mandalas for another reason – to explore grief. I drew them, I painted them, I collaged them, and sometimes I did all three together. I layered pastels on top of watercolor, then brought in clippings of wrapping paper and magazines, and worked the piece over again with markers and paint pens. The processes always seemed as layered as my grief, addressing varied emotional content with symbolism derived from my feelings of loss or from the relationship. In mandalas, I depicted the contents of K's apartment, or at least what I could remember or see in the room that she used for therapy. I depicted in mandalas the way I think that she died, and also the way I think that she lived; the way that she worked with me and how that felt. I portrayed the support I felt, and the support that I now missed. As soon as one mandala was finished, two or three more were started. I have a large collection of them now, and many remain unfinished, but waiting patiently in case I need to return to them.

Then there were the chairs: a series of tissue-box-sized scale models of her chair – the one I chose to sit in for each session. The chair itself was unremarkable except for its bright color. It was comfortable enough to draw you in for an hour, but not so comfortable that it was hard to get up from and leave. It somehow became a marker for me of K and of her office, and something that I would miss. I made a series of sculptures, all inspired by this chair. In my artwork the chair was rendered in such a way as to depict the feelings that came up for me while sitting in it; the challenges and obstacles that I faced and worked on with varying degrees of comfort. There were times when the chair hugged me, and times when the chair provided no comfort. Sometimes the chair seemed like a bottomless hole that could suck me into an endless vortex; at other times the chair was just the support I needed to sit as my tallest, proudest self.

In photos, I explored my own mortality. Photographer friends were particularly helpful in assisting me to create dramatic images. Me positioned in a 19th-century style deathbed pose, trying to lose all muscular tension. Me lying limp in a classic morgue pose with my toe tag as the only identifying feature. Me painted – seated with an intricate *calavera* or skull face, which is typically seen in Mexican Day of the Dead imagery and celebrations.

And there were journals filled with art in a variety of styles, media, and subjects. In art, I explored the memory of every other loss I had experienced; perhaps I was trying to understand how these losses had prepared me to face that of K. I drew loved ones on deathbeds; I drew memories of shivas, wakes, and memorial celebrations. I drew memories of writing obituaries, a typical journalism major entry-point. I drew memories of attempts to comfort others who had experienced loss. I drew comic-strip style panels that showcased a progressive build-up to losses that involved watching people deteriorate. I drew memories of clients who had died, and how it felt to learn of those losses. I drew my friends' mothers, who had died, and the relationships that I know my friends struggled to reframe with their mothers who were gone. And I just kept drawing. When I was feeling too much to think about drawing, I would draw myself or a part of myself. I would write about how it felt to feel loss, and I would layer images over my words, showcasing how hard it was to find the words and to find the feelings.

I even made a video that included many of the drawings and photographs and various art works that I had made. I never felt short of material that expressed aspects of loss in art. I started several altered book projects, where a book itself is the canvas on which the artist creates. Some of these projects are longing to be revisited.

It was over two years before my creative pace started to slow, and before grief in art making became a more casual exploration. It never ceased however, and as I began a more academic inquiry into grief and bereavement, I incorporated my own art into my speaking about loss. What I learned is that the experience of grief is universal, although its manifestations are deeply individual. Many are hungry for ways in which to process their grief, however, and as with anything else in life, I can offer art as a means of coping and processing all that comes up in grief. My art gave rise to ideas for how to encourage the exploration of art in my clients who were coping with grief. My art served as a model for how grief can be explored, experienced, and understood. It is now nine years since the loss of K. I am still creating, and I am still learning from my creative exploration of grief.

References

DeAngelis, T. (2008, June) 'How to Prepare for the Unexpected: Creating a Professional Will Can Help You Protect Your Patients and Put Your Affairs in Order,' *Monitor on Psychology* 39(6). Retrieved from www.apa.org/monitor/2008/06/prepare.aspx.

Holloway, J.D. (2003) 'Professional Will: A Responsible Thing to Do,' *Monitor on Psychology* 34(2). Retrieved from www.apa.org/monitor/feb03/will.aspx.

Pope, K.S. & Vasquez, M.J.T. (2016) *Ethics in Psychotherapy and Counseling: A Practical Guide* (5th ed.). Hoboken, NJ: Wiley.

Rutzky, J. (2000) 'Taking Care of Business: Writing a Professional Will,' *The California Therapist* 12(4): 44.

Steiner, A. (2011) 'Preparing Your Clients and Yourself for the Unexpected: Therapist Illness, Retirement, and Death,' *The Therapist* 23(6): 47–56. Retrieved from www.camft.org/images/PDFs/WillWriting/Preparing_ Your_Clients.pdf.

Steiner, A. (2013) 'The Therapist's Professional Will: If Not Now, When?' *Psychotherapy Tools*. Retrieved from www.sfrankelgroup.com/documents/ The%20Therapists%20Professional%20Will%20-%20Ann%20Steiner.pdf.

Zur Institute. (n.d.) 'The Professional Will,' Retrieved from www.zurinstitute. com/wills_clinicalupdate.html

Chapter 4

Monumental losses, monumental gifts

Analysand and analyst mourn the death of an analyst and friend

Vanessa Hannah Bright and Merle Molofsky

Vanessa Hannah Bright

What do you do when you are a baby whose mother dies while holding you? Do you trust that anyone else will ever really hold you again? Do you have a choice, living in the world where one needs connection in order to thrive?

My experience of losing my analyst was absolutely the worst thing that ever happened to me in my life. I'd experienced many losses in my life previously (e.g., my grandparents, grand-aunts, and grand-uncles), but losing my analyst came with a host of completely unexpected feelings and issues. In the nearly three years of working together, not only had Lily helped me to completely change my life, but also at the time of her death I was still utterly dependent on her.

In my last year of acupuncture training at the Pacific College of Oriental Medicine (PCOM) (a four-year master's level program), I began a senior internship, during which I treated actual patients with actual needles for actual health concerns. Instantly, the many issues related to the therapeutic relationship between a bodywork practitioner and a patient were at the forefront of my awareness. My insecurities flooded my awareness before, during, and after every clinic shift, when I was faced with patients who were asking for all kinds of help beyond acupuncture – both explicitly ("Can you sit with me for a few extra minutes?") and non-verbally (e.g., by taking twenty minutes to get ready to leave) – and with the many challenging situations that arose, which I felt ill-equipped to handle.

And yet no one around me seemed to be aware of any of them. On occasion, my classmates complained about some isolated concerns with a kind of "Well, what are you gonna do?" nonchalance; but they were mostly happy to be seeing real patients and getting real results from this wonderful medicine. Confused and unsettled, I found and shadowed a mentor who seemed well versed in understanding the emotional issues patients would mention. But after a few months I realized that she was not truly relating to patients as individuals, and was actually "painting by the numbers," so to speak. I was at a loss, and my insecurities mounted. No one around me seemed to be even vaguely aware of the importance of – and the challenges inherent in – the therapeutic relationship.

Enter Lily. I had taken her course, Clinical Counseling, at PCOM the previous year; in this class some of the issues of the therapeutic relationship were briefly talked about. However, the intensity of the training made this class seem secondary, and I didn't fully comprehend the essential nature of the material until much later.

A few months into my seeing patients, Lily sent out a mysterious and altogether terrifying invitation to what she called a "supervision group" for acupuncture interns. At the time, the term "supervision" had no meaning to me in this context (we had supervisors who monitored our point prescriptions, which was an entirely different procedure), but the description of the group shook me to my core: a group to discuss and work through issues of being a healing practitioner. Someone was finally acknowledging that there are real and legitimate challenges and issues that need to be addressed and worked through, and taking them seriously enough to warrant a regularly scheduled time to explore them. Despite my trepidation, I signed up, telling a close friend about how scary it felt and how that fear probably meant it was really important for me to take the risk and sign up for the group.

I had no idea just how important it would turn out to be, for this leap of faith eventually led to my becoming a psychoanalyst. As it happened, the group itself never formed: apart from me, only one other person at PCOM thought it was worth enrolling in, and even she subsequently dropped out. By then, however, I had gotten a taste of how Lily worked, and I wanted more. It took enormous courage for me to ask her to be my therapist rather than to continue supervision. She agreed, and we began to work weekly, then twice weekly, and soon three times a week. I became attached to her immediately, and felt like a starving orphan who was finally given access to a lavish buffet. My transference was apparent instantly: I felt too hungry for acceptance and care, and ashamed for showing my need. All my issues were allowed to come to the fore and to be addressed – with the overarching theme being an authentic separation and individuation from my mother. It was an utter revelation, and despite the pain of doing this work, it was an enormous relief to know that someone out there exists who could do it with me.

Through my work with Lily, I soon realized that I had been depressed for much of my life, and my depression intensified as Lily and I dug into my feelings and issues after so many years of suppression. I lived for my sessions, longed to see Lily, thought about her between sessions, and, in general, held on to her for dear life. I was so amazed by, and hungry for, her attentiveness, her presence, and her care, and I completely idealized her. She responded to my pained emails, granted my requests for extra sessions when I was in distress, and remained grounded no matter what difficult or convoluted issues I brought into our sessions. And she asked me to draw, which in itself was a revelation, and something that has led to my eventually developing into an artist. We explored my inner world in ways I never had an opportunity to do before, which was validating in absolutely unprecedented ways. In short, she finally fed me, despite my shame.

A little less than two years into our work together, Lily told me that we would need to continue our work by phone for a few months. She said she had been diagnosed with walking pneumonia and her doctor told her that she must stay at home for a few months in order to heal. I was somewhat distraught by this development, but she seemed confident that she would recover, and we were able to continue the work. For three and a half months we talked twice a week, and our sessions proceeded with her being just as present, perceptive, and caring as always. I missed her and longed for the day we would resume working in person, but I was too afraid to say that to her, afraid I'd be asking for too much.

Finally, we had our first session at the office. In retrospect, I realize that all I wanted to do was sob, but I was so anxious that

I raced through – and throughout – the session instead. I had a lot to say and filled up the available space with everything other than the one thing that was on my mind: how terribly I'd missed her and how thin she had become. I still have the image of her hand draped over her armrest, and I could see every single bone in her wrist and hand. It was hard to process, and elicited the first hint of my unconscious belief that I had somehow contributed to Lily's illness. I have always been quite overweight, and seeing Lily so thin brought up the fear that I must be careful not to take too much of her. But how could I do that when I was so, so hungry? This is what I wrote in my journal after that first session:

> The whole time I was racing – partly excited and partly fearful of running out of time. I was afraid to let myself realize what a huge deal it was for me ... or rather, I was trying to avoid myself the embarrassment of having Lily realize what a huge deal it was for me.
>
> It was weird – I couldn't really believe she was alive. The whole thing was somewhat surreal. I raced through it. I understand, though – I was more anxious than I recognized. I think I wanted to show Lily how much I've grown or something ... I really wanted her to see how calm I was. Meanwhile, I was so embarrassed to be so fat that I wished I could disappear. My turn to go away for 4 months and come back skinny.

Then, perhaps to punish myself unconsciously for a crime I did not actually commit, I stopped eating. For exactly three and a half months I became anorexic and lost about thirty pounds. I felt too emotionally hungry and too ashamed of my hunger. If I were going to continue "taking" from Lily, who was already thin, I would have to pay in some other way – and at that time I "paid" by starving myself.

Our sessions proceeded as before, in person, twice a week. Lily regained the weight she'd lost and things returned to normal. Around this time, I also graduated from PCOM, passed the national board exams, received my acupuncture license, and began my private practice as an acupuncturist. I was still severely depressed and really clung to Lily, living from session to session. However, I had also made immense strides in my capacity for self-awareness and my ability to access my feelings; I had also begun to experiment with the creative endeavors of writing poetry and painting. I brought to my sessions my tender, vulnerable poetry, and my tentative artworks, all of which were welcomed in a way I'd never experienced before. I vividly recall reading Lily my poems out loud and physically trembling with both anxiety and joy.

A year later, Lily began to change our schedule, canceling some sessions and having more and more phone sessions instead of in-person meetings. She did not tell me why, only that this arrangement was what she needed. Of course, I complied, and did not dare to ask her why. Soon, all our sessions were on the phone. Fearful that she was once again ill, and still feeling guilty for taking up her time, I had an incredibly hard time saying anything at all, but after about two months of only phone sessions, I finally dared to tell her that I missed not seeing her in person and asked if she was okay. Lily told me that she was having some health issues, but that she was working on them. I was too scared to ask for anything more. In retrospect, I can see that she was holding back a great deal, and that this was perhaps not the best way to have handled her illness. However, I also later learned that although Lily was, indeed, very ill, she fully expected to recover, and she did not want to burden her clients with this information.

On the morning of the Monday on which we were scheduled to have an afternoon phone session, Lily left me a voicemail saying that she had to cancel. She was warm and soothing as usual, yet she did not confirm our next session, saying that she would let me know about it later in the week.

I heard nothing on Tuesday or Wednesday, and on Thursday I got a call from someone who said she was Lily's colleague Anita. She told me that Lily had been taken to a hospital and that she, Anita, would henceforth be my point of contact until Lily got better. She could not tell me what was wrong with Lily, which was a profoundly frustrating experience, leading me to dreadful fantasies of the worst kind. I was completely beside myself with worry, missing Lily, feeling utterly helpless, alone, and guilty for wanting her support when I knew she had to be really sick if someone else had to make a phone call on her behalf.

I could not sleep that night, tossing and turning and having end-less nightmares. In my journals that week, I expressed a very eerie feeling, describing what felt like a bigger break than if Lily had, say, had appendicitis or something to that effect. I wrote that this rup-ture felt like an "imminent grief." Some part of me was preparing for the worst – a fear I'd had even before Lily ever became ill. Even before her first illness, every time I would see her in the waiting room to call me in for our session, some part of me was relieved to know that she was alive. Hungry as I was for plentiful holding and nourishment, I also struggled to trust that that resource would be there. When Lily was late to a session by a few minutes, I would have fearful fantasies that she had been hit by a car or had died in some other way.

That Saturday morning, I was lying in bed, surprised to have been able to rest that night. My phone rang at 9:00 a.m., and it was Anita. "I have some bad news," she said. "Okay …" I replied, lowering myself into a chair. I already knew what was coming; per-haps I'd been unconsciously preparing myself for it; but I still hoped for something – anything – else. "Lily passed away yesterday," Anita said.

Despite my internal armoring, nothing could prepare me for such news, and nothing I write can truly articulate what I felt in that moment – or that entire day (week, month, year). I stayed on the phone with Anita for a few minutes, but she was frustratingly unin-formed about the reason for the sudden passing. To be told that Lily had died suddenly, but having no reason or explanation of how or why she died, was traumatizing and unbearable.

While on the phone with Anita – I still remember exactly where I stood in my apartment – I suddenly had the thought, "It's time. I'm going to become a psychoanalyst." I was not ready for the implications of this thought in terms of what I would do or when, and perhaps at that time it was simply a comfort, a way to "be with" Lily. In retrospect, however, I see that losing Lily was a massive catalyst for the rest of my life. Given how attached I was to her, and what an enormous agent of growth and change she had been for me, it now seems inevitable that I would continue to use our connection as a way to grow – this time toward becoming a psychoanalyst myself.

Anita checked in with me again later in the day, and I told her that Lily had once given me the contact information of another therapist, who, at the time, was covering her practice while Lily was on vacation. Anita told me to try contacting her, and I did. It was a very weird experience, calling Merle that Sunday. She returned my call very quickly, and we made an appointment for that Tuesday. She brought up the fee, but at the time money had absolutely no meaning, because I wasn't going to see a therapist but rather a life raft. I wished Merle had never mentioned it (although of course she had to), and I also wish she'd never said that we should meet to see if we would be a "good fit." I was desperate and needed Merle to see me regardless of the "fit." It would be like telling a two-year-old that she was going to get a new mom – a completely meaningless statement, one to be met with vehement, rageful, excruciating resistance. I was contacting her because I was in unbearable pain, but I primarily sought her out because I knew that she knew Lily and might be able to fill me in on some of the details of Lily's death. Merle was not "another therapist" for me to see; she was my only link to Lily. When Lily gave me Merle's number just six months before, she told me that she had told Merle a little about me, so that if I needed to see her during our break, Merle would know who I was. But more importantly, Lily told me, "She is someone I really trust." Those were magic words that helped me in a situation Lily could not have anticipated herself.

Of course, I still remember that first session with Merle vividly. Walking into her office, that completely unfamiliar space, I raced directly into the bathroom, my historically safe place for containment and privacy. There, I tried to catch my breath, only to be enveloped by the utterly surreal feeling of being there. I didn't want to be there, and yet I desperately needed to be. From that point on, every time I would go into the bathroom in Merle's office, I would recall that brutal moment, only three days after I'd learned of Lily's death. It seems almost a miracle that I survived it myself.

Once I was in the waiting area again, Merle came out to greet me. She smiled at me, which was inviting, but my immediate reaction was "She is so old!" followed quickly by "How could she be smiling right now?" As we sat down, I looked at her tensely, not knowing what to say. Merle said, "This is a very unusual situation." I still remember that phrase so vividly. It described the struggle we both felt in sitting down together – the fact that she wasn't my therapist, and my desperate need both to be there and not to be there, and my absolutely insurmountable grief that I couldn't possibly feel safe sharing with her. And yet she was immediately helpful because she validated my frustrating experience with Anita and filled me in on the details of Lily's illness and death. It was then that I'd learned that Lily had had lung cancer, which first appeared a year ago, when Lily and I had those three and a half months of phone sessions. Merle also knew that Lily had fully recovered from this bout and had stayed in remission for a full year. Then the cancer returned suddenly, and quickly metastasized. I later pieced together that when Lily called to cancel that Monday session, she was already in the hospital, having collapsed the day before.

Merle also told me that Lily had not told any of her clients about her illness because she had expected to heal from it and did not think that it was as severe as it was. Initially, this news felt validating – to learn that although Lily knew she was ill, she did not actually know she was dying. In retrospect, and after years of processing and reflection, I recognize that not sharing with her clients about her illness left a devastating mark on me. Lily's reasoning, Merle said, was that she fully believed she would heal, and she did not want to intrude into the work. However, the reality was that, even without talking about it, her illness was in the room: there were canceled sessions, phone sessions instead of in-person meetings; at times Lily would be pale, and for a few weeks she also had a severe rash on her forehead, which I later learned was the result of the chemotherapy drug she was taking. Even without talking about it, I knew something was very wrong. And because she had put such a moratorium on talking about it, I also unconsciously picked up on her message not to ask her about my perceptions.

After the first couple of sessions with Merle, I found myself feeling safe and supported – we were indeed a good fit. Despite my missing Lily immensely and not wanting to see another therapist, it was hard for me not to notice that Merle was excellent at what she did. We even connected on several things that seemed uncanny. We were both poets, and we both had an interest in spirituality and seemed to think in very similar ways. But, of course, throughout this entire time I continued to struggle with Merle and without Lily. Merle held my feelings, and often she brought up the most painful truth, a truth I could never fully commit to: that I unconsciously wished that Merle had been the one to die, not Lily. Lily was only fifty-six when she died, while Merle was sixty-eight when I began seeing her. How was that fair? To make matters even more complicated, a few years prior to Lily's death, Merle had had a metastatic cancer from which she had completely recovered. What was I getting myself into? How could I possibly allow myself to trust someone else who might die, and leave me in an absolute shambles again?

I was getting myself into a therapeutic relationship I couldn't bear to be in and couldn't bear to be without. I'd lost several family members previously, the first of whom was my grandfather, whose death was particularly traumatic for me because, when I was seventeen, I was the one who found his body. Several other deaths followed my grandfather's – each with its own rather predictable cycle of grief. But losing Lily was in a category of its own in terms of trauma, an entire world I couldn't really make sense of, and which, to this day, I continue to work through in ever-deepening ways.

Psychoanalysis was a revelation, validating and encouraging crucial parts of myself – my empathic nature, my deep psychological curiosity, my creativity – which had never been acknowledged, let alone encouraged, by anyone before. Lily was the first person to really see me, and transferentially she became the ideal mother, one whose presence I had to continually secure. Given all this, it makes sense why losing Lily was the worst thing that has ever happened to me. No one around me could fully comprehend why I was so shattered by the loss of a therapist. It's sad, to be sure, but when, say, your doctor dies, you send a card and then just find another doctor. But the way I came to articulate Lily's presence in my life was to liken her to a surrogate mother in relation to an orphaned child. I felt as if I was a starving infant who finally had a mother to nurse me, only to have that mother die while still holding me in her arms.

I grew up in the former Soviet Union, where everything was scarce. My father abandoned the family before I was one year old, and my mother raised me alone. As an infant, I was often left in my crib alone for hours while she stood in lines for milk and bread, or when she took a walk to the post office to make a phone call to her parents (that was the only phone in town). Given the scarcity of resources, including my mother's time and attention, I learned that the only sure way of getting her to pay attention to my experience was to be sick or suffering. For years, I would fake illness and even stage small accidents at home to get my mother to rush to my side and offer me what I dared not ask for directly.

In my work with Lily, this theme was very much present. I felt I had to be sick or suffering, "the scared, sick little girl," as I've come to articulate it. The session in which Lily told me that one needn't be suffering in order to remain in therapy was a revelation that still stands out in my memory. I'd been convinced that as soon as I felt better, Lily would decide that I was finished with therapy; and so in many unconscious and conscious ways I continually picked at myself and made sure I was suffering in some way in every session.

When Lily died, this theme continued in my relationship to her absence. As Merle and I worked through the grief, I found myself clinging to it, having the unconscious belief that if I suffered enough, Lily would somehow see it, have mercy on me, and return. I was the infant in the crib who still believed that screaming and nearly drowning in tears might eventually bring mommy back. I had several dreams throughout in which I would be aware that Lily was "back from being dead"; I might even get a glimpse of her before she would once again disappear, leaving me even more devastated. In many ways, I continued to grip tightly to the pain of Lily's absence as a way of trying to prove that I still needed her.

And in tandem with this unconscious dynamic was my ongoing relationship with Merle, whom I both needed and rejected. As someone who grew up to be a compliant little girl, I found myself being compliant with Merle as well – putting on a smile for most of our sessions for several years, even as I inwardly rejected many of the things she said to me. Seven years into our work, I was finally able to express this dynamic in a poem addressed to her:

Dear Merle,
I write to you in need of a mirror
A soft heart to land into
I long from you some hidden wisdom
An Oracle's answer to an unspeakable question
With careful words I link my statements
Those I know your mind can hold readily
Impotently aware that each letter is literally
A moment closer to each of our own deaths
Trapped within myself, I suffer dutifully
Muffling my screams and smiling
So contained, even in my struggle
I ensure you won't suffer on my behalf
My soul screams into these pages, however carefully
You hear it deeply and you tend to it
Pouring your entire soul toward me
But I fear I already know the unknown
I am exhausted by seven years of grief
A long, bitter winter I am loathe to release
My heart, once innocently eager
Now shielded and begs to undo unbearable truth.
I write to you in desperate need of a human
But I've yet to have the courage
To once again land,
In your, or anyone else's, soft heart.
Vanessa Hannah Bright September 18, 2017

During my first session with Merle, I shared with her that I was curious about learning more about psychoanalysis, and that when I had shared this desire with Lily, she had told me, "You're not ready." Because my transference to her had been so powerful, her words held even more power in her absence. However, in that first session, Merle said something truly amazing. She softened my focus from "becoming an analyst" to "If you're interested, why not take some courses?" In fact, she even seemed excited by my interest, which was very heartening for me, and lessened the pressure for the time being.

So, aside from my processing the most unbearable grief in that first year, I was also continually thinking about analytic training.

I struggled with the question of why I wanted to do it – was it only a way to stay close to Lily and the people who knew her? Or was it my genuine desire to learn about psychoanalytic work? I was struggling in my work as an acupuncturist, but didn't know if my struggles were related to the loss of Lily or to my desire to do something else.

Unable to answer these questions fully, I decided that I would enroll in the Institute for Expressive Analysis (IEA), from which Lily had graduated and where she had taught. I did research some other programs, but I could not see myself anywhere else, partly because of the institute's creative focus, and partly because it connected me to Lily. A year after her death, I began taking my first courses at IEA.

Studying psychoanalysis was fascinating and gave me so much joy that I continued taking courses for a year. At that point, I had a decision to make: would I start seeing clients and work toward my psychoanalytic license? Lily's words, "You're not ready," began to clamor loudly in my mind yet again. Taking this step toward beginning to see clients meant that I would now be an analyst myself, which brought me closer to Lily and raised the fear that I could never "fill her shoes."

In my continued exploration of this question with Merle, I realized that I used Lily's words as a way of holding on to her as the authority and to myself as the child. If I were to recognize my readiness, I would really lose Lily. Over time the question transcended this issue (especially once I started building up my caseload) and became the question of whether I'm "ready" to be an adult. I suppose I could also see that as the question of whether I'm ready for Merle to be my analyst. To actually "land" in Merle's office and heart would mean that Lily really was gone, a reality some part of me refuses to fully accept even to this day.

Her Death

Her death did not destroy my life
Although her presence was my grace
My path, so blindingly deformed
And I despise this naked place.

Her death did not destroy my heart
Although the nightmare's grimly real

My grief and longing so immense –
A cruel wound to have to heal.

Her death did not destroy my soul
Though through her light my own could glow
My faith – disfigured, overturned
A brutal, devastating blow.

Her death did not destroy my self
Her essence – human, soft, alive,
Her love so much a part of me
That I could lose her and survive.

> Vanessa Hannah Bright (Written four
> months after Lily's death.)

Merle Molofsky

In 2010, my dear friend, Lily, an accomplished psychoanalyst, died unexpectedly. Shortly thereafter, her analysand, Vanessa, called for a consultation. We began analytic work together. Vanessa was in profound mourning. Her analytic experience with Lily was life changing. She cherished the relationship. With dismay and grief she embarked on this second analysis, working with depth and insight. We faced the challenges of mutual mourning and analyzing the necessary complexities of transference and countertransference. Naturally, she had negative feelings about me. I was not her beloved lost object. As she mourned, we had to bring her ambivalent feelings to the forefront, and she discovered that perhaps I not only tolerated, but also understood and empathized with her negative feelings, her fantasy that she would willingly sacrifice my life if it would bring Lily back to life. During this odyssey we have taken together, Vanessa herself studied psychoanalysis, graduated from the same psychoanalytic institute where Lily had been a member, and became a New York State-licensed psychoanalyst. Today, her sensitivity and depth inform her clinical practice.

Our challenges were there from the beginning, and they continue. I have found a unique and unexpected beauty in these years during which we have worked together. The layers of deep feeling, the myriad revelations during our explorations, have enhanced and illuminated my understanding of the nature of the psychoanalytic dyad, of the psychoanalytic bond.

A challenge that appeared early, and continued to be an important issue, was Vanessa's concern that her grief and mourning would trigger my grief and mourning – that she would cause me pain by causing me to remember the loss of my friend. We focused on her need to mourn and to express her grief, and on related issues that arose for her regarding her concern for my feelings. Her concern was one link in a constellation of her feelings with which we continued to work. In addition to the connections she was discovering by working with this material, her loss had a life of its own and was inseparably tied to the reality that we shared – the reality that both of us had lost someone dear to us: Lily.

For Lily

For Lily – again.
Memories of your voice,
a purity of sound
your pleasure in sound,
memories of Lily
singing
still resound.
Memories of your chosen name,
Zohar, Radiance, celebrating
your joy of womanhood
as you dance across the stage,
memories of Lily
dancing,
dance through my dancing mind.
Visions of Lily: every encounter
for open-hearted Lily
in the street with a passing child,
a shop window kitten,
a tiny dog, a chunky shaggy dog,
a wagging dog tail,
charmed you, radiant Lily,
and your delight charmed

those who caught your flash
of eternal rediscovery
of creaturely sweetness.
I miss you – a raw statement
of simple words.
I will try to deserve your trust
when you told Vanessa my name.

Our mutual loss, our mutual grief, led to an important area of self-discovery for me as well. I have a complicated response to object loss and mourning. I feel the pain of the loss, but in a somewhat dissociated way, so that I don't always feel the full impact of irredeemable loss when someone I love dies. I eventually feel the grief, sometimes years later, but by then the distance from the event continues to protect me, much as my dissociation defense initially protected me. Therefore, I was able to assimilate whatever grief was evoked in me by Vanessa's inconsolable state and by her extreme grief, a grief that for her is still as intense as ever. I have been able to contain, and hold, and empathize with her intense emotion. In so doing, I had to process my own feelings, my own sense of profound loss, in order to truly empathize and identify with her. I had to let myself feel my loss in order to resonate with her loss. It has been an important experience for me.

When I was thirteen, my dearest friend, Mina, a girl my age, who was beautiful, talented, brilliant, and loving, died of leukemia. I didn't understand how someone so young, and so wonderful, and so important to me, could suddenly be gone – gone forever. Forever. What did forever mean? It was inconceivable. And yet it was an inescapable truth. Lily, like Mina, was a very close friend, beautiful, talented, brilliant, and loving. I admired Lily so much. She had a lovely singing voice, and was a skilled Middle Eastern dancer. The similarity was striking.

On this occasion I had to confront the reality without ignoring the meaning of "gone forever." And, in identifying and acknowledging my "talent" for dissociating, for being able to "bear the pain," I was truly able to grieve in my own way, to feel my own grief, my own pain. In so doing, I had to be able to readily welcome, hold, and contain whatever feelings Vanessa was bringing to session – whatever feelings Vanessa needed to feel, and explore, and process, in a safe space, in analysis with me.

In processing my grief, and welcoming Vanessa's need to process her grief, we both were able to continue to facilitate her separation-individuation challenges, which she had been analyzing so effectively with Lily as her analyst.

A second challenge was the one we identified early on, one that was so nuanced and complex that, as we dropped the theme and then picked it up again, it proved to have a number of aspects that allowed our therapeutic alliance to evolve precisely because we both found the courage to stay with the topic, and to explore newly emerging aspects of the topic – the fact that I was not Lily, and did not "work like Lily," did not say what Lily said, did not recognize themes that Vanessa and Lily had worked on together. Did that mean I was not as skilled as Lily, not as insightful, not as attuned?

I had to identify some of the issues for Vanessa, issues she was aware of, but did not want to bring up, because she was afraid of hurting me, of alienating me.

I realized I had to put into words the conscious fantasies and fears that Vanessa thought were unacceptable, dangerous, and "bad." To do that, I also had to process feelings that Vanessa thought I would have. I had to identify my feelings of competition with Lily, any sense of inadequacy I might have felt, the possibility of resenting either Lily or Vanessa, or both of them, and I had to find some resolution. I had to count on something I truly believe, something I have always counted on, that love is stronger than hate, that love is stronger than aggression. I truly believe that negative feelings toward a dearly loved person are natural, unavoidable, and perhaps even necessary, and indeed are a measure of the depth of love, that love indeed is of primary importance.

After processing my feelings, I could easily identify and articulate for Vanessa her negative feelings toward me, so that she could discover that I would not be overwhelmed, hurt, or destroyed by them. Yes, I would acknowledge; yes, I disappoint you when I don't know what Lily knew about you, when I don't offer the insights that Lily offered you.

I am a firm believer in the saying, "Three psychoanalysts, five opinions," and I offer that saying in many situations – teaching, supervising, and, sometimes, with some analysands – and, definitely, with Vanessa. I acknowledged her feelings, and did not "collapse" into feelings of inadequacy or despair. I affirmed that

I admired Lily's depth and insights, and that I trust my own depth and insights.

Vanessa did not want to devalue me. She acknowledged that she did indeed value me. And that she felt that she needed me. Since I was able to stay grounded in my own sense of competence as a psychoanalyst, I could readily receive, hold, contain Vanessa's complex and intense feelings and thoughts about my "not-Lily" analytic self. In so doing, we could continue to explore her feelings, her anxiety, about Lily's death.

Vanessa's fears that her dependence on Lily was connected in some way with Lily's death were the third challenge we faced regarding Vanessa's devastating loss. This is where we did necessary, deep analytic work. Of course, analytic work involves exploring feelings of guilt, feelings about a flawed self, based on early childhood experiences and fantasies. This is work an analytic dyad addresses. But the work is not often centered on the death of a beloved object, and rarely centered on the unusual circumstance of the death of a very specific object, a beloved analyst. Exploring issues of guilt, issues of a flawed self, is by its very nature painful. But it is searingly painful when it is focused on such a devastating loss.

Vanessa's depth, dedication, insight, intelligence, creativity, all were heightened by her courage. Writing this chapter is a celebration of her courage. It is truly an honor to work with her.

For Vanessa

> I followed you
> from smile to smile,
> word to word to word,
> almost tears to welling tears,
> from room to room
> in childhood far away
> in distant lands,
> from star to star
> and star to galaxy,
> discovering you
> each day anew
> within my heart.

You taught me to listen.
To learn to listen
once more.
To see beyond
the truth of your charm
and feel the truth
of how you learn
to feel what you know
you feel.
You never needed to create a self.
You are.

Inconsolable grief and recovery following the death of a young analyst

Chapter 5

Birth interrupted

Lynne Jacobs

I found out on a Saturday afternoon. The call came at 4:15 p.m., just moments after the commencement of the ground war in the Gulf. "Despina died this morning," said the voice. "She awoke in pain, and she was dead five minutes later." With the news of my analyst's death, the ground gave way.

Despina left work for the last time on January 17, 1991. She thought she had viral pneumonia, and had planned to return to work in a matter of days. Instead, she was diagnosed with lung cancer, and one month later she was dead, exactly three years after our first session. When I met Despina, I was immediately drawn to her warmth and emotional responsiveness. I came away from our first session confident in her sensitivity. Within the first year I was deeply immersed in a five-times-per-week analysis, which ultimately became a six-to-seven-session-per-week treatment.

I ostensibly came to Despina to overcome my writing inhibition, but the truth was that I painfully longed to be understood and accepted at a level that I had thought impossible. I felt as if I were living always behind a transparent wall with the world on the other side. I had thinned out the wall in a prior therapeutic treatment, and had even traveled to the other side, but only temporarily. In the past year I seemed to have slipped back into isolation. I was in a long-term relationship that was solid, but my gradual withdrawal was starting to create problems between my then partner (now husband) Gordon and me.

I had chosen to interview Despina after reading an article she had written on affects and self objects. I thought that if there was any hope for me at all it rested on a therapeutic relationship in which the exploration of affect and the therapist's attunement to me were central. The article's case examples made me believe that Despina would be tolerant of my depressive affects and prolonged bouts of despair.

In the course of our work together, my intense longing to be welcomed into an intimate bond with her became evident. I had difficulty becoming aware of and articulating my longing for her because I was so ashamed of my desire, considering it to be childish and self-centered. I feared that my desire and other aspects of my personality would be repulsive to Despina. I also feared that closeness to me would prove to be toxic to her. My longing for intimacy was therefore accompanied by excruciating fear, guilt, and shame.

I also had difficulty believing that my subjective world was real and worried that I was making up my painful feelings, perhaps to gain compassion. I tended to understate the intensity of my feelings and desires, fearing that I might be exaggerating. I felt despair over the impossibility of ever bringing my subjective world into my therapeutic treatment, and felt doomed to live a split existence, divided between functioning in the "outer world" and living in my isolated and unsharable inner world.

Despina's illness was a nightmare. I had returned from a two-week break during the Christmas holiday, eager to pick up the threads of our work. We had been on a roll recently, and I felt safe and bonded with Despina, who was supporting my delicate yet burgeoning sense of vitality. I had recently turned a corner in my analysis after living in a bleak hole for eighteen months during which I recognized and processed the serious deprivations I had suffered when young. I thought my depression would last forever, and that I would never be able to repair myself and live life joyfully. From October on, my depression had lessened considerably, and I felt the beginnings of optimism and confidence. It was as if Despina had breathed her life into me, although I was still unsure if it was enough to grow by. I felt a sense of awe but didn't want to jinx myself because feeling this way was too new to be taken for granted. I wanted to explore with Despina my sense of having turned a corner in the analysis, but we never got the chance.

Despina began missing sessions due to illness, and the focus of our analysis became my reactions to what were sudden, unexpected, and confusing separations. At first she was treated for bronchitis and for migraines. When her persistent cough did not abate, doctors took X-rays and diagnosed her with viral pneumonia. Although Despina kept saying she did not feel very ill, her condition deteriorated, and she missed more work.

I was feeling strong and told Despina that if she had to take time off because she was sick, it was coming at the least disruptive point in my treatment: I finally felt able to miss sessions without painful longings and grief. Yet her illness confused and frightened me because I could see that she was becoming sicker. I feared she would never be able to recover from a serious illness, that she would be permanently impaired both physically and emotionally.

A pattern emerged: we would work together for a few days and then she would miss a few days. The last day we met, a Friday, was the day after the air war against Iraq began. She told me that she would have to take the next day off for a diagnostic procedure. I was upset by the outbreak of war and by some recent events in my life, and I told her that I was scared and wished that she could hold my hand through this frightening period. The name of the diagnostic procedure, a bronchoscopy, made me wonder if they were looking for cancer, and I asked her why they were taking a tissue sample for pneumonia. Despina said they were trying to determine which fungus or bacteria was the culprit. I said no more, fearful of frightening her.

Despina reminded me she would return to work on Monday, but I was not convinced. I felt depressed and listless all weekend. She called on Sunday night to confirm that we would meet on Monday, and she told me that she hadn't had the bronchoscopy because she had taken aspirin in the morning, not knowing that meant the procedure could not be done. She said the doctors were now thinking they might not perform the procedure after all. She laughed about how she would be fine if the doctors would just leave her alone. I was confused because she sounded light and breezy, but was taking aspirin, presumably for pain. And it was very odd to me that she called to confirm our appointment, as if she were reassuring herself by calling to reassure me. Still, I was no longer concerned about cancer and dared to feel hopeful that our regular sessions would resume.

On Monday morning Despina left a message on my work phone: her doctors had told her to take the whole week off. If she felt better later in the week she might return sooner. She also said that she knew this would be unsettling for me and that if I wanted to talk with her I knew how to reach her. I felt crushed and panicky. Her message suggested that she was receptive to speaking with me, so I called her service at my first opportunity. Her service said she could not be reached. I left a message on her answering machine, which had an unusual and disconcerting message on it. Instead of the usual, "If you wish to speak with me, call my service," it said, "If this is an emergency you may call my service." I did not know if she would check her machine for messages. I felt lost.

Despina called me late Monday night and told me that her service had not been able to reach her because she had had a fever and a headache and had turned off her house phone. She chuckled and said that she did not do well with fevers. She made it sound like it was no big deal, and yet she had taken the unusual step of making herself unreachable. I was confused and deeply distressed. Despina emphasized that she was suffering from "a nasty virus" from which she would recover. I kept frantically repeating to her that I could not be reassured until she returned to work. I told her that nothing made sense to me, and that I was afraid of a permanent change. She asked, I thought incredulously, if I was afraid she would not return to work at all. I said "No," but in truth I did not know what to think. Her incredulity led me to doubt my fears. I could not conceive of her never returning to work, and yet I was distressed, panicked, and increasingly tormented by my confusion.

At one point she said, "We have never been through something like this together before!" which seemed like a peculiar statement: I knew Despina had never been seriously ill before in her life, so I thought she was reacting to the fact that she had never been through something like this. I was jarred by her statement, and my distress and confusion deepened. At the end of the conversation, she said she thought it was important that we stay in touch that week, and she asked if she should call me or let me call her. I told her that I would call if I needed further contact, that she was sick and should not be tying herself to the responsibility of calling me. I added that I hoped I would not need to be such a bother to her.

I shared my confusion about how to reach her, and she assured me she would check her office machine daily for messages. This was the last time we ever spoke.

I spent a sleepless night reviewing our conversation, struggling to understand my enormous distress. I realized that Despina's illness was evoking fears connected to my growing up with my alcoholic mother. I was afraid something was very wrong, yet my fear was denied. There was a discrepancy between certain behavioral clues and Despina's verbal reassurances. My mother's drinking had gone unacknowledged for years despite its deleterious impact on my family. My mother had insisted that we see her the way she wanted to be seen, and I had to disavow my own perceptions and experiences.

I discovered later, after Despina's death, that she had been alternating between periods of denial and periods of terror during this time. Yet I knew nothing other than that her manner with me was unusual, confusing, and belied my own perceptions and instincts. Given my tendency to doubt my own reality, I was thrown into an agony of self-doubt. I trusted Despina and wanted to believe her upbeat presentation, so I thought my discrepant ideas and feelings meant that I was being neurotic, difficult, childish, and selfish.

On Tuesday morning I left a tear-filled message on Despina's machine, telling her what I had realized during my restless night: that although I could not be reassured about her illness, I needed to be reassured that she would acknowledge the change that was taking place, and that we could work together to adapt to her changed circumstances. I feared an intolerable distance would grow between us if she attempted to hide or minimize the changes brought about by her sickness.

I waited all day for her reply phone call. I waited into the evening as well. The next day she was to undergo the rescheduled bronchoscopy, and I hoped against hope for a call in the morning before she left for the hospital. Still no call. I felt utterly bereft, abandoned, hurt, angry, and confused. This was so unlike Despina. Why had she volunteered to call me if she was not well enough to return a call? I wondered if she had taken a turn for the worse and had been taken to the hospital. I now also felt guilty and ashamed. Guilty that I was such a bother to her, that I hadn't withdrawn and left her alone while she dealt with her illness, and ashamed of my selfish inattention to her needs.

That evening her husband Julian called me to tell me that Despina had asked him to call and let me know that she had come through the procedure and that, although they had not found the source of the problem, they had not found cancer. He sounded exhausted and emotionally drained. I could not stop myself from asking if he knew anything about why Despina might not have returned a call I made to her yesterday. I hated myself for asking, but was desperate to know what had happened. He said he thought she might have been preoccupied and anxious about today's procedure, and that although she had not said anything directly about it, he thought she would call me as soon as she felt better. Despina had never mentioned the prospect of cancer, but since Julian mentioned it twice, it was clearly a concern.

I continued to wait. The unreturned phone call loomed large in my consciousness. It had taken on tremendous symbolic power. If she didn't call, it meant the worst had happened: she was too ill and would never return to work – my world was irrevocably shattered. If she returned my call, I knew things would be all right. My entire fate seemed to rest on the single act of calling. Thoughts of Despina dominated my mind day and night already, but now my consciousness narrowed, focusing solely on the phone call. What could it possibly mean that it remained unanswered? All day Thursday, I waited for her call. Every time my phone rang, I hoped it was her. That evening, a colleague told me that Julian had canceled his study group. Despina was feeling poorly and Julian did not want to leave her alone. I was frantic with worry, and my constant and tormenting confusion intensified. Throughout the next week, I felt even more confused, tormented, lost, and alone. When I was not anxious and crying, I was listless and depressed.

On Friday morning I called the psychologist who was covering for Despina during her illness. Colleen returned my call promptly, which was somewhat comforting for me. I was so distressed that I found myself crying as I reached out to this person whom I did not even know. I said that I was guessing that Despina would not be well enough to return to work next week, and I wondered about setting up a meeting with Colleen to talk about my concerns. Colleen asked, with what seemed like a mixture of surprise and caution in her voice, "What makes you think she won't be in?" She seemed relieved when I told her that Julian canceled last night's group. I felt like she was worried I had found out something she did not want me to know. My dread deepened. She then suggested we meet the following week.

Colleen called on Saturday night and left a message that Despina would not return to work for two or three weeks. That Colleen, not Despina, called me was more evidence that she was very seriously ill. Incredibly, I was still clinging to hopes that she just had pneumonia. Even though I am pretty sure I knew better by then, in my heart I was still waiting for a return call from Despina.

I saw Colleen a few times. In those sessions I asked for health reports, told her I was afraid, and sought and received validation that my fear was understandable, especially because – at least as far as I knew – a definitive diagnosis had not been established. I was concerned that Despina was gravely ill and might die before anyone found the source of her illness! My sessions with Colleen are blurry. I remember asking what conversations she and Despina had about me; I was hungry for any feeling of contact, however indirect, between Despina and me. I felt like a young and bereft child asking if my mother remembered me.

Colleen told me during our first session, "Despina said to tell you that you are in good hands," but her message felt vague and general, and failed to reference my message to Despina. Colleen's statement disturbed me. How could I be in good hands with anyone other than Despina? I waited for Colleen to follow her statement with the question Despina would have asked: "How do you feel about what I just said?" Then I could have said what I felt, namely that I was gratified by Colleen's generous spirit towards me, but could not imagine anyone else's hands being good enough right now! But Colleen did not ask the question. I assumed – without checking – that Colleen wanted me to believe her statement without question.

My reaction to Colleen's message from Despina turned out to be paradigmatic of my experience of working with Colleen. I had two competing sets of reactions to her: I was extremely grateful for how much she went beyond the call of duty to respond to my phone calls, to set up appointments, and to keep me apprised of Despina's condition, yet I found my actual meetings with her difficult. I needed

Colleen to be Despina. Despina had encouraged me always to speak about my fears, disappointments, and hurts within the transference. She would not have made a bold statement about herself without making room for me to disagree. Despina was always on the alert for the smallest sign that I was thrown by her mis-attunement to me, and she made sure to help me elaborate fully my perspectives and perceptions.

Colleen's approach was different, yet I was trying to go on with her as if she were like Despina. She often suggested alternatives to how I experienced things, hoping that her efforts to offer me other perspectives would give me something to hold on to. Unfortunately, her efforts often left me feeling stung and ashamed, primarily because her comments were so different from what I was used to and from what I was trying to recreate. Not only was there a mismatch in our styles, but I think I believed that if I could just talk to Colleen in the same way as I had talked to Despina, then Despina would live. I suspect that there was no way for me to experience Colleen as helpful, yet neither of us was able to interpret these elements of our relationship.

Two weeks after Julian called to tell me of Despina's bronchoscopy, he called again to tell me that she had been diagnosed with lung cancer. He said that the doctors were optimistic about her recovery. They would treat her with a combination of chemotherapy and radiation, and she expected to return to work in one or two months. My heart ached for all three of us, Despina, Julian, and me. Through my tears of shock, pain, and fear, I looked up lung cancer in materials I had at home and saw that her prognosis was terrible!

I called Colleen, who was also in tears, and I raged against the ravages Despina would now suffer. I asked why chemotherapy and radiation were being used rather than surgery. "These are not the treatment of choice!" I exclaimed. "There must be metastasis." She reluctantly said there was. I said that this meant they could not really get rid of Despina's cancer, to which Colleen said she could go into remission. I protested, "But for how long?" Colleen paused, and said softly, "Well, no one can say. But she is young, strong, and the doctors are optimistic." I said that I needed to find out more information and would go to the library. Colleen blurted out strongly, "Don't believe the statistics you find! The doctors are optimistic." My stomach turned over, and I suspected that I was not being told the truth.

I arranged to see Colleen the next evening. She extended her workday to accommodate me, which was typical of her responsiveness. She always returned calls promptly, and if I needed to see her, she arranged it. Gordon drove me to the session because I was too distraught to be trusted behind the wheel of a car.

The day after Julian called me, I called the National Cancer Institute, and the person I spoke to promised to send me information. I also spoke with someone on the information hotline. From the information that I was able to piece together, it seemed that Despina already had aggressive stage 4 lung cancer, and that she could not be expected to live very long. I wished I knew who and what to believe. My best guess was that Despina was deathly ill. Colleen said the doctors were optimistic. Were they lying? Was she lying? I wished I could talk with them. Maybe they were trying some experimental drugs. Maybe Despina's youth – she was only thirty-three – really was a factor. These thoughts took their place alongside my other preoccupations: the phone call and, now, the haunting images of Despina's suffering.

Colleen was in a terrible position. I found out several months later that Julian had asked her to conceal information about the severity of Despina's illness from her patients and from Despina herself. He wanted Despina and everyone else to believe that the treatment would give her many more years of life. Yet I had been confronting Colleen with my awareness that more was going on than I was being told. She had decided it was best to confirm whatever information I came upon that was accurate without volunteering more. She answered my questions about Despina's illness as honestly as she dared, confirming my belief that there was metastasis. I was stunned, reeling, and I hurt all over, for Despina and for me. Her illness up until this point had been frightening and disruptive, but now I felt like I was living in a nightmare. I vacillated between feeling haunted and terrified by images of her suffering and my attempts to feel hopeful. I felt like a traitor when I was frightened and pessimistic. I did not sleep for several nights. Colleen told me to write down the thoughts I had while I lay awake at night so that we could discuss them. Just that suggestion helped me to feel a bit calmer because it was a task I could do despite the haze caused by my terror. I wrote of my dread of falling with no net. With Despina around, no matter how deep my despair, I felt like she was a hand underneath me. Now that hand was gone, and I was afraid that, if I gave in to my feelings, I would become immobilized with depression, as I had been in the past. I felt swept over by pain – cut off, not knowing if or when things would ever return to normal. With no access to Despina, I felt abandoned. I also feared that Colleen would protect Despina by pushing me away, that she would demean me in conversations with Despina and find my neediness contemptible, angered by my inability to adapt more gracefully to Despina's illness.

I was perpetually haunted at night by images of Despina's suffering and misery. I envisioned her tearful with discouragement and discomfort, frightened by the degree to which her life had been torn apart. I could not get the images out of my mind, for they seemed more real to me than actual physical presences. Every now and then, seemingly unendurable waves of desperate longing to be in touch with Despina would hit me. At these times I could not bear the slow passage of time. I would think:

> If only I could know that Despina got my last message and understands my fear. Can she convey a message to me through Colleen that demonstrates that she knows she did not respond to my last message, knows that she left me hanging, knows of my concern that she will act like nothing has happened?

These thoughts cycled over and over and over again, with me compulsively wondering if there was a way.

And I kept waiting for Despina's message to me, either by phone or through Colleen, saying that she was too ill to respond. Would she call when she felt better, knowing I was still waiting for a response? Or would she call only to announce she was returning to work, saving the rest of her comments for when we met in person? I waited with baited breath, needing more than anything to be released from the agony of waiting.

In our next few meetings, Colleen and I discussed my fears and concerns, but I came away from our sessions believing that she was uncomfortable with my pessimism and deep grief. I was used to exploration that focused on helping me to elaborate on and experience more fully my own perceptions and states of mind, but she seemed to be challenging me to change what I thought and felt. Her confrontations made me thoroughly doubt my instincts. Between my self-blame and fervent desire to believe the doctors' optimism, I devoted myself to trying to convince myself to be optimistic. And yet, my nagging suspicion that Colleen needed me to be optimistic to serve her and Despina's needs never left me. Within a week or so, I added other obsessive concerns to my list: What will happen when Despina returns? Will she be ill, trying to work yet needing to terminate before she becomes too ill again? If she returns not fully knowing the state of her health, how could we work in such limbo? I also knew I would feel uncomfortable speaking about my own future when hers had seemingly been so cruelly snatched from her. Wounds from my childhood paled against the backdrop of Despina's current struggle. Could I trust Despina to be honest with me about her physical and mental state? Dare I insist on honesty if she needs to feel hopeful? What will happen to my terror and despair in the face of her possible denial?

I became conflicted about what to do and where to turn. On the one hand, I wanted to stay close to Colleen because she was optimistic, assuring me that Despina would return to work. It was an antidote to the dire information I was discovering in my own research. She was also my only source of information regarding Despina's condition. On the other hand, I felt abandoned by her when I revealed my worst fears, and I felt guilty for and ashamed of being such a pessimist. I began to think of calling a different analyst, one who was not so closely involved with Despina.

I felt like a fish that had been tossed out of the ocean. I thought of all of us patients as having been tossed onto the beach. We were all squirming and bouncing around, seeking shallows to rest in until the tide returned. But we had no way of knowing when or even if the tide would come back. And the shallows were uncomfortable, cold, small, precarious – and now the shallow I was in was no longer sufficient, yet I had no confidence that I could find another that would serve me any better.

My decision to call a different therapist was made during a session with Colleen in which she described to me the relaxation exercises that Despina was doing with Colleen's assistance. During a recent meditation, Despina had exclaimed that she felt deeply peaceful, more than she had ever felt. Colleen marveled at Despina's capacity to relax so thoroughly in the face of her suffering and terror, but when I heard what Colleen said, my heart sank: the story communicated to me that Despina was close to death and that she had begun to retreat from the world. Colleen's delight at the story made me sick with lonely despair. I also felt sick with self-hatred for being so alarmist and pessimistic. Instead of telling Colleen that I was horrified by the story, I merely retreated. Ever since our first meeting, when Colleen didn't ask me about my reaction to Despina's message, I was unable to test Colleen and see if she could tolerate if I had a different reaction from the one I thought she wished me to have.

I hesitated in reaching for the phone to call Pamela, another therapist, afraid and disgusted with myself for seeking so much help. Yet my desperation overrode my disgust, and after dialing and hanging up three times, I stayed on the line long enough to leave a message. I knew Pamela from a workshop she had conducted a few years earlier, and I had liked her gentle manner and dedication to listening from an empathic perspective. I scheduled a double session so that I could both explain what my analysis meant to me and tell her about my experiences with Colleen. I hoped she could help me to assess if I should stay with Colleen, switch to an interim therapist, or wait for Despina's return. I told Pamela about my obsession with the unreturned call, and about how disappointed I felt when Colleen commented, "You sound like she is dead already!"

Pamela said quickly, "But she was dead to you – by not returning the call!" I felt relieved because Pamela immediately perceived something that I had been unable to convey to Colleen. I needed someone to understand the terrible limbo I was living in. At the session's end, I again felt relieved when Pamela said that she was glad I had called her. Her bold statements, while certainly unorthodox, reassured me because she communicated that she could listen to me without feeling invested in what my experience ought to be.

My next session with Pamela was filled with my anguish: everything had changed, and I knew continuing to work with Despina as if nothing happened was impossible. I wanted the chance to be in her presence again, to lie on her couch and feel held by her seemingly perfect attunement, yet I also wanted to give her the gift of my love. If she wanted to work, if working could bring her hope and inspiration, then my gift could be to let her be my analyst, to be her patient as fully as possible. I felt so full of love for her, and also kicked in the stomach because I realized that the honesty that had characterized our relationship would be untenable now. There was no good resolution.

The evening before Despina died I was at dinner with some friends and, despite that day's heartening health update from Colleen, I was jarred when, for a brief second, my friends' faces all turned to skulls. A moment later, their faces appeared normal, but I was thoroughly shaken. The next morning, less than a week after my first appointment with Pamela, Despina died. I had woken that morning filled with dread: something was terribly wrong – like a light had gone out in my universe. She died at about the same time I roused myself from bed to call Colleen, apologizing for bothering her again, knowing that just two days ago she had told me that Despina seemed to be feeling better.

Despina's memorial was a week later. Her patients were invited, and Colleen's eulogy mentioned the primary place Despina's patients had in her life. I was grateful that she recognized us patients, especially because I felt so adrift as I sat among people who had known her as family, friends, and colleagues. As a patient, I felt set apart from the community of mourners, with whom she had a more public relationship. Other people could trade stories and recall with each other shared times that they spent with Despina, but my relationship with her was entirely private. Not only was there no one who had witnessed my place in her heart, but also no one had witnessed the me who had emerged in Despina's presence. It was a me that I had not yet consolidated, and now my only witness was dead.

In the week between Despina's death and her memorial service, I obtained permission to visit her office one more time, something for which I am also very grateful. Colleen carefully emptied the office of confidential material, but otherwise left it intact for me.

I took with me a photograph of Despina that Julian had given me, placed her photo in her chair, and sat on the floor sobbing. I looked around trying to commit every corner of her room to memory. I tried to invoke her voice. I felt as if I were clawing at the air in the room in an effort to find her just one more time. I had collected during the previous year many of her return phone messages to me so that I could use her voice as an anchor during the most distressing and disorganized phase of my analysis. I am still so glad that I gave into what was, at that time, a shameful desire. I cherish my record of her voice, a bit of a record of our work together.

I continued meeting with Pamela, just trying to hold on until I could catch my breath and seek another analyst. In the session after Despina died, I thought I had run over my allotted time, and as I stood to leave, my knees buckled. I felt Pamela's hand on my back, steadying me so I did not fall. This gesture came to symbolize Pamela's supportive participation in my grieving. She witnessed me utterly shattered and torn open, awash in inconsolable grief for the worst loss I had ever suffered. My analysis had been my only hope for escape from the undertow of isolation and devitalization against which I swam throughout my entire life. Despina was the one person who I believed could breathe life into my dusty soul. I despaired over the prospect of finding another analyst who could pick up the threads and continue with me the journey that Despina and I had started. And yet I knew I needed to be in analysis because I was so utterly devastated and lost.

My sessions with Pamela were filled with moments of acute grief, tales of my analysis with Despina, links we made between a particular moment of grief and the loss of a particular facet of my relationship with Despina, and how my current relationship with Pamela either supported or interfered with my ability to bear my grief. Analyzing how Pamela and I were working together was essential for me because it provided me with hope that my analysis could continue. I began to experience again the analytic approach with which I was familiar and still very much needed. Although I had known that Colleen worked differently from Despina, the difference had been so jarring and shaming to me that I practically cried with relief when Pamela invited me to explore how she was affecting me.

In one session about three weeks after Despina died, I told Pamela that I had been barely able to get out of bed that morning, and that when I was deeply depressed and unable to rise during my analysis with Despina, I would comfort myself with the prospect of getting to my office, leaving a message on Despina's answering machine, and receiving her return message. For many years before my treatment, I had felt that I was waking each day in a two-dimensional world, like a cardboard box that lay flat and unassembled. It would take a great effort to experience the world as three-dimensional and able to hold me. With Despina gone, I could not soothe myself with thoughts of calling her. Being awake was horrible and being asleep was wretched – there was simply no escape. In that session, I sank into an immobilized silence, and Pamela spoke softly to me, drawing me out. She gasped quietly as I described my struggle to resist a strong inertial pull towards non-being and asked me if I had needed something from her yesterday that she had not provided. She said she was prepared to come in every day, if need be, in order to help me through this overwhelming crisis. My immobility suggested to Pamela that something was amiss, and I realized that I felt torn about leaning on her with the full weight of my grief. I wondered if I would be taking advantage of her, and she conveyed directly her interest in being with me in the depths of my grief, wherever that took us.

Pamela commented at one point on the extraordinary analysis I had had with Despina. I appreciated her words, but felt dismayed; it was as if she were saying that I could not expect to find what I needed in an analysis with someone else. I could be honest with her about my reaction and share my fear that without Despina's extraordinary capacity for affective attunement, I would be lost. That fear haunted me. Pamela and I struggled to find words and images for the intense loss I felt: Was it like losing a mother, friend, and analyst all in one? When I told Pamela about my going back to work right after Despina died, she exclaimed, "You were pushing yourself too much. You had just lost the most important person in your life!" We were both taken aback by her statement, and sat awe-struck, silenced by the truth she had uttered. I was acutely aware that Despina's husband would spend the rest of his life without his wife, while the external conditions of my life were not changed by her death. Yet Despina lived in my world in a special place, unlike any other. In some ways, she inhabited the most important place of all.

I spoke to Pamela of the shame and embarrassment I felt about needing Despina so much, confiding that I never fully understood my utter dependency. Pamela thought that I had lost Despina before my own understanding of and trust in my experiences with her were fully consolidated. Her perspective grounded me, providing me with a metaphoric rock to stand on while the torrents of grief, shame, and doubt stormed and swirled around me.

Having no community of mourners with whom I could grieve made Despina's death even harder. I think grief requires community. Despite the loving and sensitive support of people around me, including Pamela and my subsequent analyst, I do not think my healing would have been complete without having been able to share stories with a fellow patient, whom I had the good fortune to become friends with many months after Despina had died. We both had access to a particular side of Despina and shared an understanding of her that needed no explanations.

I also feel gratitude for the people in Despina's analytic community who made themselves available to me and provided me with a semblance of community. People who knew me called to offer condolences. I had one accidental communication with Despina's analyst, whom I had met prior to Despina's illness. He called my home to speak with Gordon about a professional matter, but Gordon was not home, and I answered the phone. I lingered, at a loss for words, when I realized who the caller was, and he offered his condolences, as I did to him. He said that it must have been difficult and confusing for me to have been misled, given how attuned to Despina I was. What a strangely consoling statement! I so wanted to ask him what he meant by "misled," but I thought that if I questioned him I might embarrass this kind man, who had dared to say more than he should have. Instead, I acted as if I already knew that I had been misled, commenting, "Yes, it was crazy-making, and I thought my pessimism was toxic to Despina. I felt wretched." After a few more heart-broken words, we hung up.

His comment confirmed for me that my sense of disjunction was valid. I was not crazy. I sought to ascertain what actually happened so that I could weave a coherent story and thereby gain a feeling of resolution. I felt more optimistic that I could begin to regain my sense of sanity. Despina's analyst's statement also conveyed that Despina had spoken of me and my perceptive attunement to her states of mind. I experienced pleasant fantasies of stories she might have told him. It also made me feel that my relationship with Despina was a bit less isolated from my regular world because someone had his own sense of her and me in a relationship. I felt consoled knowing that her husband had a sense of my relationship with her. Thank heavens Despina broke confidentiality enough to give me the comfort of knowing that a few people in the world had a picture of her and me together!

I came to appreciate how another person's perception of my world strengthens my own sense of reality, making it more substantial by sharing it with me rather than leaving it in my private experiential realm, where I inevitably question its validity. About one month after Despina died, I gave Pamela a letter I had written to Despina after a summer separation. I felt that if Pamela read it, all that had transpired in my and Despina's private relationship would not disappear, as Despina had.

I soon understood better my obsessive and complicated feelings about my unreturned phone call to Despina, realizing that when she spoke with me that Monday evening, promising me a phone call the next day if needed, she was no longer able to function as my analyst, despite her desire to do so. Tension began to leave my body as I realized, with enormous sadness, that she could not possibly have returned my message because she was gone in relation to me on Monday night. I am embarrassed to admit that I felt abandoned, angry, and betrayed by Despina and by everyone else who was part of the deception. Her needs had prevented mine from being fulfilled. And yet my anger and disappointment only triggered in me greater shame and guilt because I knew she had done the best she could in a terrifying situation. Over the next month Pamela helped me to feel more confident that my analytic project had not died with Despina. I decided to seek a male analyst because I worried that with a female I would constantly search for Despina.

In one of my last sessions with Pamela, I bemoaned starting anew. I was wracked by questions like, "Who can love me and welcome my needs as Despina did?" I had never felt pressure from Despina to be any different than how I was, even when my state of mind felt terribly shameful. I could not imagine anyone else having the grace that she showed towards my most ragged edges. I felt bleak, desolate, and un-held now that Despina was dead. I lapsed into another silence and eventually commented that my silence expressed desolation beyond words. After another silence, Pamela spoke of an infant in a crib who lets out only one tiny whimper, and of how she would want to go into the room to pick up and hold the baby. I felt the aptness of Pamela's description, and asked her how she knew to pick the baby up? She said that the baby was too silent. I was moved by her understanding that my silence was a statement of misery. In that moment, I felt both reassured that another analyst might struggle to know me as Despina had. I felt a sharp pang of missing Despina. I could hear her say, "Oh, I think of a baby in a crib, lying silently. It needs me to come and lovingly pick it up and comfort it." I was tormented by how much I missed Despina. I would never experience again her emotional expressiveness, hear her voice, or feel her tender and intense engage-ment. I was grief-stricken but grateful to Pamela, for I seemed to be back on track, not numb or desolate, but alive in my mourning.

In the next session I told Pamela how much I appreciated her help. Her connection to my silence brought my grief into contact with a living world, diminishing the wretchedness of disconnection that still threatened me. I felt more optimistic about reengaging in an analytic process and had gained perspective on my current-day life. I talked sadly about how Julian had expected Despina to be central to him for the rest of his life, whereas she would probably have been central to me for only a few more years. I could also see that I was beginning to make a distinction between losing my ana-lysis, which I now believed I could regain, and losing Despina, with her particular beloved qualities. Although Pamela cautioned me about starting my search while I was still so unsteady, and I had already begun to dread wrenching myself away from her, I did not want to deepen our explorations further because I knew it was time for me to find my next analytic home.

Chapter 6

Re-finding a way

Lynne Jacobs

When I told my story to Richard, through racking sobs, he said with feeling, "What a nightmare!" I found his reaction reassuring because he seemed so involved and attuned. Like Despina, Richard was emotionally expressive, and he attended to small changes in my psychic states, to his impact on me, and to my need for and fear of him.

The night after our first session, I dreamt that Richard was "Mr. Death." He was shadowing Despina, following closely in her footsteps. I watched with horror because Despina seemed unaware of what was transpiring, and yet I knew she was going to die and be replaced by Richard. I reacted to the dream with calmness, not horror, perhaps ready for Richard to step in now that Despina was truly gone.

For the first two weeks of my new analysis I cried at times with a combination of grief and fear that shook my body and choked my words; at other times, I sat mutely, feeling a bleak misery that was beyond words. At the beginning of the third week, the two-month anniversary of Despina's death, I dreamt I was a soldier in Vietnam. Rain was pouring down on my head, which was bowed as I slogged slowly through deep mud. My entire consciousness was focused in the dream on the misery of rain on my head and my feet in the mud. I had a vague sense of badness in the dream, of guilt, shame, and complicity in a terrible sham. As Richard and I explored the dream, I suggested that I had lost sight of the purpose of my analysis and was, instead, drowning in grief. Yet I also thought the dream might be an expression of something connected to my analysis with Richard. As I began to immerse myself in this new analysis, I felt afraid of once again becoming preoccupied with analysis and of losing the vibrancy of my lived world. With Despina, I had seemed to live for a long stretch of time only for the chance to be around her – barely hanging on during the interminable spaces between our sessions. My life seemed meaningful solely as experiences that I could tell Despina, and I reveled in the feeling that events in my life no longer stood apart: they gained importance when I shared them with Despina.

I had rarely cried in my analysis with Despina. Tears seemed to imply relatedness, and for me relatedness was not a given. Now that Despina had died, I could not stop crying. I felt terribly ashamed of how dependent I had been on her, and that I was once again forming an intense bond with another analyst. I was petrified that Richard would disdain my neediness while I, again, would become preoccupied with and increasingly dependent on my analysis.

Richard and I explored at length my feeling that I had somehow participated in something "dirty" in relation to Despina's illness. I realized that I felt guilty and ashamed because of my focus on the unanswered phone call, which had come to symbolize my loss of connection to Despina, and because of other "selfish" needs. I also felt I had participated in a charade when I tailored my words for Colleen's benefit and engaged in mind-bending denial in a desperate attempt to keep my connection with Colleen, who I had assumed wanted me to remain hopeful about Despina's health. Richard asked if I was being honest with him, and I told him about my sad realization that he seemed guarded with himself and less likely to feel the fierce commitment to me that I had sensed Despina felt; I believed she loved me from the bottom of her heart.

My loss of Despina permeated my new analysis. When she had been dead ten weeks, I felt like I was being dropped into an abyss when Richard told me he was leaving town to attend an APA convention. The pleasure he said he felt in working with me only caused me concern because I feared I might lose him when I became more difficult, unrewarding, and not pleasurable. I couldn't withstand being robbed of that kind of interest again. Richard reassured me when he linked his current leave-taking with Despina's death and commented on my expectation that he, too, would withdraw from me. I had feared that he wasn't keeping in mind my overwhelming grief, and perhaps felt I should be better by then.

Richard wondered if my need for his emotional presence came from a need to know that he was really there, which spurred me to describe an aspect of my history to him, which I rarely had done. It triggered within me terrible grief: all the ground that Despina and I had covered had been left hanging as if in mid-air and was still unassimilated. I wished Richard could watch a movie of my and Despina's work together, so that I did not have to tell him story upon story of my work with her. I feared that the countless stories would harm my newly forming relationship with Richard by some-how feeding off my relationship with Despina, yet I wanted him to help me assimilate my experiences with her. I was terrified that I would lose my sense of Despina if I could not make those experiences truly my own.

Through tears I told Richard that one of my quandaries was whether to tell him my original stories, which minimized my struggles, or to tell him the stories that Despina and I had developed, which I was not sure were really true. I worried that he might not respond in the way I needed him to respond, which would mean that I would have to go back into hiding.

Richard suggested during this session that I consider seeing Pamela while he was gone. I had wanted to scream to him,

> You don't understand! I don't want to see anyone else when you are gone. I have bounced around, told my story to three different people since January. I want to stay with you. I want to suffer while you are gone, if I must, and deal with it with you!

Richard understood immediately that I did not need relief from my suffering, but wanted a particular other person with whom I could suffer, and he was that person now.

I sobbed tears of fear and grief, feeling that the loss of Despina meant the loss of my inner reality as well. Richard asked about the physical sensations of my grief as he noticed me struggling for breath. I told him I felt like my chest had been ripped apart and was hanging open with blood, muscle, and bone dangling raggedly. He suggested that if Despina had helped me to flesh myself out so that I was no longer a "ribbon person" (i.e., a person with no substance, who appeared in a sketch I had showed him), then parts of me were torn away when she died, as if my inner world, which I had finally been able to share with her, had either been buried with her or brutally shoved back inside of me and made unreal once again. Richard seemed moved by what I said during this session, and we both recognized how important it was for me to feel that he was affected by me, so that I did not feel like a ribbon person; it seemed that if he could feel the emotional weight of my experiences, they could again become real for me.

I broke down, crying that Despina had died too soon, and now Richard was leaving too soon, too: fear, pain, and feelings of excruciating loss were coming in almost unbearable waves. I was on a roller coaster, and a new wave of grief came with every meaningful exchange between Richard and me. I was flung between extremes of hopefulness and devastation, and this roller coaster ride lasted many months.

Richard and I confronted innumerable times an inevitable and ever-present problem: he was without doubt my second-choice analyst. Yet Richard handled his second-place status with remarkable graciousness, humility, and generosity. He focused on supporting me to articulate my losses, however they took shape and as fully as possible. He was ever cautious during our first few years not to say anything that I might construe as pressure to feel (as he presumably felt) that I could survive my losses and benefit from analysis with him. We were necessarily negotiating rapidly shifting configurations: at one moment I needed a clear signal from him that he welcomed my most disheveled and grief-stricken yet tentatively hopeful self, while at another moment I needed his open-hearted validation of the enormity of my loss of someone who could not be replaced and had no equal, a loss that might leave me forever shattered.

I knew that Richard had seen Despina present her work and had participated in clinical discussions with her. He quite openly admired her evident talent for on-going attunement and empathy. His separate experience of her was confirming to me because it made me feel like he knew what I had lost. For a long time, I was afraid that I still needed the degree of attuned listening that Despina had provided. I believed I would have to make do with Richard, who could only help me to build scaffolding on top of an already severely cracked foundation. But Richard was particularly alert for moments when he thought I was trying to accommodate what I perceived as his limitations. He often used my mood and my dreams to look for my subtle accommodations to what I perceived as his limits. I told him he was only "episodically attuned," which eventually became a sweet joke between us. Initially I did not believe that Richard could care for me in the way I needed, commenting to him that I had great confidence in his ability to respond to me with sensitivity after he dropped me, yet I was concerned that if I landed on my head and shattered my skull, it would be too late! Eventually, I came to feel that Richard's commitment to acknowledging and exploring the meanings of his failures at attunement provided a holding environment that was "good enough" for me.

Richard told me a year into my treatment with him that he was glad that I had had a prior analysis with Despina; he admitted that he may not have been able to hold me in the way I initially needed to be held. During my treatment with Despina, I felt like I had a "fetal self," a self that had not quite finished being born when Despina died, but which could now breathe on its own. Because I had achieved this, I could work with Richard despite never feeling the seamless and total molding around my body that I had felt with Despina, as if she held me so utterly that even air gaps could not exist between us. I felt like I had been torn from her womb, and landed like an infant kangaroo in his open pouch. The distance from her womb to his pouch felt like an awful abyss.

With Richard, I also confronted my feelings of disappointment with Despina, who I felt had swept me into her denial. I had a picture of Despina, which she gave to me after I had asked Colleen if it would be possible to get one. While feeling at the time that my request was monstrous, I treasure the photo. Despina signed the back of the photo and wrote, "I'll be back, better than ever." It had broken my heart to see that note because it was so far from any imaginable reality. The pressure on me from both Despina and others to deny the severity of her illness felt like a horrifying repetition of a childhood filled with the denial of my mother's illness, and my participation in the pretense with Despina remained a great source of anguish and shame for years to come.

Navigating a new treatment after Despina's death was often fraught. I felt intensely needy and was terrified that no matter how hard he tried, Richard could not provide me with the perfectly attuned holding I so desperately sought. I often felt bereft and forlorn at a session's end, especially when it was the last session of the week, and I then felt heavy with despair, knowing that I would not get the emotional holding I still needed, much to my shame. I told Richard one day that I could act like I was getting better, but worried that if I did that I would move forward as an empty shell. I did not want to be dead but felt deadness creeping into me. This was different – more final – than being "un-alive," the feeling I had had in treatment with Despina before she helped my un-alive fetus to be born. In order to continue living, my fetus-self now needed proper and constant holding or it could die, just like Despina.

During that period, I felt in shock and kept expecting to wake up from my nightmare. I experienced stabs of searing pain when I woke in the morning and realized that this was my actual life, not a dream. Occasionally I became afraid of Richard because of his mis-attunements, and I consoled myself with the thought that I would soon feel safe lying on Despina's couch; but then reality crashed upon me with a sudden thud, and I remembered that Despina was dead.

In sessions with Richard, I felt held by him in my grief, and yet I was never secure in the solidity of our connection. Did he not know that babies had to be held in special ways? That babies had to be set down gently or sometimes not at all? I worried about the depth of his understanding of me and about his seeming inability to stay consistently attuned to me. I told him how Pamela knew that when I was too silent it meant that I needed to be "held," and Richard came to understand that my silence signaled intense feelings of alienation and misery, feelings that Despina had welcomed and bore. He became a witness of my treatment with Despina, recognizing how she held me "just right," knowing when I could not articulate what I needed to say, and sticking with me until I felt the sense of attuned togetherness I needed to feel safe.

In retrospect, I know it must have been hard for Richard – filling the shoes of an idealized dead analyst is no easy feat. Yet he did not shy away from asserting his differences from Despina, telling me directly that my silence signaled to him something different from alienation and despair, and that he believed babies move between different states – they whimper, fall silent, feel despair, make do, etc. – and the person holding the baby learns if he is doing it correctly through an interactive relationship with the baby itself. I was moved by Richard's finely attuned attentiveness to my silence, but I also lamented that he referred to "the person," rather than to himself. Was he reluctant to personally hold me? His distancing language upset me, but I appreciated our ability to have these honest exchanges.

The relationship between Richard and me went through many ruptures and repairs. For example, I left on a Friday in tears, desperate for his acknowledgment that he knew I felt dropped at each week's end. I assumed his silence meant that he did not want me to be so reliant on him. I then mustered up the courage to tell him about my experience, and he affirmed it, acknowledging how bereft I felt and that he had left me stranded. My confidence was restored because I felt like he was trying to find a way to hold me despite how challenging it was. His effort made me cry again, with a mixture of deep despair and of terror, which often swelled within me when I spoke of needing to be held. Richard ended this particular session by stating gently and seriously that my leaving in terror was a very difficult thing for me to have to endure. And his response – his ability to hear me and shift according to my needs – heartened me and made me eager to use my analysis with Richard as more than an opportunity solely to grieve.

Despite my efforts to analyze new material with Richard in order to forge a relationship with him that was free of Despina, my grief swallowed up my efforts to explore. I sank into a depressed lethargy: with Despina dead, I, too, felt dead rather than merely "un-alive," as though my fetal self had become just barely viable while working with Despina, but now perished from "failure to thrive" syndrome. I feared that Richard needed me to be beyond infancy, and we explored together why I experienced this pressure as coming from him.

I told him that he did not use attunement as his primary mode of engaging me, as Despina had done. Richard responded, "She melted around you," and I replied, "Like a hot water bottle on the couch with me." Richard said, "When you are cold." I told him something I had told Despina: that if he waited for me to start before he began conforming to my shape, I would have to leave my deepest vulnerability – my baby self – behind in order to jump across the huge gap to find him. I explained how in my childhood home I was often overlooked, as if I weren't there. Richard suggested that my being overlooked while being in pain surely contributed to the unreal quality my pain often possessed.

Increasingly feeling that Richard could hold my pain, I ventured to tell him stories about how Despina and I worked together to help me grapple with feeling so vulnerable and abhorrent. For months, I had experienced myself as a repulsive werewolf, dragging my depression onto Despina's couch. In one session, I referred to the movie *An American Werewolf in London* and said that I was like the unwilling werewolf, who – because I was alive – was a danger to others, whom I was unable to protect. Despina replied, "His buddy knew differently. His buddy loved him!" To which I responded, in anguish, "But the werewolf begged to be shot so that he wouldn't cause more harm, and his buddy shot him, as he should have!"

A few weeks later, I again felt like the werewolf and, in a session, described myself to Despina as sitting with my back to her with my hair matted with mud and blood. Despina, ever attuned, moved close to me and wrapped a blanket around me. She gasped, and said, "Oh, Lynne, someday you will see how un-monster you are!" For the first time in our thirty months of working together, I realized that we saw things differently. Until that moment, I had really believed that she saw me as I saw myself. I was so startled to find that she did not see a monster, although she could see that I saw a monster. The timing was exactly right for me because I had "dragged" her through my monster life; I knew she knew me well, and I could see that despite her knowledge of who I was she still did not see me as a monster. For the first time, I could see a horizon before me. What felt like my eternal damnation was now understood as a particular perspective rather than as an absolute truth.

Richard listened closely to my words, and then commented on how I was currently holding myself. I had my arms across my chest and my fists clenched tightly. I told him that I had sometimes held myself this way with Despina because I had not wanted to lean on her too much. Yet Despina always seemed willing to provide exactly what I needed. I used to call her answering machine and leave messages, and she would leave return messages, which would give me something to hang on to between sessions. Richard asked if I felt cautious about calling him, and I told him that I was. He wondered if I had felt dropped because he hadn't brought up my not calling him despite his knowing about my frequent phone calls to Despina. I nodded yes, that I wished I could call but worried that he would be annoyed and withdraw from me. I actually worried about everything I told him because so much of it had to do with how perfectly in sync Despina was able to be with me, and I did not want Richard to adapt to me in a way that was not right for him. Richard interpreted that I was not asking him to replace Despina, who was irreplaceable; I was describing my needs with the hope that he could both welcome and respond to them as himself. I left that session feeling deeply mournful, but less wretched because I felt a glimmer of hope. His recognition that I needed him to broach the topic of my calling him felt like a "holding" interpretation, which was free of harsh judgments about my neediness and wish to be brought out of myself.

Four months after Despina's death, Gordon and I visited Mount St. Helens while on vacation. The devastation on the hillsides matched my own inner landscape. I read a sign that asked visitors to walk with care because volunteers were spending hundreds of hours working to restore the mountainside. Gordon remarked that the volunteers seemed so passionate about restoring the mountain to life, and I wondered if Richard could ever feel that degree of passionate dedication toward restoring me.

That night I had a dream: I was supervising a young therapist. I sat behind a one-way mirror. She was telling her somewhat naïve client that she (the therapist) was dying of cancer. She had thought that over the summer she had gone into remission, but her symptoms had returned and she would die. Her client looks baffled, tearful, and asked in a quiet, plaintive voice, "Does this mean I am to leave you now?" The therapist at first begins to say no, but she then says, "Well, yes. Little children need to have a mother, and I can't be yours – you must find another." The patient looks increasingly distressed and baffled. I told the therapist that while it's important to explore the patient's feelings about leaving the therapist, the patient also needs permission both to stay and to explore her feelings about staying. I also said that perhaps the patient believes she cannot leave her because she – the "child" – does not want to be sent away from the "mother/therapist" she already has.

I awoke and thought immediately of a story I had told to Despina in the autumn before she died. I was immersed in grief related to my unmet longings for responsive mothering from my own mother, to whom I felt quite loyal despite her severe alcoholism. The story was of a woman and her two young children, all of whom had been dragged into the woods. The mother was killed, and the children were found hours later sitting with her dead body. What else were they to do? Where else could they go? Despite the enormous sadness I felt after the dream, I also sensed it was a turning point: I knew there was somewhere else I could go.

The 23rd day of each month still ushered in an anniversary reaction of deep sadness. On June 24, I spoke to Richard of missing Despina deeply, and of wishing there was some kind of observance I could perform, such as visit a gravesite. I told him that just weeks before Despina stopped working, I had had the desire to apply to a newly forming psychoanalytic institute. I had told Despina of my decision and fantasized of a future in which we would both be analysts, "tearing up the institute" as new faculty members (she was in analytic training herself at the time). Richard enjoyed the image of us reveling in each other's talents and accomplishments.

A few days later I woke up thinking about how I had believed that Despina had hated everything about me in the early months of our work together. During my session that day, I told Richard about a time when Despina and I both showed up as guests at a relatively small dinner party. For reasons that were still unclear to me, I reacted with a surge of self-hatred, which, despite Despina and my best efforts to understand, did not abate until Despina admitted that she had not known what to do at the party, having never experienced anything like that before. I, then, recalled that I had a dream of sitting at the dinner table at the party, naked from the waist up, wishing Despina would give me her sweater; but Despina seemed unaware that I felt so exposed. Despina interpreted that she had left me hanging, not knowing what to do. I now realized that I had needed Despina to say something similar when she was ill: instead of her saying, "We have never been through anything like this before," I needed her to admit, "*I* haven't been through anything like this before. I am confused and overwhelmed, and I do not know what to do."

In treatment with Richard, I was better able to understand how Despina's own lack of clarity about her illness impacted me. I was left feeling simultaneously pulled in and blocked out, and I felt terribly confused by her last phone message to me: Was I supposed to call her or to leave her alone? I also felt incredibly ashamed that I had tried so hard to speak with her after she had left work – that I was not able to ascertain the reality of her situation and withdraw sooner. I had clearly overstayed. After she died, I felt like a confused child, fearful that I had somehow worn out Despina and killed her. I needed to be reassured that people don't die from being worn out by those who need them. The parallels between Despina's illness and my mother's alcoholism were lost on neither Richard nor me.

Even a year later, I continued to go over in minute detail the misleading information Despina, Colleen, and Julian had given me. I could not let it go. The perceived injury of being so thoroughly abandoned seemed to necessitate a viable explanation. I even played for Richard the confusing last message that Despina had left me, perhaps so that he could fully understand the reason I was so unsure.

During this time, I was ever aware of what I perceived as Richard's inability to tolerate my despair, and I often felt dropped by him when I sensed that I was "too much." For example, Richard conjectured one day that my current sense of deadness was particularly strong because I had taken in my dead mother. I instantly felt dropped and told him that I thought he was telling me not to feel despair anymore, that there was a dynamic explanation that would reveal the cause of my suffering and help me to resolve it. Richard understood and interpreted, instead, that I simply needed him to welcome and hold my suffering.

Despina was integral to my transference to Richard because I so often measured him against her. I had felt secure in her interest in me and protected myself from Richard's lack of interest, feeling skittish with him and worrying that he only wanted to hear about my early life. I wanted to tell him more and more about my history with Despina despite my anxiety: as far as I was concerned, my development had started when I entered into treatment with

Despina. Richard reassured me that he wanted to listen to whatever I wanted to speak about, which reassured me, once again, that he was aware of his impact on me. I felt safer knowing that he was keeping track of my reactions to him, knowing that his awareness made it less likely that I would try to accommodate a particular version of me that I thought he desired.

His reassuring comment enabled me to explore other reasons as to why I was skittish: I feared "nestling in," becoming dependent, and then losing him; I did not want my analysis to loom so large that I again lost the vividness of my "real" life. I told Richard how my life had revolved around my analytic sessions for my first two years of treatment with Despina. My lived world was meaningful only insofar as what it meant in the telling of it to her. During that time, I had utterly lost what thin connection I had had to my life. Only during the last few months of treatment had I begun to feel that I was a person who was living an *actual* life. Richard understood, commenting, "That is one aspect of your loss when Despina died ... No, that is an understatement." I agreed, and we discussed how wonderful it had been to have both a vivid life and a vivid analysis, and to share them both with Despina. I was desperate not to lose my life again.

Richard thought that my life became vivid when I could confidently carry Despina within me as an interested presence in my life. Her death took that feeling away, leaving me empty and forlorn. I became nauseated by Richard's words, and he suggested that my sense of having a vivid life had not yet gelled. He thought that I centered my life around my analysis with Despina because it was there that I felt vitality; by carrying within me Despina's interest, I could feel more alive wherever I was. I experienced a surge of hope when I made a connection between what Richard was saying in our current session and how shattered and lifeless I had felt without him when he went away. I had thought I needed to keep distant from Richard to persevere with my life, yet he was suggesting the opposite: I could remain vital by moving closer to him! And he did not seem repulsed or daunted by the prospect of closeness with me.

I went away for a few weeks at this time, and Richard also spent time away on vacation. During the difficult (but not excruciating) separation, I had the following dreams.

(1) Despina returned and she wanted us to set up some appointments. I was befuddled. I felt betrayed and confused. After all, I had been told she was dead! Now here she was, acting as if we could continue our analysis. I ended up having two sessions with her. I told her she could not be emotionally available to me anymore. She insisted that she could be. I started to say something about how horrified I was by the ravages of her disease. She put up her hand as if to silence me and said, "Do I want to hear this?" I said, "See what I mean? You can't be open to my experience of things." She insisted she could be, and tried to argue the reality of her situation.

Between sessions I was in torment. I knew she would be dead soon, so I was caught in a mess. I did not want to give up my sessions with Richard; it had been difficult to rearrange my schedule to be able to see him in the first place, and I might have to start from scratch again if I stopped temporarily. But I wanted to see Despina if I could! And now I had patients scheduled during what had been my session times with her. And I certainly could not afford to see both of them. I was angry at being thrown into such a bind.

(2) I found myself driving Despina's car. She got out and started walking to a building. When I got out, I noticed papers falling from the back seat of her VW Bug. This was a sign to me that she was not functioning well. I moved to clean up the fallen papers, and found an envelope meant for delivery to her psychoanalytic training institute. It had been returned to her because she had addressed it improperly. I was dismayed to see just how far gone she was. Then I found some childhood pictures of me that I had loaned her. I chased after her, worried about her disorientation.

She was talking animatedly, asking how we might get to Connecticut, or maybe we were already in Connecticut, because she had a doctor's appointment to get a proper diagnosis. "After all," she was saying, "maybe I don't have lung cancer." She thought maybe she had uterine cancer, which would be worse because she could live another twenty years if she had lung cancer. Or maybe she had breast cancer. She pointed to her breasts hopefully. She was reaching for any straw of optimism. I was crestfallen and horrified. She then said to me, ruefully, "Maybe I have AIDS." She was sounding crazy to me. I wondered how I might gently ask for my pictures without increasing her sense of doom. The pictures were one of a kind, taken from my mother.

After our break, Richard and I discussed my dreams, both of which seemed filled not only with my feelings of loss, betrayal, and confusion, but also with my wish that someone would have stepped in, picked me up, and made things better. They also revealed my ongoing distress about the confusing messages I got from Despina. The pictures seemed to suggest my efforts to reclaim myself, so that my experiential world would not disappear with her.

On the six-month anniversary of Despina's death, I had the following dream. I was running errands ordered by Colleen on Despina's behalf. Gordon walked into an office and saw Despina's bed with a lit cigarette next to it. I was appalled. She did not tell me she smoked! I saw her in the hallway, but I hung back so she would not see me looking at her. Her hair was bedraggled, her cheeks sunken, her pallor gray. She was dressed all in black.

It seemed clear to me when discussing the dream with Richard that I was still wrestling with regret that Despina could not admit to me the severity of her illness. I remembered a dream that I had while still in analysis with her. In it, she was smoking cigarettes. I had the dream after I had sensed during a session that she was agitated. I had been worried about her and asked her if she was okay or if something was bothering her. She said she was fine, and we limped through the session, but I never really settled in. It did not occur to me to doubt her perception of her state of mind, and I thought I must be mistaken. That night I dreamt that I came upon her by surprise, and she quickly tried to hide a cigarette in her purse. I had no idea what to make of the dream, but when I told it to Despina, she immediately said that she had been wrong to say that she was not in distress the day before, but she had only realized later that she was upset about a friend who had been at risk during the earthquake that had occurred in San Francisco. I had the odd but not unfamiliar sensation of relief that my perceptions were accurate: I was not crazy. And yet I also felt guilty because my perceptiveness seemed so intrusive.

I grappled continually with my feeling that Despina's efforts to give me what I needed depleted and ultimately killed her. I felt I should apologize to Julian for killing his wife. I knew I was special to Despina and sometimes sensed the pleasure she felt in our work.

My feeling was confirmed after she died, when someone who knew her told me that I had, indeed, been very special to her. I told Richard not to let me become a favorite patient because he would be killed too. My needs seemed toxic for Despina because she was so inclined to give. My mother had been worn down by the needs of all her children, and it had been my duty, as the eldest daughter, to protect her from the weight of this burden. "Richard must know his own limits," I would repeatedly tell myself. Yet I also believed that if Richard protected himself from my toxic needs, I would likely die from malnutrition.

During a session with Richard, I thought about a specific moment during the summer before Despina died, a moment which had signaled a subtle but permanent change between us, yet it was never fully addressed. I was in an acute depression, which had been increasing in intensity over the prior six months. Despina was about to leave for a week's vacation, and I felt like I might not survive emotionally without her. She told me that I could call her, but I felt tearful, anguished, and frightened. I wished desperately to be able to leave her alone, but I needed to stay in touch with her. She asked what would be so awful about my calling her, and I burst out with, "But I would need to call you every day!" She said absolutely nothing in response. Ordinarily I might have burst out with a statement of need, and I would feel her attuned welcoming of my needs, which would help me to settle down and make use of the emotional exchange between us without taking further action. But in the face of her unusual silence, I assumed she had changed her view both of me and of what was appropriate for our work together. I imagined she felt that I should no longer need her to such a degree. I tried to adjust to the change in the atmosphere in the room. Eventually, over the summer and fall, we talked about the change I sensed because Despina could tell that I had been thrown off-track. But despite exploring my sense that she had changed toward me, I never mentioned the actual moment of her silence. I thought of it often. I felt terrible about it because it was the only memory I had of hiding something from her.

I told Richard that I could not mention that moment to Despina because her response of silence left me feeling too humiliated. He wondered, since I had been able to mention other moments when I had felt humiliated, if I had said nothing because I did not want to expose her and myself to her failure – that I had needed to protect her from the reality that she was not quite up to par, perhaps because she was already suffering from symptoms of her illness. Richard's interpretation brought to mind a sickening moment when I had heard a thud behind me. I later understood the noise to be Despina's head suddenly falling on to the back of her chair. At the time, I did not comment on the noise, cautious not to intrude, and went on as if nothing had happened.

I explored in depth with Richard the final months of my treatment with Despina, and became even more cognizant of the times I had picked up on her illness long before it entered into my conscious awareness. During the fall and winter before her death, I was absorbed with images and imagery of my mother dying and leaving me alone. I'd envisioned my mother lying in a grave, with autumn leaves falling upon her. I was desperately trying to keep the leaves from covering her up completely so that I wouldn't lose her entirely. Although Despina and I discussed this material, relating it to my mother's emotional deadness and my sense that I had somehow lost Despina, I could never bring myself to speak of the moment when she remained silent in the face of my need: I suspect that its unusualness signaled to me that something was radically wrong. Rather than confront that prospect, I suggested that she had perhaps grown bored of me, and I hoped that this was a temporary condition.

When Colleen shared with me that Despina's first symptoms included frightening and painful migraine-like headaches, which began over the summer, my experiences in the last months before she died began to make more sense. I had noticed that she had lost weight and started continually to suck on lozenges to suppress a cough. Although I brought up her coughing a couple of times, I perceived that she became uncomfortable in response to my comments, so I stopped commenting and never dared to mention her weight loss. The first time Richard coughed in a session, I burst into tears.

By late August, I had occasional spates of sessions that were not dominated by my grief, and I felt as if I were better able to feel consolidated in my life. Sometimes these phases would invigorate me, while at other times they would usher in a melancholic sense of loss, which reflected my sadness that I really was going on with my life without Despina and there was nothing I could do to alter this horrific truth. Two years after Despina's death, I felt deeply saddened because I realized that I would never have a new memory of her. It was as though I had collected all the memories I could and had gathered them like berries into a basket, thinking that once I had filled the basket I could continue to collect new ones in a fresh basket. When there were no new berries to gather, I felt shocked and stricken – as if she had died all over again.

Despina died repeatedly in unexpected ways, as when someone asked me for a referral for a therapist, and I thought of her because she would be an ideal therapist for that person. For a brief moment, I actually thought of giving this woman Despina's name, still thinking of her as alive, out there and working. In my mind, I had been prohibited from seeing her because I was toxic to her, but she was still able to see other people.

In early September I was scheduled to go to a meeting of fellow Gestalt theorists to discuss and work on various writing projects. I had been anticipating the trip with excitement and mild trepidation. Before my trip, I had a dream: I was leaving on a long journey, but I could not find the special milk I needed to prevent myself from wasting away.

I told Richard that only Despina had the special milk I needed. We spoke of Despina's "holding attunement" and how I could voice my distressing and shameful feelings within the holding environment she provided. Richard suggested that my intense shame might prevent me from articulating what I needed from him in the face of our impending separation. My dream from the previous night came to mind: I was dying from AIDS and could not find something I needed. In fact I didn't even know what I was looking for.

I paused, trying to find my way through a moment of confusion. I told Richard that I was not seeking something from him – I was missing Despina. But while saying those words, I knew they were untrue. The feeling that I didn't know what I was looking for seemed to reflect a transitional space between my attachment to Despina (from whom I needed "special milk") and my attachment to Richard (from whom I needed things I hadn't yet articulated or understood). My recognition of my growing attachment to Richard both relieved and mortified me. I imagined that articulating what I needed from him would be met with disgust. Even using language like "special milk" filled me with embarrassment. Yet Richard persisted in exploring my fear of turning to him for my needs, and I experienced a growing closeness between us and an increased sense of our shared pleasure in working together. This pleasure was a double-edged sword for me: I felt that the closeness somehow sullied both Richard and me, as if we were engaged in something sinful and bad, yet the exploration of those feelings with Richard seemed to be proof that I was truly in analysis with him and not just mourning Despina!

Richard, thankfully, took my inevitable comparisons between him and Despina in his stride, and he was also able to use them therapeutically to deepen our work. Setbacks occurred often. For example, despite feeling closer to Richard before my work trip, when I returned a couple of weeks later, I experienced him as unable to hold or be attuned to me. He seemed bent on analyzing me, which felt very distressing. I woke up in the middle of the night anguished and crying because I knew only Despina could hold and be utterly attuned to me in the way I required. I felt completely lost without her.

During our next session, I felt deadened, depressed, and despaired that Richard forgot my cardinal rule: Attunement first (then we can analyze, if we must)! I revealed to him that I ached for him to be more mommy-like and hold me, not daddy-like, which meant waiting for me to be my more mature, analytic self. In the session, I was holding myself, sobbing deeply, and drowning in what felt like bone-shaking misery. In a voice and cadence that was at once reflective and intent, Richard told me that he'd recently had an image in his mind of a small fetus, which had been taken from its dead mother's womb and placed in a cold and sterile petri dish. The fetus was being watched, but it needed to be held, so great were its feelings of grief, loss, and despair. My sobbing escalated with both relief and anguish. I admired Richard's ability to see himself as the cold scientific watcher, which I had experienced him to be, and I knew it couldn't be easy to bear witness to the extremity of my pain. I felt grateful that he could both tolerate me and understand my experience.

He was, of course, right. I had come to life in Despina's womb, where I reveled in getting the right nourishment. I then lost her prematurely, before I was born and able to breathe and live on my own. Only during my last four months with Despina had despair not been part of my life. Those months were the first depression and despair-free months I had ever experienced, and their loss felt catastrophic.

Epilogue

While writing this chapter, I struggled with what felt like my own inability to portray adequately the quality of Despina's on-going attunement, which was conveyed by her tone of voice and the sounds that she made, rather than by the words she spoke. Both Pamela and Richard used words to reflect their attunement, but Despina felt like the proverbial "good enough mother," who felt her way into me and never needed words to experience what I felt or to heal me. Yet I appreciate more and more fully that each analyst worked with me under what must have been incredibly difficult circumstances. I admire their ability to stick with me through attunements and mis-attunements, and I am grateful for their attempts to understand my idiosyncratic needs. Because of their help, I could consolidate the gains I had made with Despina, and then continue to grow in the ways I so desperately desired.

Over the last few months of my first year of treatment with Richard, my analysis took a shape of its own. However, as the first anniversary of Despina's death approached, I spiraled into desperate waves of grief and despair. Richard was scheduled to leave for a brief holiday on January 17, the exact anniversary of my and Despina's last session. Before he left, I had a dream: Richard abandoned me while I was holding a large painted picture of Despina. He was working with another patient, trying to persuade the patient of a particular view of "reality." He was responsible for me and for the portrait, and I needed him to help me get where we were supposed to go. I felt terribly lost and fiercely protective of the portrait. It needed to go with me to our destination.

Richard wondered if the dream reflected guilt I might feel about leaving Despina behind and moving on in a new analysis. This perspective didn't seem right because there were too many moments when meaningful events in my analysis with Richard were followed by swells of grief and mourning that stemmed from my desire to share these new experiences with Despina, to celebrate my moving on with her. We came to understand the dream as instructive: it conveyed that we should use my experiences with and memories of Despina as useful guides, compasses that would help us know when we were on track. In the dream, Richard had been off-track with another patient in the very way I felt he had been off-track with me the previous day.

On the anniversary of the first day that Despina took off due to her illness, I was knocked off my feet by grief and disorientation. I dreamt that Despina was back to meet with me for one week. I told her how, in order for me to feel whole, I needed her to be in emotional contact with all the various dimensions and emotions of my inner world. I was in agony because it seemed unbearable to have to give her up again.

On the day before Richard was to leave on his trip, the first anniversary of my and Despina's last session, he told me that, on that particular day, as much as I wanted his words to be meaningful, I could not permit them to be. I replied, "Your interpretations only matter if we are in the middle of a process. But the process ends today: our last day. Since there is no tomorrow, what is the point?" Richard then said something that was stunningly affirming and reorganizing for me: "That is what you needed to say to her. In some sense you knew she was gone to you on that last day." His words matched a memory that had come to mind when I told Richard our work was over: I was sitting on my friend's porch, agonizing over the impossibility of resuming my analysis with Despina even if she actually was able to return to work. Her condition would be too changed. I thought of how often I had ached to return to her warm, enveloping presence, and how many times I rued that Richard, despite his genuine, tender reactions, could not envelope me as she had. And with this thought, I realized that in my imagination, even before Despina had died, returning to my analysis with her would have been impossible because the inevitable changes that she had undergone in response to her illness would have made it impossible for her to envelop me as she once had: I would have lost what I needed most. This realization helped me to recognize that Despina was not the only person who could help me feel vital.

Richard told me that I was growing legs and arms, growing viability. No longer was I just looking to be understood and held. Instead, I found myself enjoying both my own sense of agency and my ability to build a new and different kind of connection with him. My relationship with Despina also continued to change as the dynamics among the three of us shifted. Around this time, Richard offered me an interpretation that enabled me to settle in with him more fully. He wondered aloud if I had been interpreting his imperfect attunement as punishments and rewards: when I was unworthy, he was not attuned to me; when I was worthy, he was. The correctness of his interpretation helped me to see that I was blaming myself for what was probably a stylistic difference between Richard and Despina – Despina led with attunement and Richard did not. I was finally able to enjoy Richard's way of working because I did not experience it as judgments on my goodness or badness.

And yet a few weeks after the anniversary of Despina's death, I told Richard that although I was grateful beyond words for our first year of work together, and knew I had landed in the right place to go through my bereavement, I did not know if he was the right analyst for the next phase of my journey. I hated to say this and was petrified of his response, but I had to admit that I still had grave doubts about whether I could go where I felt I needed to go in the face of what I believed to be his merely episodic attunement. I also felt that now that I was no longer struggling solely to stay afloat, I needed to take time and consciously choose my next analyst, even if that analyst turned out to be Richard. Richard responded that although he enjoyed our work together, he was prepared to say goodbye to me if my path took me in another direction, and that it was most important for us to understand my doubts wherever those doubts would take us. I almost re-chose him right there, on the spot!

While Richard was gone, I had a dream: I was dying. I offered my patients the choice of setting up a termination session, knowing that would mean that they would leave me before I was truly gone, or they could wait until I had to quit, but then they would not get a chance to finish with me; there would be no notice of the ending.

I went to visit Despina in a cancer ward. I was carrying information about lung cancers. The ward was overcrowded and miserable. Colleen left me alone to find my way to Despina's room. I never found her.

When I told Richard the dream, he suggested that my information about cancer concretized how gravely ill I knew Despina was, and that I also knew I was carrying unwelcome information that nobody wanted to discuss.

Later in the month, I had another dream: I had returned to Vietnam, where I had once been a soldier. There was a soft rain falling, and I was riding in a jeep with another person. I was searching for a beautiful hamlet that I had gone to. I knew the hamlet was gone. It had been blown to bits by our bombs. But I still searched. I felt no great urgency to find the hamlet but was propelled more by wistful desire.

The dream seemed to suggest that I did not need to find Despina any more, that although I still missed her and her loss would be a permanent part of my landscape, I was healing. The dark storm clouds of grief that had been encircling me since Despina had died progressively lifted, and I entered a calm, almost sunny world. The dream was especially surprising to me because I had felt intensely miserable and distraught in the days leading up to it. The dream was such a potent shift that I ended up transforming it into a poem, the writing of which worked to solidify my sense that I was, indeed, healing.

To Despina, One Year After
A song played at your memorial.
A favorite of yours,
A song of bereavement.
Words to your mother, perhaps?
"You can go now," it said "I'm all right."
No! I railed. Not you, not now.
I'm not all right.
Dreams, since your death,
of horror, trauma, loss.
Always in Vietnam,
my psychic war zone.

Pouring rain and mud,
blood and mangled bodies.
Then a *gentle* dream.
In time for your Yarhtzeit.
My yarhtzeit tribute to you;
A dream of going in search of a special hamlet.
I had passed through it once before,
a gentle and serene paradise.
I longed to find it again, yet
I knew it was gone.
Bombs had fallen,
The hamlet disappeared.
I knew that, yet
I had to go and look.
Light drizzle as I began.
I felt mournful, wistful,
and strangely at peace.
See, I did not need to find you.
I just wanted to.
This is the healing.
You knew.
I miss you. I always will.
But I no longer need you.
You can go now. I'm all right.

(February, 1992)

Making room for death within the treatment setting

Chapter 7

After the first death, there is no other[1]

Maria K. Walker

My time with M began in death and ended in death.

I went to my first therapy appointment with M in 1999. I was nine-teen years old. I was not quite sure what I needed, whether I could trust her, or what it meant to be in therapy. M welcomed me into her office with bright eyes and a careful voice. It was the summer, and I was living back home in Cambridge, Massachusetts for my college break with my father and step-mother. M was just beginning her own private practice. I met with her for a couple months, and then left in August to return to college for my sophomore year, with no clear plan of seeing her again.

Shortly thereafter my life changed profoundly. A week after I return-ed to school, my father was diagnosed with pancreatic cancer. Baffled and terrified, I made weekend trips home to Cambridge to be with him. By the end of September, we were told he had just weeks to live. I left school and moved home. I started to meet with M again. My father rapidly declined, and two weeks later he died.

My father was an artist. He laughed easily. He held our family together with abundant love. With his death a heavy darkness fell. My stepmother, four months pregnant at the time, gave birth to my brother in the spring. He and our father never met. My sister, in her last year of college, returned to Atlanta after our father's death to finish her last year of college and pass the first of many milestones he wouldn't witness. Wanting to be home and away from college, which seemed for-eign and irrelevant, I decided not to return to school that semester.

I wandered, numb, between my father's home in Cambridge and my mother's in Ohio. Through those days of pale sadness, I continued my therapy with M. I met with her in person when I was in Cambridge, and otherwise we had phone sessions – a ritual that continued for the remainder of our years of working together. Those early sessions often felt stilted. I'd cringe when it seemed that M said too much or not enough, or when I felt that she herself was overwhelmed by the situation. Regardless, we continued to meet, and despite the imperfections I perceived, M's loyalty and reliability were unwavering. She was a witness without judgment who saw me and heard me in my aloneness. Week after week, month after month, I continued talking with her, even when I was speechless and felt there was nothing more to say.

Grief is a non-linear Jacob's ladder of sadness, confusion, and clarity that folds in on itself. It normalizes, then fades, and then springs forth again. M and I talked through the cycles of grief that ebbed and flowed like tides through the months and years after my father's passing. We talked as I negotiated family and personal relationships and when I made the decision to travel abroad to Nepal in my last semester of college. We talked as I decided to become an artist myself. We talked as the end of college approached, and I decided to stop our sessions. I felt ready to move forward on my own, and for two years our paths parted.

When I reached back out to M, she had started to practice Lacanian analysis, and our phone calls followed a new structure: twice weekly for twenty-five minutes, instead of forty-five minutes once a week. Trusting our history, I followed her lead as we progressed to a nuanced practice of listening and speaking. All the while, life continued. I studied painting in Philadelphia and moved to New York. I married my college love. I kept a regular studio practice and began to show my artwork. I went back to school to study art therapy. Later, my work as an art therapist grew from the values I had learned in my work with M: a belief in the ability to know one's self and to follow the grounded needs of the soul.

M and I brought our best selves to our work together. Each week she returned realigned, ready to listen, even after sessions of dissonance. She was thorough, thoughtful, circling back to earlier threads, honest and humble about her own uncertainties and growth. Her commitment heightened my commitment, motivating me to continue to engage, listen, and move forward.

My work with M is the closest experience I've had to making art: a cool early morning in the studio with time and quiet ahead, the sun low with wood and canvas before me. The pain of feeling stuck, of a clogged head, the avoidance of a difficult painting. The careful listening, sitting, watching, and the shifting of the artwork, which becomes a compass, reorienting and guiding my mind and process. My work with M brought me clarity and centeredness. The core of my paintings paralleled the core of our work: slowing time, finding balance, making space for light.

We talked through dreams. She taught me the way a dream can be cracked open, illuminated, listened to, relieving unseen tension and uncertainty, revealing optimism and ability. As a self-possessed leader, she followed my lead and marveled at the places the dreams would take us. Over our years I had a recurring dream, each time set in a different context, but always with the same essence: M walking away from me, or unavailable, or dismissively booked with another patient, or available but without privacy. I connected the dreams with the value I placed on my therapy, and my fear of losing her commitment. Retrospectively, I also see that the dreams may have been connected to her death, perhaps drawing on a prescient anxiety I had. Even after we knew she was sick, and our work continued, we did not make this particular connection, or at least not explicitly. Perhaps we were too close to see it.

At certain junctures I considered stopping our practice, wondering how long was too long or too much. As we talked through this idea, I consistently returned to the decision that as long as I gained from therapy, I would continue. And so, I always continued.

By the time I found out about M's illness, about ten years after we began working together again after college, the reality of her personal life, around which she had always kept impeccable boundaries, had crept into our sessions. She started to cancel sessions with little prior notice, and then took an uncharacteristic break from working for a month. She addressed the change early on, telling me that a close family member was sick. I accepted this, sympathized, and thought about the stress she was facing.

When she returned to work, we resumed our regular rhythm. But then the cancelations began again, and I felt a hint of distance in her engagement. Rather than following M's philosophy that words are oxygen, neither of us spoke about it. I silently personalized the strain I felt in her. With her withdrawal I also withdrew, feeling unsure of what exactly was happening and why. I wondered if I was somehow the reason for her change, or if I was being oversensitive, sensing a shift when, in reality, there was none in her at all.

Eventually I gathered myself, took what I had learned from her ethos and our practice, and I spoke to her about the change. Usually it had been M who made sure we addressed everything, particularly in difficult times; but I knew it was necessary for us to speak. Looking back, she seemed relieved and not surprised. Perhaps she didn't realize how the changes in her were affecting me, although I imagine she was, more likely, unsure about how to navigate this new territory, while still honoring both her privacy and our honesty.

M agreed that things had been different. She proceeded to share that it was she, not a family member, who was sick. She was experiencing a relapse of breast cancer from when she was younger. She verbalized her uncertainty about whether to share this with me, and to what degree. As she talked, she reflected on my sensitivity to our communication, my history with my father's illness, and the need to speak with me more truthfully and directly. I did not feel anger or resentment that she had lied. I was anxious about her health and prognosis, but I was also relieved to know the truth and to understand the reason for what I had perceived. I was saddened to think of her distance, and the massive complexity of life she was facing beyond our sliver of time together.

After M told me about her illness, our relationship shifted slightly. M continued to maintain her carefully set therapeutic boundaries, but she was also more honest about the state of her health and the times when she needed a break. This provided relief for me and, I believe, for her as well. I never felt strain and withdrawal in her again, even when she faced the end of her life. M provided as-needed information when her care affected our sessions, and when she alluded to setbacks or new treatments, she reassured me of her trust in her medical providers and her progress. In this context, I accepted cancelations or changes without personalization or resentment. In fact, her reassurance was always so adamant that I rarely worried about her prognosis, and for the next two years I often forgot about her illness altogether.

After those two years, M began to require more frequent treatment and her health problems became more evident. M remained optimistic about and committed to her work, though the reality of her mortality began to set in. After my father's death, I had lived with an ongoing anxiety about the loss of other loved ones. In fact, even before my father was sick, I worried about his death. I spoke with M about this, but not specifically in relation to her. To talk with her about my anticipated suffering after her death felt like an imposition, and even inappropriate. Regardless of her strength and professionalism, I felt in her the vulnerability of a person facing the end of life.

There are values that we follow in life, including values within therapy and analysis; and then there is the unknown reality of dying. In the shadow of her illness, there were conversations that M and I did not have. I wondered and worried about what it would be like to lose her after so many years of working together. I feared the loss of a mentor for whom I cared so deeply, and the loss of our practice, and how that would affect me. I did not speak all these thoughts, and she did not directly offer space for these feelings and questions. Unlike before, when our silence was an absence and an avoidance, it was clear that M was giving her best to her work. Talking about my life after her death, however, lay outside this realm.

As a result, I experienced a new kind of solitude while M was still living. Sadness and anticipation settled upon me, an experience of unspoken grief before actual loss. Our practice, however, remained vital and kept me in the present. Our sessions continued to re-center me, not least in relation to my anxiety around her health, even though we didn't speak about it directly. Outside of therapy I also found strength in my art, my family, and the muscle memory of the years of work we had already done.

The penultimate time I saw M in person was during a visit back to Cambridge in January 2016 – back to the town laden with the spirit of my father – about eight months before she died. Despite her illness she was still working, as she continued to do until about a month before her death. We met for three sessions that weekend. On the first evening we lingered, facing one another in conversation, something we didn't usually do. She spoke more personally about an upcoming treatment. She was animated, working through her thoughts, and appeared grateful for our conversation. She said of her path, "I choose life." She reflected that she did not want to live just to be alive. As long as life continued to be dynamic and giving, she wanted to continue. I admired her clarity and felt a mirroring strength in myself.

That night, however, I had a haunting dream. M and I analyzed it the next day, and what became clear was that the conversation outside of the parameters of our usually contained practice had left me cautious and confused about returning to our practice. I hated to acknowledge this, because it had felt so good to talk candidly with M; nonetheless, it was clear that that level of intimacy outside of our designated boundaries interrupted and halted the therapy. M received this heedfully, and as we proceeded into the months ahead, we returned to the parameters and routine of our analytic/therapeutic relationship. This meant stepping back from that candid closeness, but also staying closer to the life of the work, which had in itself an invaluable and incomparable closeness to it.

M and I continued to meet for our phone sessions, and the weeks and months continued to pass. Her illness was a reality, but she continued her work, engaged and committed. In July of that summer, I learned I was pregnant. I was filled with joy to share this news with M.

At the end of August, just a month later, a colleague of M's called to tell me that M had to cancel for the week. The woman had a lovely accent and kept the conversation brief. I thanked her and felt questions rise in my chest and stomach. M had never had someone else call me before. No one else had ever entered our shared space. I rationalized that a treatment had come up and we would return to normal the following week, but I also had a sense of foreboding.

The next week the colleague called again. Or was it M who called? Grief works like that, time folding in upon itself. Yes, it was M who called. Her voice was faint, but clear. She said to me, "I thought it was something small. Things got worse quickly. I am in hospice care." I thought about my father. *Here we are already. It has come so quickly.* M proceeded to say, "We won't be able to terminate."

What does it mean, not to be able to terminate after seventeen years of work? Without realizing it, I had a picture in my mind of M's death: a gradual decline, the analytic decision to end our practice, all with time and peace, including a conclusive termination. I felt anger followed by guilt at my anger, which really was helplessness and fear. I wondered, *Why did she let us continue for so long? Couldn't we have prepared better? Wouldn't it have been better to have ended sooner rather than to come to such a blunt end-point?* We had been so committed for so long; to face an end like this robbed me – robbed us – of closure to our years of work and to so complex and exceptional a relationship.

When I found out that my father had just weeks to live, I cried and raged: a teenager powerless, desperate, flooded with love and fear – as though my anger at the injustice could change the course ahead. I remember the sadness and resignation in my father's face. Here I was, now with M, full of feeling and with so little time. It was time for acceptance.

I think back, and I wonder what it meant to M to tell me that we couldn't terminate. The loss, the disbelief that in the tenacity of her commitment to her work, and in a way precisely *because* of that tenacity of her commitment to her work, she couldn't formally end her practice as planned. I remember a similar retreat in my father as he faced the limitations of death about a month before he died. He said to me and my sister, "I won't be able to be there for you through this," and for years I held on to these words as a form of desertion. *That is it. He is leaving us.* Though I could continue to talk with him and see him and love him, an initial tie had been cut. In her final year of life, perhaps knowing better what my father may have been experiencing, M offered a different perspective of admiration towards those words of my dad. He had known his limits and spoken them. He was brave enough to put his helplessness into words. In the face of his inevitable, rapidly approaching death, perhaps he felt the awe of not being able to give beyond himself to the daughters he loved so much. And he wanted us to know.

All this feeling; all these memories; I was still on the phone with M. I tried to wrap my head around her words and just as I was about to ask, she said, "You can come and say goodbye."

With that, the door that had just closed with hollow darkness reopened. What had just been taken away from me was returned. We agreed that I would come the following week. I awaited with excitement and dread. I would see her again, and it would be the last time.

After the phone call that weekend my husband and I took a bus to Cambridge, back toward the ghost of my dad, back to the town where I first met M. We borrowed a car and drove down a windy road to a large, white, farm-style hospice house, surrounded by trees. There, M welcomed me to her still room. Once more with her careful voice, her kind eyes, she let me in. We sat together, and she shared her precious time.

We talked about our work. I expressed my gratitude for our practice, my admiration for her, the ways the work shaped who I am. We talked about the beauty of her room, surrounded by windows. She got to see my growing belly. I told her the names my husband and I had chosen for our baby, something we shared with no one else before the birth. I brought with me the jade stone she gave me when I was nineteen to carry with me to my father's funeral. She returned to me the pale peach prayer shawl I had brought her from my study-abroad program in Nepal.

She wondered aloud if she had pushed me too much to stay in therapy at those junctures when I thought about stopping. With surprise I heard her speak about the ways she had learned and grown from the practice with me. I reassured her, *I continued on my own; the work continued to give.*

I gave her a small artwork of painted lace stretched over wood that could stand on her windowsill: the only painting I gave her in our years together. She was generous with her time. We used more than a regular session, then she grew tired and it was clear we had reached our end. So many words, then simply, *I will miss you.* She led me to the door, her face peeking around the frame as I left, just like our sessions in person back in Cambridge.

I left with my husband, who never met M, but had known of her since college. We drove back home through the trees. I thought, *now I am alone, as we all truly are.*

The days and weeks went by. I thought about my last meeting with M. I had been surprised to recognize death in her face, in her breath, in her voice. Despite this she was so giving. She didn't say, "I can't do this." I didn't have the opportunity to reflect with my father the way I did with M. The afternoon she had given me was a gift. Perhaps not a technical termination by the analytic book, but I could not have asked for a more peaceful, thorough ending. It softened my mourning ahead. With time I realized that the meeting was for M too. She needed our goodbye as well.

I often thought about M in the days and weeks that followed. Had she passed? When? How would I know? The call came just under a month later, from the same kind colleague, who had the honorable task of calling M's patients one by one by one. She was professional and caring. She was grieving herself. She asked me kindly if I had a referral. She told me about the memorial service and invited me to attend. Talking with the colleague, I wanted to hold on to her, the first and only being in my path who had also known M. But I also knew and respected the limits that came with the work. The undercurrent of our words was our knowing and loving M.

Part of the painful beauty of grief is the coming together, remembering together, holding the spirit of the loved one alive in a collective memory. There are memorial services, anniversaries, toasts at holidays, stories for later generations, tearful phone calls after finding a scrap of paper with old handwriting.

No one else in my life knew M. Although those close to me knew of her, understood the importance of the work to me, and knew about the sessions twice a week and the years of practice, the loss that came with her death was solitary. I had support when I cried, but no one was crying with me. I had lived through grief before, but the person who had helped me through that grief was now the object of my grieving, and I was without her to work my way through it.

In the privacy of a relationship with a therapist or analyst, that other person is a key witness to your history, your thoughts, your dreams. The therapist embraces these parts of you in confidence, in security, and from that interpersonal distance you see yourself more clearly. The other person holds these treasures of your self in all their complexity and messiness and longing. And when that person dies, that witness is gone.

I felt anxious without our practice, and my anxiety grew with the fear that without our weekly work, I would become mentally stiff, hunched, and jumbled. In our final meeting M addressed finding a referral, and I told her I wasn't planning to continue with someone else at any time soon. She seemed relieved only because she had tried to identify a good match, but she could not find someone. Even in the grief after her death, I did not consider finding a new therapist. My mourning was about me and M, and I did not want to bring another person into our relationship. I was not ready for that kind of new beginning.

There is a difference between the death that started my relationship with M and the death that ended it. Was I weighed down by her absence after she died? Yes. Did I shake with sadness and feel the emptiness of the time I would have spoken with her? Yes. Especially with the birth and growth of my baby, I longed to speak to her through the kaleidoscopic complexity of motherhood that threw me into a vertigo of looking back to my childhood and ahead to my own death. This was compounded by the pressure of time that comes with parenthood, including less time for painting. Less time to sit and listen and watch in the studio.

I miss M. I can hear her voice and see the light of her face. The soft warmth and smell of her office. I can feel the openness, the relief, the clarity that would come after we would meet. But, unlike the years of darkness that followed the death of my father, the time after M's death has been lighter. The grief has folded back into life more easily. M taught me this. Because of her, because of all the work we did together, I could bear her death.

My time now is full. It is different. There are no blocks of time set aside for my phone calls with M. I have a son. We drive together in the quiet early morning and, as he sits in the back of the car and watches the trees pass by, I talk through a dream under my breath.

There have been so many dreams. Shortly after she died, I dreamt of a child, alone, walking home through the empty park across the street after it rained. I try to honor our work and work through the dreams that come. When I do, I can taste the clarity I used to feel with M. So many other dreams, though, have come rapidly in a strong current, passing by me and continuing on, downstream. Especially in the months after M died, I would watch them pass, sealed and coded, and I mourned them too.

I can still hear M's questions and reflections. I worry I will lose her voice, and I know I cannot fully embody her objective ear. But if I still myself and listen, there I am. I know this practice; it is part of me, just like the studio. Here I am now, me with me. I associate, and slowly the chemistry of my body shifts. I can see the trees more clearly. Here I am in my body, my boy in the rearview mirror. I go forward into the day.

Note

1 Thomas, D. "A Refusal to Mourn the Death, by Fire, of a Child in London." *The Poems of Dylan Thomas.* Ed. D. Jones. New York: New Directions Publishing Corporation (2003), p. 221.

Chapter 8

The gift of goodbye and the invisible mourner

Iris Hellner

My analysis started as a once-weekly treatment, when I began a doctoral program in clinical psychology, and my analyst embarked on her psychoanalytic training. It later turned into a three-times-a-week analysis that lasted for many years, then became a twice-a-week therapy, and returned to a once-a-week treatment as my life became fuller and busier and, even more importantly, as my progress was palpable. I learned a great deal from my analyst not only about living in general and living my own life in particular, but also about saying goodbye. Deep into this long-term analytic relationship, my analyst was diagnosed with cancer, had chemotherapy, and went into remission. A few years later, the cancer returned and took her life. In an ironic twist of fate, I had entered therapy to address issues related to unresolved losses, one of which was especially complicated because it had allowed no room for goodbye; the death was especially tragic and sudden. When it was clear that my analyst was dying, this irony was lost on neither me nor her: I had found a therapist in order to address issues of loss, and that therapist was now dying.

As I am someone who is rather private, writing this public, personal chapter was a move out of my comfort zone. I tend not to share intimate details with those who are not close to me, and I am reserved about what details I reveal about myself to my patients. However, the painful therapeutic journey made with my own analyst during her illness and death was so remarkable that I felt compelled to capture parts of it. I believe there are lessons to be learned from the extraordinary ways in which she dealt with her illness and impending death. This chapter is also an effort to pay tribute to her.

In this chapter, I will focus mostly on her illness the second time it occurred, as that episode is the stronger memory for me. I will share anecdotes about my analysis with her during her illness; how we discussed the possibility and then the probability of her death; our final goodbye; and thoughts about what it is like to be a grieving patient. There is a dearth of literature written by patients about their ill and dying analysts, and even fewer papers about their bereavement. I hope that this chapter expresses aspects of experiences that others have had, and I hope that it offers insights about how best to support patients who face this unique loss.

I wrestled with the question of whether or not to disclose my analyst's identity.[1] Wishing to honor her, I was drawn to name her. However, I also wanted to protect her privacy. After much deliberation and helpful discussions with colleagues, I decided to keep her identity private. Firstly, I wanted this chapter to reflect my experience as her patient. Secondly, out of respect to her, I decided I did not feel comfortable publicly sharing intimate details without her consent. Interestingly, I found that keeping her identity private also allowed me more fully to focus on my experience while writing this chapter. Here, I will call her Dr. A.

Disclosure and knowing

During both bouts of cancer, Dr. A. was forthcoming with me about her illness. Before undergoing surgery after the initial finding, she explained briefly by phone what was happening. She was clear and to the point, explaining the circumstances and also letting me know when I could expect to see her again, which was in less than two weeks. In both the first and second episodes, she shared the diagnosis and prognosis with me, briefly mentioned the course of treatment, and explained how it would impact my therapy. She did not wait for me to ask any of those questions. I cannot say if this was how she handled things with other patients, of course, but Dr. A. knew me well and recognized that information was something I needed in order to cope; a lack of information would have ratcheted up my anxiety. I appreciated knowing, as much as her condition worried me. In not waiting for me to ask, Dr. A. gave me the green light to discuss her illness. Had she not invited this discussion, I might have felt it was a taboo subject or feared intruding on her privacy. My own propensities aside, I cannot imagine having evidence or a sense that one's analyst is very sick over a prolonged period of time and not having that illness articulated at all. I recognize that for others such a disclosure by one's analyst may have felt burdensome. For me, however, being kept in the dark would have been onerous.

Since Dr. A. was direct and frank with me, we could both be honest while navigating what was in the room and in our relationship, from both a logistical standpoint and a psychological one. She let me know when to expect her absences; I asked about how much time she would need and why, and she briefly explained the need for recovery time after her chemotherapy treatments. I learned that she had thoughtfully planned the timing of her treatments for late in the week so that she had time to recover over the weekend, which minimized disruption for her patients. I was aware that there was much detail that was left out but appreciated and found helpful what she did share. It felt like enough to help orient me, but it was without extraneous details.

Mortality in the background and foreground

Dr. A's cancer went into remission, only to return a number of years later. It felt unimaginable to me that her cancer could return. During her remission, my worries about her illness and the possibility that she would not recover receded with a triumphant feeling that she had "beaten it." Dr. A. regained her health and seemed like her old self. The therapy focused less on her illness over time. It was as if the experience of her sickness had been cast out of my mind and out of the therapy room. When she became ill for the second time, I was stunned. It hadn't occurred to me that her cancer could return, and with its return came strong worries that this time Dr. A. would not beat her illness.

My awareness of Dr. A.'s mortality moved between the foreground and the background of my treatment at different times. For a while, my experience of her illness, of potentially losing her, and of how these two issues related to my own dynamics about attachment and loss were the exclusive topics of sessions. We talked about her cancer returning and about my sadness for her and for me. She invited these feelings and I spoke openly about my anger that her illness had entered my treatment again. I voiced my feelings of disbelief and anger that she was sick again. It felt terribly unfair. I shared openly and emotionally about how worried I was about her and how much I feared that this time she would die. This second time around, the prospect of losing her and my wished-for relationship – a relationship free from a legacy of loss – was the focus of the treatment. It was a potent time spent working on these issues, which had such a powerful resonance with my own history. While cancer was not a part of my own history, the fragility of life, mortality, and the reality and finality of loss were.

The treatment was fundamentally changed because Dr. A.'s ill health and its concomitant needs entered the treatment in profound ways, ways that no one would hope for in any therapy. While there was much time in the treatment when Dr. A.'s illness was in the foreground, I felt that she continued to prioritize my experience. Dr. A. deftly kept the focus on my history, my struggles, my internal world, and my experience of her and her cancer. I could speak directly about her illness and about her. Early on, in addition to telling her how very sad I felt because she was suffering, I also expressed how conflicted I felt about discussing other aspects of my life. How could I speak about issues that seemed mundane and trivial when she was facing a battle for her life? During one rare personal disclosure, Dr. A. said that she found her work to be engrossing and deeply engaging and that it took her mind away from her cancer. She expressed what she felt in a matter-of-fact tone, without much emotion. I knew that she was letting me know how helpful the work was for her. I felt that she was also telling me that she was very much with me, and I took her disclosure to be a communication that my speaking about other things was fine; there was room for me and for things not cancer-related. It proved to be a very powerful experience for me. To hear explicit confirmation that Dr. A. could create and prioritize space in her own head for me, despite her immersion in her own awful experience, was monumental and provided me with a healing contrast to experiences earlier in my life when my needs were overshadowed by those of others.

At a later juncture, I did not focus exclusively on her illness. She would make links to how my comments related to her illness when she perceived a connection that was unconscious to me, but she did not otherwise draw our attention to her cancer, and it receded to the background of my treatment. I resumed talking about other parts of my inner and outer life. Both not feeling overshadowed and feeling able to speak about other things were possible for me because I could feel Dr. A.'s presence and engagement; she felt to me like her normal self, and continued to leave space open for me: for my feelings, thoughts, fantasies, and memories.

At other times, Dr. A.'s illness and mortality would inevitably be jolted into the forefront of my treatment. When Dr. A. greeted me one day with a wig and noticeably missing eyebrows and eyelashes, I felt like I was punched in my gut. When I saw her looking very tired and, later on, very thin, I was overwhelmed with sadness and worry. With these overt reminders of her battle with cancer, I was grateful to be lying on the couch; not seeing her provided me with tremendous relief. For a while, starting and ending sessions became more difficult as I found myself covertly checking Dr. A.'s appearance – Did she look thinner? Was she more gaunt? I often tried to gauge how ill she was. Dr. A. asked me about my experience of her physical changes, and I was able to speak about the impact of seeing her this way – of the shock, fear, and pain I felt. It is remarkable to me that she remained so available and grounded, and that she was able to allow me to speak so directly about my reactions to her physical alterations. While experiencing and sharing my terror about losing her, I felt held by Dr. A., despite the fact that she herself was facing worries similar to mine.

While there were changes in our schedule, with a few sessions missed for chemotherapy, for the most part the frame stayed solid, which helped keep us in the "business as usual" mode. However, there was one session when Dr. A. didn't show up, and I found myself wondering if the time had come when she would never return. There was no note on the door and no message left, which was unusual for her. I didn't know what to do with myself while standing outside her office. At that moment, I realized how present and real the fear was, the "waiting" for that moment. Dr. A.'s spouse soon arrived and told me (at her request) that she had been delayed at an appointment and would not be back in time for the session. I realized then so palpably the degree to which I had been living with the question of how much time she – and we – had left.

My concerns about how much longer we would have were the focus of many subsequent sessions.

A couple of times, Dr. A. had asked if I wanted a referral to another therapist, and we explored the pros and cons of my continuing with or leaving her. I know that some of her patients did leave, while others remained. I wrestled with the decision in discussions with Dr. A. and also with others close to me. I chose to remain because I felt that there was still productive work going on. Dr. A. continued to feel emotionally available to me, and she was not noticeably different from how she had been before her illness. I felt that the work was also quite deep. I knew that I also opted to stay because of my attachment to, and my love for, her: I was not yet ready to say goodbye. On some level, I recognized that working with her while she was ill was an opportunity to address and work through my issues related to loss, as painful and challenging as those were. Not surprisingly, there was a complicated mixture of motivations, only some of which I was aware of at the time.

Saying our goodbyes and confronting death

With her health worsening and a poor prognosis, Dr. A. announced that she would be continuing her cancer treatment but closing her practice. She explained that it was too difficult for her to continue at that point. We prepared to end the long treatment and to say goodbye.

Dr. A.'s illness and the possibility of losing her had been painfully difficult to talk about; discussing the likelihood of her death was surreal. Loss and death had been on my mind for quite some time; my preoccupation with them had long predated therapy. To be able to speak so frankly and starkly about my feelings relating to loss and death was new for me, and helpful. Giving voice and deep emotion to what had previously seemed unspeakable and unsharable – expressions that could not be received or tolerated by others – felt groundbreaking. Dr. A. encouraged me to speak about my thoughts and feelings about the probability of her death, always keeping space open for me to share what I was going through. I expressed my concern about the impact on her of my talking about her dying. While I recognized that I was only able to speak about it because

Dr. A. invited me to do so by creating a climate in which my discussion was welcome, I was nevertheless worried that what I was saying would hurt her or make her sad. After exploring my worries about hurting her, Dr. A. remarked in a soft tone, "You discussing it isn't what makes me sad. I am sad about the possibility that I may be dying. You bringing it up and talking about it is not what makes me sad." Her response was direct and felt generous. Dr. A.'s ability to draw clear distinctions between her experience and mine was immensely powerful for me. That conversation was also terribly sad.

We had often discussed the possibility of her dying over the course of her long illness, but it was now heart-wrenchingly real. With our last session scheduled, there were many new questions: Did I want to know if she got worse? Did I want to know when she died? How did she feel about my knowing? Did I want to go to her funeral? How did she feel about my attending her funeral? Would I begin a new therapy? Most of these questions I asked her directly, while a couple were posed by her.

Dr. A. asked me if I wanted to be notified if her health worsened and if she died (however directly we discussed her dying, I don't think either of us was able to use the words "when" instead of "if"). As we always did, we first explored my thoughts and feelings about what she had brought up. We discussed what I wanted to know, what I did not want to know, and why. I was clear that I wanted to know both when she took a turn for the worse and when she died. I asked Dr. A. what her wishes were – if what I wanted was OK with her. She told me that I would receive a phone call from her colleague, whom she had already asked to call me. I promptly forgot the name of the colleague. Dr. A. added that her ability to control the situation would no longer be there, and that while she would make these arrangements and give my name and number to her colleague, she couldn't promise that these arrangements would work out as planned. It was helpful to know that there was a thought-out plan in place. While I recognized that the plan was not foolproof, and while I appreciated her reminder to that effect, I became worried about the idea that, if all did not go as planned, I might not learn about Dr. A.'s death; or I might learn about it in a public way, from colleagues or through the grapevine. These possibilities were difficult for me to imagine. To have had such a personal and intimate relationship with Dr. A. and not to be notified of her death, to learn about it in an impersonal way, or to be denied the opportunity to attend her funeral: all these possible scenarios felt alienating and akin to enduring another kind of loss.

Dr. A. and I discussed whether or not I could attend her funeral. I remember feeling trepidation before asking her. I found it incredible that we were talking about that topic. It again felt surreal and also a relief, scary, and achingly sorrowful. Dr. A. asked me what I wanted, and I was clear that I wanted to attend. I wanted to honor her and felt that I needed to have a final goodbye. I also had a burgeoning sense that I would need to participate in a ritual with others who were grieving so as to feel less alone. Dr. A. took time to think about it and told me that it was fine with her if I attended, but she made a request that I not approach her young children at the funeral. When she mentioned her children, Dr. A.'s voice cracked. In that moment, I think the brutal reality hit us both very hard. I had young children: one, only a year younger than her eldest. Her request was unbearably poignant to me, especially as a mother. It was a rare glimpse into the pain she felt while facing the fact that she would be leaving her children. I felt such pain for Dr. A. and for her family. I was struck that in that dark moment of trying to protect her children, Dr. A. was also striving to attend to my needs. I can't imagine how she had the presence of mind, strength, and groundedness to be able to tend to my needs at that moment as throughout our goodbye process. Her ability to move through our goodbye process in such a present and attentive way felt loving and courageous. I felt grateful to be able to express my own wishes and to know hers.

We recounted the many years of our relationship, what we had gone through together, and what had changed in me and in our relationship. Dr. A. shared her thoughts and reflections about the ways in which I had grown during our time together. I also noted what I had seen change in Dr. A. I expressed how much I would miss her and our relationship, and what I imagined my life would feel like without her. I wrote her a letter to tell her what she meant to me and what impact she and the analysis had had on my life, and I shared that I could see her in my work as a therapist, in my marriage, in my relationships, and in my mothering. The treatment and Dr. A. had permeated my life. In our last session, while acknowledging that we saw changes in both of our lives throughout our long relationship, Dr. A. remarked, "You were there at the beginning of my career as an analyst and you are here at the end." These conversations were overwhelming, meaningful, and tearful for both of us.

The invisible mourner: the funeral and beyond

Dr. A. died three months after our last session. Her colleague did call to notify me of her death and gave me details about the funeral service. I have a strong memory of being on the call, though I cannot recall the words of the conversation or the voice at the other end of the line. Despite knowing it would come at some point, I was shocked to receive the dreaded news. I realized that my fantasy and wish had been that Dr. A. would have a much longer time than she had. The pain was intense and the grief deep.

I attended the funeral service with my spouse and a friend. I felt fortunate to be able to go to it and to have close support by my side. As I had anticipated, the funeral was an important means for me to say goodbye and for the reality of her loss to be cemented. It was especially helpful to be part of a formal mourning ritual and to participate in honoring Dr. A. with others who knew her well. To be among a sea of mourners who loved and admired her was moving, and their sorrow mirrored the depth of my own mourning. Because I joined in the communal grief, my pain and loss felt shared and recognizable. The funeral provided a much-needed physical space in which I too could be a mourner, and taking part in it felt validating and comforting.

Attendance was overflowing and the numerous eulogies were warm and effusive. My impressions of Dr. A. as a strong, giving, and remarkable person were affirmed by her close family and friends. The confirmation of my perception of her as a person, outside of the transference, was also comforting.[2] Dr. A.'s funeral reflected her and provided me with elements of comfort and validation. Had it been poorly attended, or had the eulogies been impersonal or cold, the funeral would have felt incongruous with the person I knew; had that been the case, I imagine I would have felt saddened and confused.

While I found it validating and very helpful to be at the funeral, I was also aware that I was an outsider. I was an unacknowledged and unknown intimate, which made me feel that my grief was, in a sense, invisible. I could not speak at the service or approach others directly with my sorrow. I became excited when I saw a patient whom I recognized. She had had the session right after mine, and for years we nodded to each other in acknowledgment when passing in Dr. A.'s hallway or outside on the street. When I caught a glimpse of her at the funeral, I wanted to connect with her, at least to nod in shared mourning and loss. I ran after her but lost sight of her in the crowd. We did not interact, and I'm not sure what it would have been like if we had interacted. My great disappointment illustrated to me just how much I needed to connect with another person who, I imagined, was feeling the depth of grief I was experiencing: someone who knew Dr. A. in a similar way and was currently in a position similar to mine. As a patient, my grief felt very lonely. The lovely eulogies that had praised my analyst's commitment to and passion for her work did not explicitly mention her grieving patients. While I understood this omission (the speakers were in their own deep pain and could hardly be expected to think of her patients), this lack of recognition also contributed to my feeling like an invisible mourner.

My feeling of invisibility became more acute in the weeks and months after Dr. A.'s death. I felt as if my grief was closed off from a larger community. Aside from the funeral, there were no other formal rituals in which I could participate. For example, I could not attend Dr. A.'s shiva or visit with others who were mourning her. I longed to speak with someone who had known Dr. A. and with whom I could exchange memories of her – such an opportunity would have been so meaningful a part of my mourning process. I wished to join in as part of a group that reminisced about her sense of humor or marveled about her astute and intelligent insights. There were no photos to look at or mementos to hold and remember her by; both would have been a comfort in coping with her death. Despite the central role Dr. A. played in my life, I could not mark this significant loss with a mourner's custom of my own, such as sitting shiva myself. I was, however, very fortunate that I could turn in my grief to my long-time peer supervision group.

They created a space for me to share my feelings and memories and provided me with much holding. I was fortified by their ongoing support and, especially, by their understanding of what a loss of one's analyst means to a patient. I can imagine the additional pain, confusion, and invisibility a grieving patient might experience if her grief were not met with recognition and a deep understanding of the gravity of such a loss.

During this period of time, I felt great pain and sadness. In trying to acclimate to this new reality, questions arose for me about Dr. A.'s finals days. When exactly had she taken a turn for the worse? Did she know she was dying when we stopped? Did she suffer? Did she die at home? I was aware that these questions were out of the bounds of the therapy relationship, and that I could not seek answers to them. I was alone in my attempts to create a narrative of the end of her life. Creating this narrative seemed important to me at that point, I think, because actively thinking about her experiences offered me a link to Dr. A. in the months during which we did not see each other after our last session. Of course, I had also cared deeply for her and wanted to know how she had been in those final months. The experience of being left with lingering questions that would remain unanswered highlighted for me the finality of the loss of Dr. A. and of our relationship. This was a time of intense emotions. I suffered from disrupted sleep and difficulty concentrating while I continued to confront and increasingly acknowledge the reality of my loss. Interestingly, my clinical practice with my own patients was especially deep and intense in this time of grief. I felt access to deep, raw states in myself and in my patients, which led to very rich work. Indeed, like Dr. A., who had shared that her work both absorbed and comforted her, I found myself having similar experiences in my own work as a therapist.

In the year following Dr. A.'s death, I also struggled with how to think about our relationship and how to forge a new, ongoing connection to her despite her death. Perhaps as long as one's analyst is alive, the connection might feel sustained after treatment ends not only in the patient's mind, but also because the patient imagines that she is still held in the analyst's mind (even if in its recesses), and that the connection could be re-established with a phone call, email, or visit. When the analyst's mind no longer exists, sustaining a sense of connection is radically challenged and lies only in the patient's mind. For a while, it felt to me as if all we had done and known together had died with Dr. A. As she was the only other person who intimately knew our connection, my own hold on the relationship felt elusive to me at times. She knew my most intimate thoughts and feelings; she knew me from the inside out in ways that few, if any, know me. I entrusted her with my most delicate secrets, which she literally took to her grave. Dr. A. also took parts of me with her: parts of myself that only emerged when I was with her and parts of me that could only exist in our private dyad. I found myself wondering: What becomes of those parts? They felt suspended or sometimes lost. While we can say as much about anyone close to us who dies, a deceased loved-one who is not one's therapist often maintains a presence in our lives because other people who knew the deceased help us to sustain the feeling of connection with the dead, to affirm the importance of the past relationship, and to facilitate a new and ongoing psychic relationship with that loved one after death.[3] I believe that this aspect of mourning and moving forward can be more challenging for the grieving patient whose reminders of and connectors to the relationship are often almost exclusively internal. I had chosen to pursue psychoanalytic training at an institute different from Dr. A's. At that particular stage of my mourning, I wondered about the ways in which being in the same community as she might have offered me some solace. For a brief time, when I encountered colleagues from Dr. A.'s institute, I fantasized about asking if they knew her and then announcing that I had been her analysand. I was also aware that having external links to Dr. A. in this way might have been painful.

When we ended therapy, Dr. A. had a couple of referrals for a new therapist ready for me, one of whom she had spoken with about working with me. During the process of saying goodbye to Dr. A. and subsequently grieving her, I could not fathom the idea of starting a new treatment. I was also not convinced that beginning a new therapy was what I needed to cope with the loss. My grief felt natural and necessary. As time passed, however, and as I entertained the idea of starting a new therapy, I became aware that beginning with a new analyst felt like it would signal the ultimate goodbye to Dr. A. and to the analysis I had with her. I felt conflicted not only because I would be taking a painful step toward putting Dr. A. and our relationship firmly in the past, but also because it would be an active step I chose to take. If someone else were to become my analyst, what would become of Dr. A. and our relationship? I had to face, and to reconcile myself with, the idea of letting go.

Years later and moving forward

My grief, most acutely felt in the early months after her death, came in waves and abated over the course of a year. Three years after Dr. A.'s death, I felt ready to and interested in beginning a new analysis. I decided not to work with the therapist she had suggested. Again, I chose someone who was not from my institute, but also not from Dr. A.'s. Choosing someone from outside both our realms felt like a fresh start because the person would not have a link to her. The beginning of this analysis was difficult. Trusting and engaging in a new analytic relationship was frightening. I was afraid that my new analyst would get sick and die. I asked him in the initial consultation if he was healthy, while also pointing out that I knew all too well that his good health was no guarantee. New themes relating to Dr. A.'s death, as well as older themes, became the focus of my new treatment.

This new analysis ushered in another phase of mourning. I processed and explored complicated feelings about Dr. A.'s illness and death. I revisited my profound sadness and anger; yet I now expressed anger at Dr. A. – an anger that (I only then realized) had been more reservedly expressed to her. I reflected on the costs of having stayed in the therapy as Dr. A. was dying: the fears, anxiety, and great pain. I explored both our joint decision to keep working together for as long as we could and my motivations for staying in the treatment until the end, and I also pondered what her own motivation could have been. I wondered what it would have been like if I had left sooner. I became more aware of my desires to take care of Dr. A. and that staying with her was something I could offer her, as I had known how gratifying and helpful our work was for her.

Despite these costs, my experience with Dr. A. was enormously therapeutic for me. My prior fraught relationship to loss was profoundly changed by my experience with Dr. A., who handled her illness and death so openly with me. I had entered treatment initially because death and loss were at the forefront of my consciousness, distractions from my daily life. Treatment helped me to understand why death and loss were such central preoccupations, and how to relegate them to a different, less prominent place. As my analysis evolved, death and loss again moved to the forefront of my experience, thrust as they were to a most painful place *in vivo*. As much as I would have preferred not to go through this pain and tragic loss, I feel grateful to have been able to experience impending death and loss so differently with Dr. A. After our process together, I was left with little I didn't get to say or ask about her death and my loss; having that opportunity to say goodbye felt like a gift. By facing her death together, I was fortunate to have been able to ask questions about her wishes and to express my own preferences, to reminisce with her, to ready myself for her death with her, and to prepare for my life without her: in a sense, I could begin to mourn with her still there.

Prior to my experience with Dr. A., it would have been counter-intuitive for me to believe that such a painful experience in a treatment could be therapeutic for anyone. I appreciate that my own experience is not necessarily the right experience for all patients, nor is it the right approach for all analysts. Dealing actively with one's own analyst's death is so much to bear for each member of the therapy dyad. I feel great admiration and gratitude for Dr. A.'s incredible strength and courage; for her capacity to remain present and to keep my experience at the forefront of the treatment; and for the ways in which she was able to invite, tolerate, and work with my intense feelings about her sickness and dying while dealing with her own illness and impending death. Understandably, not every analyst can address their patients' responses in this way while also confronting their own death.

I want to suggest that for some patients, as it was for me, facing illness and death honestly and directly with their analyst might be reparative, provided that the analyst is able to create an experience that places the primary focus on the patient's experience while managing his or her own feelings about dying.

From time to time, I reflect on what I remember of Dr. A. and my treatment. I remember much about the process – what I learned from her, what I experienced and grew to deeply understand about myself and my history, major themes, and challenges. I know how profoundly I changed with her help. I think that much that we did has become a part of me, floating in and out of my conscious awareness. I have found it especially interesting to discover over the years the things that I find myself remembering: I hold a bittersweet memory of Dr. A.'s laugh in my ears. I think of words that she said with an unusual pronunciation, with her own particular and subtle twist. I picture her face and can hear her voice greeting me at the door at times when I open the door to greet my own patients. At other times, I find myself using words with a patient or offering an insight that I later recognize grew out of my treatment with Dr. A. A feeling of great warmth emerges when I pause to realize how my internal connection with Dr. A. is sustained in these ways, and how I can now miss her with a smile.

Suggestions

My experience of my analyst's illness and death was, of course, unique to my analyst and me, as is the case with every therapeutic dyad's relationship. I do not think that there is a universal approach to use in addressing very difficult situations with patients. However, from my vantage point both as a patient who endured an analyst's loss and as an analyst myself, I would like to propose some concrete suggestions and questions for analysts to consider. These suggestions stem, of course, from my reflections about my personal experience; some of my proposals might be appropriate and meaningful to some patients and analysts and wholly inappropriate and not meaningful to others. While I offer these ideas for consideration, I hope that they represent only a few suggestions among many, as our analytic communities increasingly confront how to address our own illnesses and prospective deaths. I have been pleased to participate in this volume and hope it fosters ongoing dialogues.

- *Acknowledgment of grieving patients.* While I was making the final edits to this chapter, several colleagues died and were honored in email chains of various professional listservs I am on. The messages were heartfelt and touching; they described colleagues who meant so much to their professional communities, and they acknowledged how much the deceased gave to the field and to their patients. What struck me is the frequency with which patients were not referenced in these expressions of condolences, which is interesting given that so many of our patients are in the field and probably on those listservs. Acknowledging that patients might be in attendance at funerals or memorial services or might be reading condolence messages might help grieving patients feel less invisible. Explicitly stating that condolences are extended to family members, friends, colleagues, and patients would be helpful.

• *Supporting ill and dying analysts.* In recent years, I've seen and heard numerous discussions in our analytic communities about professional wills, an important step in our attempts to plan for our own deaths and to protect the needs of our patients. We need to discuss how to support ill and dying analysts when they are wrestling with these very difficult decisions (e.g., whether or not to disclose one's illness to patients; when to end with a particular patient or patients; how to say goodbye; how directly an analyst should discuss his or her impending death; when an ill analyst should close his or her practice). We need to provide support and to encourage ill and dying analysts to reach out for support for themselves. Perhaps the establishment of formal and dedicated entities or forums to sponsor and facilitate outreach and support could be helpful.

• *Decisions about funerals.* Agreeing to have one's patients attend a funeral or memorial service is an analyst's personal preference. As is clear from my account above, it was very helpful for me to know that Dr. A. was fine with my attending her funeral, and it was extremely meaningful for my mourning process. For some patients, though not all, this might be an important question to discuss with their ill or dying analyst, if the analyst is able to engage in so challenging and emotionally charged a topic. In preparing for the event of an unplanned death, the analyst's wishes about whether patients can attend their funeral or memorial might be important for analysts to detail in a professional will. I am not advocating that all patients should attend funerals or that all analysts should feel compelled to allow patients to attend. I also recognize that, for some families, the attendance of patients could feel intrusive or inappropriate at such a very private, painful time. And for patients, some funerals and memorials could be too upsetting or even traumatic to attend. I raise this issue to bring the question of funerals and memorial services into an open dialogue so that the question does not feel taboo.

• *Fostering immortality.* I think many patients have a fantasy of the immortality of the analyst that is often inspired or supported, wittingly or unwittingly, by their analyst her or himself. The ability to return to one's analyst after treatment has ended, whether for a tune up, a check in, to resume treatment, or to establish a future reconnection, is importantly offered to patients when we end treatments. I do so myself. At the same time, given my experience of losing Dr. A. and the fact of mortality, I wonder whether we can modify this promise without arousing terrible anxiety. I suggest that topics that our field needs to examine and discuss further include how we talk to our patients about our future availability and incorporate into our patient's treatments a recognition of our own mortality.[4]

• *Supporting patients.* I believe it is important to think about how to support bereaved patients, those in the field who have a community, and those who are not in the field, who might feel even more invisible. How did they learn of their analyst's death? What kind of support is needed after a death, and who may provide it? How do we create a holding environment to support the depth of their grief? How do we think about former patients who are no longer actively in treatment – are they notified or not? We often refer patients to therapists to begin a new treatment. That is certainly helpful for many, but not for all. As I described above, I needed time to grieve before entering a new treatment. Perhaps bereaved patients could benefit from drop-in groups, where a community and a physical setting in which to mourn can be created, and with recognition and support provided by a therapist or a lay leader knowledgeable about the range of grief reactions relating to the loss of a therapist. Additionally, opportunities for recognition of the magnitude of the loss of one's therapist are much needed because they are not always understood and provided in the larger culture.

- *Concrete remembrances.* When someone we love dies, we often have mementos, photos, and concrete objects to hold on to that are connected to the deceased; the grieving patient often lacks such remembrances. A photo would be the easiest way to offer patients a concrete remembrance. For example, printed programs with a photo of the analyst could be handed out at funerals or memorial services, or an obituary with a photo could be made available. A website or online presence that has an image of the deceased analyst could also be maintained in memoriam.
- *Expanding our knowledge base.* We need to continue to educate ourselves as a field not only about the experiences of ill and dying analysts, but also about the experiences of patients of ill, dying, and deceased analysts. This book is an important contribution toward meeting that need. My own story reflects a planned ending with an analyst who invited both illness and death into the room and into the relationship. For me, this thoughtful and explicit process provided healing and a significant new experience. We need to know more about the impact on different patients of the various ways in which illness and death have been addressed, avoided, planned for, or neglected in treatment. Similarly, we need to know more about the impact on patients whose loss of a therapist was abrupt, whether because the death was sudden or because the terminal illness was not known to the patient. Most patients' accounts of losing their analysts are from clinicians. We need also to hear from patients who are not in the field. Additionally, insight into how best to support analysts during such trying times could be gained by (1) learning from analysts about what was helpful and supportive to them when they were dealing with potentially life-threatening illness while they still worked as analysts; (2) hearing personal accounts of how analysts grappled with and made difficult decisions concerning their illnesses; and (3) learning more about the different ways in which illness and dying were handled and addressed with particular patients who had particular diagnoses and transferences. Exploring the ways in which institutions, such as training programs, institutes, and regional associations, communally address loss might help communities to create mourning rituals and support for grieving patients and colleagues, and may also provide support for and guidance to ill and dying colleagues.

Generating dialogue through conferences and workshops, and possibly creating task forces to study analysts' and patients' experiences and needs, are all possible steps which could help our communities to think about how best to care for ourselves, while also considering the individual needs of both ill and dying analysts and their patients.

Notes

1 I made the decision not to disclose my analyst's identity before it was determined that all names in this volume would be anonymized.
2 Rendely (1999) asserts that the loss of one's analyst represents not only the loss of the analysis and a transferential relationship, but also the loss of an intense and personal *real* relationship.
3 Gaines (1997) writes that mourning entails both detaching from and maintaining an inner connection with the lost object. He also highlights the important role of others in facilitating this process of "maintaining continuity." Deutsch (2011) poignantly illustrates her process of developing an inner connection with her deceased analyst.
4 Numerous authors have described what motivates the analyst's denial of his or her own mortality as well as the clinical implications of fostering an illusion of mortality. Papers include Dewald (1990), Junkers (2013), Denis (2013), and Pinsky (2014). Traesdal (2005, 2013) advocates that the analyst work through his or her own fears of dying and discuss with patients their concerns about the analyst's death as a potential reality.

References

Denis, P. (2013) 'Psychoanalyst: A Profession for an Immortal?' in Junkers, G. (Ed.), *The Empty Couch: The Taboo of Ageing and Retiring in Psychoanalysis*. New York: Routledge, pp. 32–45.

Deutsch, R. (2011) 'A Voice Lost, A Voice Found: After the Death of the Analyst,' *Psychoanalytic Inquiry* 31: 526–535.

Dewald, P.A. (1990) 'Serious Illness in the Analyst: Transference, Counter-Transference, and Reality Responses and Further Reflections,' in Schwartz, H.G. & Silver, A-L.S. (Eds.), *Illness in the Analyst: Implications for the Treatment Relationship*. Madison, CT: International Universities Press, pp. 75–98.

Gaines, R. (1997) 'Detachment and Continuity,' *Contemporary Psychoanalysis* 33: 549–571.

Junkers, G. (2013) 'The Ageing Psychoanalyst: Thoughts on Preparing for a Life Without the Couch,' in Junkers, G. (Ed.), *The Empty Couch: The Taboo of Ageing and Retiring in Psychoanalysis.* New York: Routledge, pp. 3–6.

Pinsky, E. (2014) 'Mortality, Integrity, and Psychoanalysis (Who Are You to Me? Who Am I to You?),' *The Psychoanalytic Quarterly* 83(1): 1–22.

Rendely, J. (1999) 'The Death of an Analyst: The Loss of a Real Relationship,' *Contemporary Psychoanalysis* 35(1): 131–152.

Traesdal, T. (2005) 'When the Analyst Dies: Dealing with the Aftermath,' *Journal of the American Psychoanalytic Association* 53(4): 1235–1255.

Traesdal, T. (2013) 'Analysis Lost and Regained,' in Junkers, G. (Ed.), *The Empty Couch: The Taboo of Ageing and Retiring in Psychoanalysis.* New York: Routledge, pp. 82–90.

Part II

Practitioners

The post-death analyst

Chapter 9

Defenses, transferences, and symbolism after an analyst's death

Jerome S. Blackman

From my experience in treating a few people whose prior analysts had died, I have developed certain understandings. These dynamics most likely do not apply to all analysands who lose their analysts to death. Different analysands' premorbid personality structure, childhood/adolescent/adult history, and specifics of their relationship with the first analyst are bound to be different. One of my purposes in writing about my work with Maria, one analysand of mine whose prior analyst had passed away, is to demonstrate some of the reactions that are likely to occur in people whose pathology does not include deficits in major mental functions (i.e., deficits in integration, reality testing, and abstraction ability) or deficits in the establishment of self and object differentiation (no splitting, fusion anxiety, or disorganized attachments) (Blackman, 2010).

Maria's symptomatology was essentially based on unconscious conflicts deriving from unresolved oedipal issues during latency and adolescence. These problems were exacerbated by a trauma: the death of her father when she was twelve years old. Nevertheless, her adult adaptation had been satisfactory until a series of difficulties in her marriage occasioned the development of panic attacks, horse and airplane phobias, and sexual inhibition. The death of her male analyst after a year of analysis for those problems became symbolically linked with those unconscious conflicts, as was her transference to me after he died. Much of our work together involved understanding how the death of her first analyst had caused an exacerbation of her symptoms, and why. It was then necessary to integrate dream material, her transferences to me, her childhood history, and the traumatic death of her father in order to unravel and relieve her symptomatology.

More specifically, Maria's reactions included (1) rather easy transfer of a good analytic alliance; (2) a wish to condense me with her lost analyst as a defense against grief; (3) conscious grieving; (4) stunning unconscious guilt over entirely unconscious fantasies of having killed her first analyst because she had harbored unconscious wishes, prior to his death, of castrating and killing him; (5) identification with the aggressor, where the deceased analyst was unconsciously experienced as having abandoned the patient – leading the analysand to engage in rationalized behavior of abandoning the professionals who attempted to help after the first analyst's death.

The subsequent analyst must also face conscious and unconscious reactions to the death of a colleague, which may engender empathy with the analysand or produce countertransference disruptions of the later treatment. I also attempt to describe some of these complicating factors as they entered into my treatment of Maria.

A bit of theory

From my vantage point, the death of the analyst, first, is a reality loss of a confidant with whom the person has shared many intimate, and often secret, thoughts and feelings. This loss (Blatt, 1992; Spitz & Wolf, 1946) necessarily creates an "anaclitic depression," or in the vernacular, grief. The dependency on the emotional support of a relatively nonjudgmental therapist is also lost, as is the opportunity for a frequent "analytic toilet" (Anthony, 1970, p. 854) for relief of overwhelming affects (Bion, 1962) needed to foster clear interpretive understandings. The time, money, and effort the person has put into the prior analytic work also seem lost, as the person must "start from scratch" with someone new, especially if the presenting problems, and/or newly clarified problems that arose during treatment (Volkan, 2011, chapter 16), are still unresolved.

What I have found, under favorable conditions, is that there may be an immediate displacement of trust and a continuation of the analytic alliance. My concept of the analytic alliance involves elements of what Greenson (1965) called the "working alliance," whereby the patient is clear with the analyst about a chief complaint, and agrees to attend sessions, to attempt to free associate, to respond to the analyst's interventions, to arrive and leave on time, and to pay the fee. Secondly, the analytic alliance (Adatto, 1974) comprises elements of the "therapeutic alliance" (Zetzel, 1956) summarized in (Blackman, 2013), where the patient develops basic trust in the analyst, is able to understand both positive and negative transference, verbalizes and understands resistances, and reports integrative shifts as well as shifts in defensive activity (see also Brenner, 1975). In Maria's case, the analytic alliance was shifted to me, so in a sense I could pick up "in the middle" without entirely having to "start from scratch." Transferences, in general, in such patients, are more varied. Regarding Maria, we examined multiple displacements and shifts of transference to me, the "surviving" analyst, as well as several other analysts she consulted, after the tragic loss of her first analyst, before she got to me.

These relatively predictable reactions to the reality demise of the analyst are regularly complicated by the person's individual history and dynamics. Conscious awareness of the "triggering" (Solms, 2015) of certain affects from the past is routinely encountered. Some ego regression caused by overwhelming affects, such as a transient decrease in abstraction, secondary process (time sense), or integrative functioning, is not uncommon. So is libidinal regression to an "oral" dependent stance engendered by often-conscious shame and guilt (Bergler, 1954). So, the new analyst is typically faced with a "mess," requiring some flexibility in technique.

If the patient's pathology involves object relations deficits (Blackman, 2010; Kernberg, 1975; Volkan, 1995), the new analyst will likely find distancing defenses, affects overwhelming the capacity for affect regulation (Bretherton, 1992), and recrudescence of anxiety about object constancy – especially fears that the new analyst might disappear, especially if the patient utters any hostility about the prior analyst's death (Akhtar, 1994).

When there have been traumatic losses in the person's life, of course, the death of the analyst is experienced as a new trauma and adds to anticipation of further trauma. The affective reactions to a new loss can produce a variety of pathological defensive operations. Aside from identification with the aggressor and identification with the lost object (reviewed in Blackman, 2003), other defenses may include suppression, isolation of affect, counterphobic "diving in" to a new treatment, intellectualizations about the nature and certainty of death, or exaggerated empathy for the departed analyst's spouse (reaction-formation and projection). For example, one patient consulted me after her first analyst had died in a boating accident. For two years, she did not associate to this loss. Finally, as her suppression and avoidance were linked with other material, she recalled a long-forgotten depression that occurred when she was transferred, at age four, from the loving care of her grandparents to her busy, workaholic parents.

Finally, I would like to share what I consider a bit of psychoanalytic common sense. Losses are almost never just losses. Losses usually have multiple meanings, and these meanings will vary from case to case (Brenner, 2006). The complex activities of the mind add symbolism to just about everything (i.e., a cigar is never just a cigar, which may be the joke Freud intended if he, in fact, ever made that quip). Losses may be experienced as a punishment. Losses may be experienced with glee (one patient, after her mother passed away, sang me the chorus of "Ding, Dong, the Witch is Dead" [Arlen, Harburg & Harburg, 1939]). Losses may be felt as a loss of control, and thereby engender anger. Losses may be experienced as a loss of self, producing "aggressive breakdown products" (Kohut, 1971), which are sometimes turned on the self, causing depressive affect and, in some cases, suicide attempts (Menninger, 1933). Losses may be taken as an omen of bad things to come. Losses may be thought of as a confirmation that nothing ever good happens (in depressed patients). Losses may cause anxiety of various sorts. Finally, losses may be unconsciously associated with a wish to castrate or seen as the result of a castrating wish.

In Maria's case, as I mentioned above, there did not appear to be object relations pathology. She did not suffer with anxiety about basic trust; her self-image was well defined. Rather, the case turned on specific dynamics during her current marriage, her first genital phase, and her late adolescence (Blum, 2010). It was not until she was in her late thirties, after her husband was injured, that she had sought consultation with Jeff Rodrigue, a past analytic supervisor of mine, for acute phobia of horses and airplanes, panic attacks, and sexual inhibition. After a year of analysis with him, he died from a myocardial infarction. That's where the story begins.

The prequel

I knew a little about Maria before I saw her. I also knew quite a bit about and had feelings toward the professionals whom she had consulted during the week after Jeff, her first analyst, died. Jeff had been a talented supervisor of mine. He had also helped me get involved in teaching by getting me to work with him at Charity Hospital in New Orleans when I finished my residency. When Jeff had been supervising me on the case of a sixty-year-old, never-married, lonely, depressed woman, I once mentioned that I did not have any history of her sexuality. Jeff remarked, "She's probably jacking off once in a while." During the long slog of residency and analytic fellowship, that type of ironic comment kept me afloat.

Symbolically, Jeff most certainly represented the big brother I never had (and could have used). To add to that symbolism, Jeff had obtained his training analysis with Hank, who had also been my training analyst. During my analysis with Hank, I had come to realize Jeff's importance to me, both in reality and fantasy. Consciously, I was never aware of any rivalry with Jeff. It was no doubt submerged in the extensive gratitude I felt toward both him and my (our) analyst, Hank.

Maria had seen two other psychiatrists after Jeff died, before I saw her. One was Algernon (another of Hank's analysands, I later learned), a hilarious, sarcastic guy who had also supervised me. He, like Jeff, had acted as an antidote to my many frustrating experiences with other supervisors. I remember during one of my early meetings with Algie, I mentioned that one of my new patients had seen many previous therapists and received different diagnoses. When Algie dryly commented, "Well, you're smarter than all of *them,,*" I got a belly laugh that lifted my spirits for days.

The other psychiatrist Maria had consulted was Mark, with whom I had been friendly for a decade; Mark and I shared a waiting room. We were both single at the time, had commiserated about our problems with dating, and ate lunch together at least once a week. He had also been analyzed by Hank.

These were some of the factors I had to consider during Maria's evaluation and treatment. For example, it was hard for me to hear of Maria's unconscious hostility toward Jeff, since I had felt so grateful and warm toward (and unconsciously competitive with) him, and was myself grieving. I had to think hard about my reaction to hearing Maria idealize, express gratitude for, and mourn her one consultation with Hank after Jeff's death – parallel reactions I had had when I finished my analysis with Hank, without whose analytic input I would never have become a relatively symptom-free human being.

There were sizable oedipal countertransference dynamics I was forced to confront in myself so that they would not interfere with my handling of Maria, who was in great distress (Marcus, 1980). I experienced guilt about Jeff's death and sadness about losing him. I experienced (sibling-based) guilt that my friend, Mark, had been unable to handle Maria, and that I "won" her as a patient. I was also aware of internal pressure to perform, to show Hank, my former analyst (and now friend and colleague), that I was up to the job. Fortunately, I decided to get some assistance from one of my favorite supervisors from analytic training. His input helped me to avoid the unconscious landmines that could have destroyed the analytic work.

From Hank, who had referred Maria to me about a week after Jeff's death, I learned the following about Maria: She was thirty-nine years old and had been married for fifteen years. She and her husband were both from Argentina. Her husband was a physician who worked for an international medical organization (something akin to the World Health Organization), and was stationed in the U.S. for three years, with an option to renew for another three years. Maria had an undergraduate degree in English but had not worked since they had arrived in the U.S. about a year previously. They had two daughters, one in fourth grade, the other in high school, both doing well. The husband traveled frequently. Both Maria and her husband, Jorge, were equestrians.

Maria had first consulted Jeff, her first analyst, soon after arriving in the U.S. She had not had prior treatment. Her chief complaint was a fear of riding horses that had developed after an incident where she and Jorge had been riding together. Jorge was thrown by his horse and broke his femur. After that, Maria could not even get near a horse. In addition, she developed a fear of airplanes to the point where she could not go to the airport (to see off her husband on his frequent trips). She also lost interest in sexual activity, and when she attempted sex with her husband, she did not become stimulated.

During her analysis with Jeff, Maria had become aware that there was a link between her husband's injury and her father's death when Maria was twelve years old. Maria and her father had been riding on a buckboard ("*calesa de cuatro ruedas*") in the Pampas on vacation (one of their favorite mutual activities) when one of the wheels hit a rut and the buckboard overturned. Her father hit his head on a large stone, and unfortunately died several days later from the cerebral hemorrhage he had sustained in the fall.

With that background, I agreed to continue Maria's analysis.

Evaluation and transition to the second analysis

Maria was a neatly, conservatively dressed woman, who was immediately engaging. She showed excellent reality testing, abstraction ability, and capacity to organize her thoughts. She had never had suicidal ideation. During the evaluation session, she sat and recounted to me pretty much what Hank had told me. She added that when Jeff had died about a week previously, she had cried, and was still grieving. She asked me if I had known him, and I acknowledged that it had been a shock to all the analysts in the community. She then related to me, in more detail, what had happened after Jeff's death.

Jeff's wife had retrieved Jeff's office materials and referred most of his patients to Hank. Hank had triaged many of them, including Maria. He had evaluated her in his office, and then initially referred Maria to Algie. Algie consulted with her but didn't have time to see her, so he referred her to Mark. Mark, a dynamic general psychiatrist, saw her for a consultation, diagnosed her with panic and phobias, and prescribed a low dose of diazepam (Valium). The night after Maria saw Mark, she took the Valium, and within an hour had a severe panic attack, causing her husband to bring her to the local Emergency Room. The ER physician referred her to a psychiatrist at the psychiatric hospital next door, and she stayed overnight. Mark visited her. The next day, when Maria was discharged, she called Mark. He recommended that she continue analysis. To that end, Mark had called Hank, who in turn called me.

After explaining all this, Maria expressed a wish to continue her analysis. She had been getting better while working with Jeff, and hoped she could resolve the panic attacks, phobias, and the sexual inhibition that had cropped up after her husband's injury. Accordingly, we set up a four-times-a-week schedule and Maria started using the couch in session two.

Maria at first talked a great deal about Jeff, how smart he had been, and how he helped her understand that her phobia had occurred not just because of Jorge's broken femur, but also because of her father's death, which had involved horses. Although the dynamics of all that were not clear, Maria was optimistic that the connections could be found – as was I.

Her first dream while in treatment with me was "You are reading Dr. Rodrigue's notes, but they are covered in blood." She associated to Jeff's death being bloody: he had had a myocardial infarction while he was driving. He, therefore, had sustained bloody injuries after his death. We understood she wished that I had seen Dr. Rodrigue's notes (I had not). When I pointed out that she saw me as like Dr. Rodrigue partly to relieve the pain she felt over his loss (bloody notes), Maria cried. She was horrified at how "bloody" the scene must have been, though neither she nor I knew the exact facts.

Soon after that, she reported another dream: "I am wearing a dress with a corsage, but the middle of the corsage looks like Dr. Rodrigue's pen, and the pen is bloody." She thought again of how she wished to avoid the grief over losing Dr. Rodrigue, and of where his pen was pinned, as part of a flower accessory, to her dress; other dynamics of this dream took over a year to figure out.

Maria's "story"[1] and her analysis with me

During her roughly 400 psychoanalytic sessions with me, two alternating yet connected foci appeared in Maria's associations. One of these concerned the problems in her marriage. The other concerned her conflicts surrounding her relationship with her father and the meaning of his death. Elements of both these conflictual areas were also periodically displaced or transferred onto me.

I worked with Maria actively, so there was much discussion. Maria's major defensive operations were repression, symbolization, externalization, displacement, avoidance, inhibition of critical judgment, and transference. There was little isolation of affect, rationalization, or intellectualization, and virtually no concretization. Our interactions were therefore affect-laden, and symbolic discussions flowed with some ease, although they were at times painful. Resistance did not appear until two years into her treatment, when it arose surreptitiously and became a critical juncture.

Emotional closeness did not produce distancing defenses, and pre-oedipally based mistrust did not seem to be an issue. After Maria's father died, her mother became withdrawn during Maria's adolescence, which, we figured out, led to her somewhat exaggerated hunger to attract boys' attention. Later she experienced conflicts over wanting her husband to be more "maternal" in his attention and more caring than he had been. Because of guilt, however, Maria had been "easy-going" about her husband's many travels, and had denied or minimized any frustration and anger about how his idealism interfered with her wish for more closeness and affection. She didn't want to "damage" his career.

When Maria was in college, she had strongly disliked Ani, a highly seductive and attractive female drama major. Ani was dating Jorge, a medical student and "an older man," who seemed out of reach; this provoked Maria's competitiveness. She dolled herself up, made a point of interesting Jorge, eventually seduced him, and was thereby able to steal him away from Ani. Maria knew that Jorge was an idealist, out to "cure the world." Although Maria had at first admired Jorge's values, through analysis we recognized that, over the years, Maria had been using reaction-formations and rationalizations to help her minimize how much Jorge's travels annoyed her. He had not even been present at the births of their two children – he was busy doing surgery on indigent children. Any anger she felt toward him for his absences immediately caused her to feel guilt: could she compete with indigent children? And if she insisted he come home, she imagined her demand would "demasculinize" him, which made her feel even worse. We could see that her relative passivity in relation to Jorge was a defense against this castration guilt.

Maria's fear of airplanes was also connected to repressed matters regarding Jorge. When she could not get on a plane, she caused him the same type of "abandonment" that she felt he had perpetrated on her – identification with the aggressor after the fact (A. Freud, 1936). She simultaneously punished herself, as she was left lonely. Maria's loss of sexual interest, similarly, reflected an unconscious (destructive) wish to repel Jorge, so although she periodically allowed sexual intercourse, she did not give him or herself any satisfaction: both of them ended up symbolically punished.

Although Maria began to understand with more clarity why she felt guilty in relation to the frustrations with her husband, and how that guilt had caused her to become anxious and defensive, her symptoms persisted until we could integrate the various compromise formations (Freud, 1926; Waelder, 2007) which had unconsciously made her susceptible to such defensive activity in the first place.

Over the next two years in analysis, Maria shared many memories of her childhood and adolescence. Although they did not appear in chronological order, I will relate them that way for the sake of clarity. She recalled feeling close to her mother as a child. Her mother was warm and loving, and did not favor Maria's older brother. In fact, Maria adored her older brother, who in reality had been loving and protective toward her. Maria became a Daddy's girl during the first genital phase. As best as she could remember, she also adored her father, and loved doing things with him. He was a warm, gentle man, whose work did not interfere with her time with him.

As she was discussing, with some tenderness and sadness, her feelings toward her father, Maria recalled an "exception." There was an incident, when she was approaching six years of age, when she had had a nightmare and wanted to enter her parents' bedroom. Her parents, who apparently did not suffer from the separation anxiety so common in today's parents regarding their children, had locked their bedroom door. Maria's reaction to finding the door locked was not to knock. Instead, she got angry, and recalled the thought: "I hope that my father dies! That way, if I can't have him, no one can!" I pointed out (a reconstruction) that "no one" was a generalization that must have shielded her from facing competitive feelings toward her mother (Loeb, 1982). Maria at first laughed. She then agreed and remembered something else: when she got angry at her father (and mother), she ran and jumped in bed with her brother, who did not object.

As we worked in analysis, we could trace this pattern: when Maria felt excluded by a man, she rejected him and jumped to another. Something like that had happened after Jeff's death. She saw Hank and then Algie, but both rejected her. Then, Mark accepted her, but something strange happened when she took the Valium he had prescribed. Instead of calming her, the Valium had caused a severe panic attack with ego regression, and she had needed to be hospitalized for a day. The panic attack represented a compromise formation: taking Mark's Valium symbolically orally castrated him (see below), and she ran to another doctor. By needing hospitalization, where she had to see yet another doctor, she unconsciously rejected Mark just as she had been rejected by Hank and Algie, that is, she jumped in her brother's bed. That hospitalization and her paradoxical reaction to the benzodiazepine could only be analyzed later (see below).

When Maria's husband frustrated her, she associated that perhaps she had wished to leave him and find another man. This heretofore unconscious fantasy had caused her so much guilt that she could not go near an airport for fear that she might get on a plane, go find another man, and never come back. Thereafter, she feared she would be punished by losing her husband, who represented her father. The idea of punishment by loss was massively exacerbated by her father's actual death.

I now heard more about the accident in which her father had died. She and her father (but not her mother nor her brother) loved horses. They often rode together. When the family vacationed in the Pampas, it was quiet and serene, and she and her father enjoyed riding together. Her father was taking her to the store in town on the day of the accident. They were planning on spending hours together, and, for a while, he let her handle the reins of the horse pulling the buckboard. They were having fun talking and her father was "driving" (i.e., he had the reins), when a wheel of the buckboard hit the rock. Now, in treatment, we could tie the guilt that Maria felt to her competitive feelings toward her mother at the time when she had attempted to enter the parental bedroom years before, and her childhood thought that if she couldn't have her father, she wished he would die. At age twelve, she had partly reacted as though her competitiveness toward her mother had brought about her father's demise as a punishment. In addition, right after the accident, she partly reacted as though her five-year-old homicidal fantasy toward her father had resulted in his death, and that his death represented her punishment for that wish.

How was this connected to Jeff's death? To the extent that Jeff symbolized Maria's father, she had harbored possessive feelings toward him. Jeff's friendly personality and warm expressiveness elicited that transference, and the patient had been aware, during her work with Jeff, that he had become a father-transference figure. She had been enjoying her work with him when he passed away, so the connection to the buckboard trip with her father seemed clear. But now Maria mentioned something which I had not known about previously. About two months into her analysis with Jeff, he had his first coronary. He was out of the office for about a week, and when he returned he had told her he had had a mild heart attack. At that point, Jeff had given Maria the option of continuing her analysis with a different analyst. She had decided to stay in treatment with Jeff.

We now deconstructed that decision. Maria had stayed with Jeff for several reasons, including (1) she liked him, in reality, and thought he was smart and helpful; (2) she unconsciously felt guilty about her anger toward him for getting sick and would have felt guiltier if she had "killed off Jeff" by leaving him; (3) unconsciously, she felt guilty over her competitive feelings toward his wife (this was later reinforced when Jeff's wife had been so nice in helping Maria find another analyst after Jeff passed away); (4) she wished to master the death of her father, and thereby hoped that Jeff would live so that Maria would not have to mourn; (5) unconsciously, Maria felt guilty over a wish to kill Jeff, transferred from her father, because he was unavailable to Maria (oedipal guilt); and (6) she forced herself to repeat the loss of her father with Jeff so that she would not have to think of her complex reactions to her father's death.

But Maria's transferences didn't arise only from first genital phase conflicts. Maria was also depressed and angry that her mother could not soothe her after her father died. Her mother was inconsolable for several years. During adolescence, Maria had eventually turned to boys defensively, as a salve for the loss of her father and as a substitute for soothing from her mother. Maria's intense competition with Ani, Jorge's prior sexpot girlfriend, also involved an intense wish for maternal soothing that had become repressed and then sexualized (what Volkan, 2011, has called "reaching up").

The pressure for maternal soothing had been unconscious at the time Maria married Jorge, but we could see that in some ways he represented a maternal figure because of his wishes to take care of children around the world. Maria had projected herself onto those needy children to avoid the pain and shame regarding her mother. There was, however, another dynamic thread that helped us put the pieces of Maria's complex web of symptoms together.

About eighteen months into her analysis with me, Maria reported a dream regarding my friend, Mark, the third psychiatrist who had seen her after Jeff's death: "He gives me the Valium. Then I am eating the Valiums, but they are pennies. I keep eating the pennies." Maria's associations to this dream first involved Mark, and how she felt grateful that he had been "supportive" by giving her the Valium and even visiting her after she was hospitalized by a different psychiatrist. She then gasped. When I inquired about this gasping, Maria told me "I can't believe it." She then explained what she had been thinking: in English, with her Spanish accent, the way she pronounced the word "pennies" was exactly the same as she would say the word "penis" in Spanish. As she recounted this, she experienced a mild panic attack on the couch.

We immediately addressed her associations about that panic attack. She felt guilty about Mark: she had not given him a chance. As she mentioned the guilt, the panicky feelings subsided a bit. But her thought of eating a penis required more analysis. I reconstructed that this must have been her childhood fantasy when she was angry at her father because the bedroom door was locked. When she wished him dead, Maria was biting off his penis (a form of castration wish). She also associated to something about her husband. Maybe she wanted to castrate him, too? "Yes," she thought, "if he were a woman, he would have been with me when my daughters were born!"

I interpreted that her guilt over anger that her mother "was not there" for her after her father's death may have also led to a fantasy of emasculating her husband to (symbolically) make him more maternal; however, her severe unconscious guilt over wishing to "demasculinize" him caused her to repress that thought. Instead, she took care of everything, did not put pressure on him not to travel as much (inhibition of aggression), and stayed punished. That unstable equilibrium had broken down after her husband broke his leg. The broken femur, so close to the genitalia, unconsciously symbolized her wish to castrate him (to make him the mother she needed from adolescence). Moreover, Jorge's accident "could have killed him," a near miss that brought Maria's unconscious wish to kill Jorge and her father (and Jeff) too near to reality, causing massive guilt reactions, and the resulting panic attacks. Maria's recent inability to enjoy sex with Jorge had similar dynamics.

The critical juncture

After doing so much work on understanding her complex reactions both to Jeff's death and to the other psychiatrists she had seen – as well as on how those reactions were unconsciously connected with her dreams, childhood fantasies, and adolescent memories – Maria had reported relative freedom from the symptoms that had begun after Jorge's accident. Her character had also shifted from (passively) accommodating and loquacious to more cooperative and forthright. Now Maria associated that she had been similarly passive a couple of months previously, when Jorge told her that he wanted to return to Argentina after his three-year stint in the U.S. was completed. Maria had wanted to finish her analysis with me, but now saw that she felt that, if she had pressured Jorge to stay in the U.S., she would have felt guilty about "damaging" his career. Although we now knew the origins of her guilt, Jorge had already applied to return, and his request had been granted. Maria then asked me if I thought she should ask Jorge to rescind his acceptance (for the return to Argentina) before they had to leave in a month.

I felt quite conflicted about the situation and about Maria's direct question to me. Consciously, I felt it would have been ridiculously grandiose of me to suggest that Maria and her husband put his career on hold for another three years just so that she could see me. There were, of course, plenty of psychoanalysts in Argentina. In retrospect, I realize that I also had unconscious countertransference reactions: I felt guilty about possibly competing with

Jorge (representing my father), and guilty about having "won" my oedipally tinged sibling rivalry with Mark (Hank had eventually referred Maria to me). These unconscious factors, which I did not think of until sometime later, caused me, at the time of Maria's request, to be relatively passive with her about this (as a defense). I later saw that at the time she brought up the problem of residence, I intellectualized matters by suggesting we try to understand what had happened: perhaps her question to me was related to the dynamics we had understood thus far.

In what follows, I will describe some of what we understood during that last month. But after Maria left for Argentina, I felt somehow self-critical, and over about two years, as I rethought the ending, I realized that unconscious factors had led me to avoid telling her my true opinion, which was that she should have finished up what we had been working on, and that Jorge staying in the U.S. a while longer would not damage or kill him. The reason she asked my opinion was that she wanted absolution for her wish to stay with me – in order to relieve her guilt about numerous transference factors. However, my musings, associations, and self-criticism were eventually useful (see my Epilogue, below).

In the approximately sixteen sessions we had left before Maria returned home, she expressed sorrow and guilt that she had not told me about Jorge's application when it occurred. We understood that she had been in conflict: her wish to stay with me symbolically represented some way in which she was "cheating" on Jorge, who apparently did feel some competitiveness with me (see my Epilogue, below). This wish was parallel to her anger at her father when she was five, anger that led her to jump into her brother's bed: in this compromise formation, I represented the brother. She had also anticipated that we were nearing the completion of her analysis, and had taken control of that loss by rejecting me first – also leaving me before I could die, as Jeff had (identification with the aggressor before the fact: A. Freud, 1936).

There was a transference to me not only from her father, but also from Jeff – whereby she symbolically killed me off and destroyed (i.e., castrated) my "analyzing instrument" (Isakower, 1992). In addition, as in adolescence, she avoided the dependency on me (as a mother) by leaving and staying with her (father-)husband. In fact, their sex life had improved dramatically, so the use of sexualization as a defense returned.

A new factor arose during the short, forced "termination." Maria was relieved to finally be "going home." In her dreams, she was returning to the Pampas on vacation. Her associations ran to a wish that her father had stayed home with her instead of taking her on a ride on the buckboard. As her guilt about Jorge had been analyzed, she had realized that she had been angry at him for dragging her to the United States to begin with. She had left her mother and many friends at home. Maria also longed to speak her mother tongue again (Cao, Blackman, & Guan, 2018). As I represented her father, she was killing me off and jumping in her brother's bed (now symbolized by her husband).

Two weeks before Maria ended her analysis with me, there was a long holiday weekend. When Maria entered my office, she said to me, before getting on the couch, "I hope you and your wife had a good holiday." I did not tell her that, at the time, I was not married. Instead, after she reclined on the couch, I pointed out that she was very nice to say so, but that we knew that sometimes, when she was so nice, it was to avoid guilt. She then suddenly developed spastic paralysis on the couch. Her hands and feet froze; she could not move. Her hands took the appearance of claws (Berthelsdorf, 1988). She asked me what to do. I asked her for her associations (to the acute conversion symptom).

She thought of using her hands to hurt someone. I linked this thought with her reaction-formation in wishing me a good holiday with my wife. She said she did not know my wife, and did not want to hurt anyone. We then discussed her guilt over any aggression, whether toward my wife (competitive aggression) or toward me. She began crying.

Maria thought she felt guilty about leaving me. She had not told me early enough. That wasn't fair. We linked her not telling me with her own losses, which had not been fair or predictable. We could note her identification with the aggressor, undoing, and turning passive to active. Her paralysis disappeared.

During the last week of her treatment, I got some names of psychoanalysts in Argentina and passed them on to her. She thanked me for my help, and we said *adios*.

Epilogue

Three years after Maria had said *adios* to me, Jorge called me. He was back in town, in the U.S., and requested a consultation with me. I told him I couldn't tell him anything related to Maria, but I would be glad to hear his thoughts and input. He came to my office a few days later. I was surprised at how shy Jorge was, considering his globe-trotting medical activities. He told me Maria had asked him to say hello and to thank me for my work; she also thanked me for finding an analyst for her in Argentina.

Jorge then told me that he felt a little guilty about interrupting Maria's work with me, but he had been quite fearful that he would never get a stable, home-based position in his organization. There was competition, and he had been concerned that a non-physician administrator would take the position he wanted. He said his return to Argentina had been helpful, and he now had the leadership position. He was not traveling much at all, and Maria's panic and phobias had not returned. He expressed some gratitude. I told him he was quite welcome, and I was glad to hear that Maria was doing well.

Two years later, that is, five years after the somewhat abrupt termination of her analytic work with me, Maria returned to the U.S. (to visit a relative) and called me. She wanted to see me. By this time, I had given considerable thought to the treatment, its surprise ending, my countertransferences, Maria's acting out, and the visit by Jorge. I gave her an appointment.

When Maria entered my office, she immediately said she did not know quite why she had called me. I said to her, "I think we have some unfinished business." She smiled. She said, "That's exactly right. I was thinking something like that this morning. Unfinished business. What is it?"

I responded that I had some ideas, but first I was interested in what had happened with her over the past five years. Briefly, she filled me in. She and Jorge were doing OK, although they had not returned to riding horses. Maria had returned to work teaching English in a high school. Her children were on track. She said she had spent two years with an analyst in Argentina, but that that analyst "never said much," and they had not gotten into "what we worked on." She then asked me what my ideas were. I decided to tell her.

I told her that when she had asked me whether she should ask Jorge to rescind their return to Argentina for another year or two, I had made an error: I should have told her to ask him to rescind it. She asked me, "Why didn't you? I think I wanted you to tell me so I wouldn't feel bad about it." I told her I had not previously encountered the problem she presented, and so I was not sure how to handle it. But I agreed with her that she was feeling too guilty about telling him she wanted to stay in the U.S. I should have pointed that out, and supported her decision more. By not doing so, I thought I must have reminded her of how her mother had "not been there" for her after her father's death. She agreed: "Right. I remember wanting you to be more reassuring. I ran away from you like I ran away from my mother when I was a teenager."

She told me Jorge had wanted to meet me. She thought he felt somehow competitive with me and with her analysis. She said she knew at the time they decided to return home that he was also a bit annoyed with her personality changes – she had become less inhibited about her aggression with him, more openly desirous of his time, and more insistent that he curb his roaming the globe so that he could spend more time with his daughters. She didn't want him to be mad at her. When I asked her what she was afraid of, she thoughtfully said, "Of losing him. That's ridiculous. He would never leave me. Is it punishment again? Damn it!"

We then got back to the termination, itself. We reviewed how she felt guilty about staying to finish analysis with me because she still felt it would somehow injure Jorge. The issue of guilt regarding me or Jorge had not been worked through with her subsequent analyst in Argentina. They had focused more on loss. In Maria's opinion, Jorge would not have been injured had they stayed in the U.S. a bit longer, although he had rationalized to her that it was a good thing that they had returned. There was never any reason for him to feel worried about his job. People loved him. They could have waited another year or two (or three) with no problem. Her guilt about injuring him had been aggravated by his anxiety.

I reminded her of how her guilt toward Jorge was actually a remnant of her guilt over her father's death and her death wish toward her father when she was little. She remembered. "Right, and the castrating dreams. I remember. I remember getting paralyzed on your couch." We then discussed how her leaving me turned the tables, and represented both the punishment for Jeff's death and her father's death, both of which had reified unconscious castrating fantasies represented in her dreams of the bloody pen-corsage and of eating pennies-penis. She said, "Right. I did all that when I left you, like Dr. Rodrigue and my father had left me. It's crystal clear."

Summary

I have attempted to sketch out, in this chapter, some of the things I ran into when Maria's analyst died and she was referred to me for continuing treatment. I hope that the summary of her analysis with me demonstrates the complexity of the loss. I have also endeavored to describe my reactions, countertransference, and otherwise to my loss of an analyst-mentor and friend, and how that complicated the whole situation.

In particular, this case report and my thoughts about it may be instructive to my colleagues who encounter a situation where the death of the patient's analyst is layered with compromise formations. Maria's case, I believe, illustrates what can go on in the mind of people who suffer from symptoms, trauma, unresolved oedipal fantasies, and precipitating adult marital situations. Perhaps some of the findings are generalizable, perhaps not. But Maria helped me understand the power of interpretive technique in the aftermath of a first analyst's death, when conditions for that type of treatment are present. It is my hope that I have been able to pass on that understanding.

Note

1 Volkan and Fowler (2009).

References

Adatto, C. (1974) *The Analytic Alliance*, Personal Communication.

Akhtar, S. (1994) 'Object Constancy and Adult Psychopathology,' *International Journal of Psychoanalysis* 75: 441–455.

Anthony, E.J. (1970) 'Two Contrasting Types of Adolescent Depression and their Treatment,' *Journal of the American Psychoanalytic Association* 18: 841–859.

Arlen, H., Harburg, E., & Harburg, E.Y. (1939) 'Ding Dong, the Witch is Dead,' www.youtube.com/watch?V=rhjoj9iqekg. Sony/ATV Music Publishing LLC. From Baum, F., Langley, N. & Ryerson, F. (1939), *The Wizard of Oz*. www.imdb.com/title/tt0032138/.

Bergler, E. (1954) 'Post-Analytic Misuse of Pre-Analytic Symptoms,' *Psychoanalytic Review* 41(2): 191–196.

Berthelsdorf, S. (1988) 'Ambivalence towards Women in Chinese Characters, and its Implications for Feminism,' *American Imago* 45(2): 229–237.

Bion, W.R. (1962) *Learning from Experience*, pp. 1–116. London: Tavistock.

Blackman, J. (2003) *101 Defenses: How the Mind Shields Itself*. New York: Routledge.

Blackman, J. (2010) *Get the Diagnosis Right: Assessment and Treatment Selection for Mental Disorders*. New York: Routledge.

Blackman, J. (2013) *The Therapist's Answer Book: Solutions to 101 Tricky Problems in Psychotherapy*. New York: Routledge.

Blatt, S.J. (1992) 'The Differential Effect of Psychotherapy and Psychoanalysis with Anaclitic and Introjective Patients: The Menninger Psychotherapy Research Project Revisited,' *Journal of the American Psychoanalytic Association* 40: 691–724.

Blum, H.P. (2010) 'Adolescent Trauma and the Oedipus Complex,' *Psychoanalytic Inquiry* 30(6): 548–556.

Brenner, C. (1975) *Alterations of Defenses during Psychoanalysis. Kris Study Group Monograph*. Edited by B. Fine and H. Waldhorn. New York: International Universities Press.

Brenner, C. (2006) *Psychoanalysis: Mind and Meaning*. New York: Psychoanalytic Quarterly Press.

Bretherton, I. (1992) 'The Origins of Attachment Theory: John Bowlby and Mary Ainsworth,' *Developmental Psychology* 28: 759–775. www.psychology.sunysb.edu/attachment/online/inge_origins.pdf   (accessed December 2018).

Cao, L., Blackman, J., & Guan, E. (2018) 'Societal Change and Language Change in China: Language-Switching during Multilingual Dynamic Psychotherapy,' *Psychoanalytic Psychology* 35: 224–230.

Freud, A. (1936) *The Ego and the Mechanisms of Defense*. New York: International Universities Press.

Freud, S. (1926) 'Inhibitions, Symptoms and Anxiety,' *Standard Edition* 20: 5–176.

Greenson, R. (1965) 'The Working Alliance and the Transference Neurosis,' *Psychoanalytic Quarterly* 34: 155–181.

Isakower, O. (1992) 'Chapter Five: The Analyzing Instrument: States of Consciousness and the Dream Psychology of Dr. Bertram Lewin (A Further Expansion of the Concept of the Analyzing Instrument),' *Journal of Clinical Psychoanalysis* 1: 204–208.

Kernberg, O. (1975) *Borderline Conditions and Pathological Narcissism.* New York: Aronson.

Kohut, H. (1971) *The Analysis of the Self.* New York: International Universities Press.

Loeb, F. (1982) 'Generalization as a Defense,' *Psychoanalytic Study of the Child* 37: 405–419.

Marcus, I. (1980) 'Countertransference and the Psychoanalytic Process in Children and Adolescents,' *Psychoanalytic Study of the Child* 35: 285–298.

Menninger, K. (1933) 'Psychoanalytic Aspects of Suicide,' *International Journal of Psychoanalysis* 14: 376–390.

Solms, M. (2015) *The Feeling Brain: Selected Papers on Neuropsychoanalysis.* New York: Routledge.

Spitz, R.A. & Wolf, K.M. (1946) 'Anaclitic Depression—an Inquiry into the Genesis of Psychiatric Conditions in Early Childhood II,' *Psychoanalytic Study of the Child* 2: 313–342.

Volkan, V. (1995) *Six Steps in the Treatment of Borderline Personality Organization.* New York: Jason Aronson.

Volkan, V. (2011) *Psychoanalytic Technique Expanded: A Textbook on Psychoanalytic Treatment.* Charlottesville, VA: Pitchstone Publishing.

Volkan, V. & Fowler, C. (2009) *Searching for the Perfect Woman: The Story of a Complete Psychoanalysis.* New York: Aronson.

Waelder, R. (2007) 'The Principle of Multiple Function: Observations on Over-Determination,' *Psychoanalytic Quarterly* 76(1): 75–92.

Zetzel, E. (1956) 'Current Concepts of Transference,' *International Journal of Psychoanalysis* 37: 369–375.

Chapter 10

A patient's and analyst's self-experiences with shared loss

David Braucher

Introduction

Nichole was a young adult struggling with the sequelae of a traumatic childhood with a psychotically disturbed mother and a depressed father. After two suicide attempts and subsequent hospitalizations in her teens, she failed to find a clinician with whom she did not feel too overwhelmed with shame to openly reveal herself. In her early twenties, a friend's analyst referred her to Dora, who would become the first analyst she would "ever trust." After ten years of treatment with Dora, Nichole's life was beginning to stabilize when Dora died in a traumatic accident. As Nichole sought recognition for the unique relationship she had lost, the analyst charged with closing down Dora's practice rebuffed Nichole as one among many, including herself, who were suffering a tragic and precipitous loss. Recalling that Dora had spoken to her about a supervisee of hers with whom Dora had discussed Nichole's case – yes, Dora had discussed her case with her supervisee and mentioned as much to Nichole – Nichole set her sights on finding him. At the memorial service, Nichole asked around until she found me. She asked if I would talk with her. With perhaps too much beginner's enthusiasm and willingness, I readily agreed.

Nichole initially refused to accept me as her new analyst. Her traumatic past with a psychotically intrusive mother and a depressively absent father rendered her incapable of mourning – of tolerating the paradoxical experience of the presence of an absence. Consequently, she attempted to replicate with me the experience she had had in her treatment with Dora. Unaware of what I was signing up for, I found myself involved in a treatment in which I had unintentionally agreed to receive supervision from a patient who also set the frame. In a way, we replaced Dora for each other. I became her analyst, and she acted as my supervisor – a very rigid and demanding one, I might add.

Through what often felt like a "wild" analysis, I experienced myself as a type of transitional object – as a substitute for Dora with the same alleged power to comfort Nichole as Dora had had, but ultimately as an object within Nichole's illusion of control. I found myself in the paradoxical gap between feeling that *I* was all-important to Nichole, and yet without agency – a divine ruler ruled by his subject.

Over the course of this treatment, the pressure to be ever available forced my personality flaws to the surface, and I repeatedly failed Nichole's expectations. This shortfall not only revealed how I was in fact a distinctly different analyst than Dora, but it also helped me to extricate myself from Nichole's illusion of control. Once I was established as a *useable object*, Nichole began to learn to relinquish her prior need for magical control over others in her life. It also created an opportunity for her to own her aggression, giving way to a working-through process in which she began to reveal her previously disowned capacities. In the interpersonal crucible of our two personalities, Nichole was able to have a new self-experience – one that inspired her to learn to tolerate internal conflict, self-soothe, and ultimately develop the capacity to mourn, allowing her to internalize as a part of herself all the good that she had initially received from her work with Dora.

Dora introduces Nichole

As a relatively new analyst, I was perhaps too flattered to question my supervisor's practice of asking for my input on her own cases. While it felt a little peculiar, I was so honored to experience myself as one of her colleagues – not quite an equal, but certainly on my way to becoming one someday. I remember discussing the young woman, Nichole, who was trying to negotiate having a threesome with her girlfriend. As a bisexual woman, Nichole wanted the security of being in a committed relationship with a woman, while not having to forgo the desire to act on her heterosexual impulses. While ostensibly acquiescing, her girlfriend sabotaged their efforts at a threesome by choosing only the most undesirable men to join them. I remember wondering aloud to Dora whether Nichole's purported need to act on her heterosexual impulses wasn't actually a way to create space in her romantic relationship, the space typically created by a third – in childhood, the fathering one.

Dora and I discussed Nichole's childhood; how her father's depression rendered him an undependable attachment figure for the few years of her life that her parents remained together. Her mother, on the other hand, was ever present and physically and verbally abusive, and she seemed to have been frequently motivated by her own psychotic process, trapping Nichole in a traumatizing mother-infant dyad, which must have resembled more of a prison than a holding environment. It seemed to me that the intensity of Nichole's romantic relationship, as Dora described it, might have been reminiscent of feelings associated with being trapped in her mother's psychotic world. Dora went with my insight but added a concrete twist of her own. She thought that maybe the absence of a penis created a certain amount of hysteria in lesbian relationships – that women were prone to merger and therefore required a penis between them. I would later discover that Dora shared this idea with Nichole, mistakenly crediting me as its author.

Over the course of my supervision with Dora, I bonded with her mainly over our shared intellectual curiosity. Our supervisions typically revolved around discussions of various psychoanalytic theories. And yet her intellectual prowess was counterpoised by the quiet, almost syrupy way she spoke to me. It was as if she were always talking to a wounded child. Whereas many of my colleagues found her voice soothing, it always rang a little saccharine to me. At the time, I was working mainly with aggressive preadolescent boys, and I remember wondering how a patient could ever express anger towards her – she presented as so sweet and soft-spoken.

A few months after discussing Nichole's case with me, Dora died in a tragic accident that was apparently the result of a psychotic break – a potential side effect of a powerful antibiotic she was taking for an intractable pneumonia. My community was shaken. *How could this happen? Could it have been a suicide?* The accident was so public, and she was such a private person – a suicide seemed impossible, and yet the gossip continued. A witness on the street reported having seen Dora in her pajamas run into oncoming traffic as if she were attempting to escape a pursuer. Apart from the basic horror this event inspired, my identification with Dora as a supervisor at the beginning of my career left me feeling traumatized, vulnerable, even somewhat endangered: if this could happen to her, it could happen to anyone.

Nichole introduces herself

At the reception following the memorial service, a colleague informed me that there was a young woman, a former patient of Dora's, looking for one of Dora's supervisees who was in the process of getting his doctorate at NYU – I was the only one who fit this description. Then a young attractive woman introduced herself. Nichole informed me that Dora had spoken to her about me. She made a point of telling me that Dora had referred her girlfriend to me but that my number had been lost before a call was made. Feeling exhausted after the emotional tribute, I gave her my number without much thought.

Walking home that day, I was grateful to be reminded that Dora had referred her patient's girlfriend to me. It felt like a vote of confidence that Dora had wanted to *share* a family case with me. Again, I didn't question the motives for the referral other than that this esteemed colleague considered me competent – a self-experience that was confined but barely tarnished by her passing. After all, Dora had been the one to encourage me to start a private practice. She referred my first patients to me; she even lent me her office for a number of months to help me to begin my practice.

The beginning

Soon after the memorial, Nichole began telephoning me; I took her phone calls. At first, we were just two people commiserating over a shared loss; Nichole seemed to just want to talk about what happened. As for myself, partly emboldened by Dora's confidence in me, but also vulnerable due to the traumatic loss, I welcomed these talks. However, it soon became apparent that Nichole really wanted to talk about her experience with the clinician closing out Dora's practice – an experience that left her feeling humiliated and diminished.

It was important to Nichole to talk to someone who knew Dora, but more significantly, to someone who knew her through Dora. Ostensibly, she wanted someone to honor her special claim to Dora – someone to honor the self-experience she had with Dora – to treat her perhaps more like a daughter in mourning than as a patient. After a few weeks, Nichole began to attend sessions with me in my private office. However, she was clear that she was not looking for an analyst to replace Dora – Dora was irreplaceable: the mere idea of accepting anyone as her analyst felt too disloyal, not only to Dora, but more importantly, perhaps, to the unique and profound loss that she was suffering. So, although Nichole attended sessions with me, she would not bestow on me the moniker of "*my* analyst" for a number of years.

Nichole was particularly preoccupied with finding some instructions about her treatment that Dora said she would leave in the eventuality of her untimely death.[1] I knew of no instructions that Dora might have left behind, nor did I know all that much about their work together. But I did want to help, and I did want to feel that I could do some good in the wake of a tragedy that had traumatized my professional community, inducing in so many of us a sense of powerlessness. So, I listened to Nichole's interpretation of Dora's instructions, which – although apparently never written down – would soon assume a fixity, as if they had been engraved in stone.

At the time, following a developmental arrest approach, I gave primacy to my patient's subjective reality regardless of what I believed the objective reality to be. I believed the treatment was to shore up a patient's sense of self in order to facilitate the release of their own natural developmental strivings. Nichole's interpretation of Dora's instructions was just an aspect of her subjective reality that it was my job to privilege.

On the other hand, I was unaware of how susceptible I could be to a sweet, needy woman in distress – how her dependency would work synergistically with my own counter-dependency. At the time, I also had a more objectivistic and functional perspective on treatment and believed that one therapist could easily replace another. I was comfortable with the idea that my personal *self* was not an essential part of any treatment. I believed that the treatment happened in the patient's head, with the latter's transference fantasies expressed for the two of us to experience and understand.

Practiced in play therapy, I was trained to allow the child's play to organize the session and to let them fill the room with their fantastic realities. In this way, accepting Nichole's version of Dora's instructions into the treatment was no different than participating in any other patient's creative play, at least in theory. Whereas my plasticity was very helpful in engaging a child in play therapy, it is important to keep in mind that there was always a responsible adult to take the child home after the session. In working with Nichole, this plasticity quickly got me into a fix: there was no adult to take her home, and so for a number of years I felt like I had to take her home with me, at least psychically.

Nichole's interpretation of Dora's instructions

According to Nichole, the most important edict she learned from her treatment with Dora was that she was to call Dora "ten steps" before her distress grew to the point of developing into suicidal ideation. Nichole talked about her late night chats with Dora, and how they soothed her; they made her feel like she was at home with Dora, a part of her life, and not just another patient relegated to formal office visits. And so I too was called on to have many impromptu phone sessions with Nichole as she struggled with persistent suicidal ideations triggered by one interpersonal crisis after another.

Nichole had initially told me that Dora had developed a new technique for her work with her and that Dora was trying to find a way to make up for the mothering that Nichole had been deprived of in childhood. I assumed that Dora was using techniques common to developmental arrest models like Winnicott's Object Relations or Self Psychology: that she was trying to find a way to give Nichole the mirroring one typically receives from an empathic therapist who provides the patient with a holding environment that they can then internalize and be fortified by. I never imagined what I was actually signing up for.

One incident that clued me in to what Nichole had in mind occurred when she had to cancel a session in order to attend a family gathering. Later in the evening of the day of the canceled session, I was inundated with phone messages from a distraught Nichole. When I returned her call, I was informed that I should have known that she would need a session on the day she would be spending time with her family; they made her feel so awful. Dora would have realized that she needed the session and would not have agreed to cancel it or, at the very least, she would have called to make sure she was OK. What I did was humiliate her – shame her by putting her in a position to have to call me and ask for help. It occurred to me that the self-experience she had in her treatment with Dora was nothing short of *primary maternal pre-occupation*. Dora attended to her the way one attends to an infant, incapable of expressing their needs. As proof, Nichole showed me postcards Dora sent her when she was away on vacation. They were from various cities in Europe and written in Dora's inimitable handwriting, each closing with, "Your mother in the sky."

Given the demand for my availability, it soon began to occur to me that Dora might have been attempting literally *to be the mother Nichole never had* – to actually parent her. It also began to dawn on me that what Nichole was describing in her treatment with Dora was an attempt to create the experience for Nichole of being on the receiving end of a *primary maternal preoccupation* – of someone who is so attuned to Nichole's needs that she would almost magically attend to them without Nichole having to suffer the shame of finding the words with which to express them; Nichole would not have to experience the helplessness that might inspire one to ask for help.

Dora hadn't been employing techniques of the developmental arrest models. She was attempting to provide something akin to a *corrective emotional experience* by putting herself in the position to actually parent Nichole. By the time I had realized this, it felt too late to renege on agreeing to work with her; the persistence of her suicidal ideation made me feel that I could not abandon her as

Dora and so many others had. Also, the more she maintained contact with me, the less I feared her acting on her suicidal ideation, and so like a pair of exhausted boxers we clung to each other for fear of the blow that would follow letting go.

Symbolic equivalent to Dora

Nichole became anxious when I made any attempt to help her to self-soothe. She insisted that Dora had wanted her to rely on her instead. Soothing herself left her feeling truly alone in the world; it was confirmation that she could never have the mother she so desperately wanted – *needed?* If I attempted to get off the phone too soon, Nichole would press for a time later in the day when we could talk again. If she got any indication that I was feeling put-out by her phone calls, she would explain to me that Dora always knew just the right thing to say, and that she could calm her down with one sentence. The implication was clear: as bad as it was for me, it was worse for her, and I only had my own incompetence to blame. Working with preadolescent boys, I was used to what Epstein (1999) refers to as "the bad analyst feeling": I knew how to stand my ground against an angry onslaught. But I was out of my depth in dealing with a patient who had such a persistent and bewitching need for me to help her. I had never before felt *that* necessary to another's wellbeing.

Whereas I had conceptualized the treatment as an attempt to help Nichole internalize the holding environment that Dora had provided for her, Nichole was trying to actualize a replacement, or to fashion me into a symbolic equivalent – someone who was to be Dora in her stead. Nothing and no one would replace Dora, but the instructions could provide the blueprint for creating a suitable clone. As Ogden (1992) explains, when a person is unable to mourn, or to accept the presence of an absence, they are compelled to recreate the lost love in a substitute. I was being groomed to become a proxy, or a stand-in for her *mother in the sky.*

As I failed at this task, I would try to commiserate with Nichole about her loss, readily admitting that I was no Dora. And yet every struggle, every pain, eventually led Nichole to remind me of what Dora would do. Clinging to me, she would insist that she still needed the type of care she got from Dora. Simultaneously, I felt reprimanded and cajoled, pressured and yet oddly empowered. My inexperience with this type of clinical challenge left me *flying blind* with Nichole, and blinded as to my own path.

As her *mother in the sky*, Dora seemed to have fashioned herself as an ever-present, primal mother in the eternal sky, immune to the weathering effects of time. In Freud's myth of the primal horde, the murder of the primal father transforms the father into a totem that represents his rules and prohibitions (Freud, 1913). Similarly, the death of Dora transformed her into an unmovable object – a set of rules that could not evolve – that could not be altered. Freud (1913) teaches us that death transforms the object from someone who can die into someone who can never die.[2]

What I initially thought of as a treatment focused on providing a mirroring experience that would eventually facilitate mourning was becoming one in which I was being inculcated into the cult of Dora. Although I don't believe that I was purposefully deceived, I know I did feel coerced by the persistent presence of Nichole's suicidality, which at the time signified to me a suffering so great that the drive to protect her felt like nothing short of a moral imperative. Her damsel-in-distress demeanor called forth in me a valiant knight setting off to save the princess from a nameless and faceless dragon.

During these early sessions, I felt like I had been empowered and burdened through some categorical connection such as I imagine it might feel to wake up one day to discover one had royal blood and was burdened with taking care of a previously unknown and dysfunctional kingdom. Nichole had a way of making me feel absolutely essential to her – unique, and yet stripped of agency. Her desperate neediness inspired in me a wellspring of confidence, but a confidence devoid of competence, perhaps not unlike how an adult child caring for an ailing, needy, and help-rejecting parent may experience themselves as simultaneously compelled to help yet impotent to effect the necessary changes.

Nichole's disowned abilities

Nichole disowned her abilities in general and her ability to think clearly in particular. Frequently, she would ask me what I thought a lover meant by something they said. Disclaiming any ability to read another's mind, I would attempt to resist her entreaties. But with a pitiable persistence, Nichole would assure me that I had the power to help her. "I just want to know what *you think*. Dora used to tell me. She knew how confused I can get." Rationalizing that this was a form of lending Nichole the ego she lacked, I would inevitably acquiesce.

If what I thought was what Nichole wanted to hear, and it eventually turned out to be "right," I was once again her personal seraph, and that much more essential to her wellbeing. If it turned out to be wrong, she would react as if I had betrayed her. With innocent incredulity, she would say, "But you *said* …" as if somehow I had purposefully misled her. Then the shame of her pain would become mine.[3] If what I was thinking was not what she wanted to hear, Nichole would angrily accuse me of putting negative thoughts in her head – "Why did you say that? I don't want that in my head." Then she would either resist leaving the consulting room, remaining on the couch in a slump after I announced the session's end, or she would later inundate my answering machine with desperate pleas to call her back.

Despite my failings, I felt essential to Nichole, much as a parent can feel simultaneously discarded by and indispensable to a young child. In this way, I knew how her girlfriends could feel seduced by her powerful need for them and repulsed by her need to control them. I also knew how it felt to just want to say what she wanted to hear, and so to be freed of her persistence, of her need to get me to agree with her, even if it afforded just a short respite from the handcuffs of her tenacity.

For Nichole, any difference of opinion or desire could be experienced as a rupture and an implicit threat of abandonment, and so differences were rarely tolerated, even if it was little more than the expression of a wish. For words, even just spoken, had a concrete, magical quality; she held onto them like a life vest when lost at sea. Once, when a girlfriend expressed a desire to make chicken soup like her mother used to make, Nichole was catapulted into anxiety. "She told me she was a vegetarian!" I wondered, "Is she not entitled to change her mind?" The answer: "I would have never gotten involved with someone who ate meat. She can't just change the rules." Another time, upon discovering that an ex-girlfriend had begun dating, Nichole was dejected and confused: "She told me *I* was 'the love of her life.'"

Compromise formation between impulses and interpersonal realities

Nichole's intense anxiety centered on the loss of another and extended to the loss that attends the curtailment of desire by forgoing acting directly on that desire. She insisted that inhibiting her desire filled her with a sense of deadness. Consequently, she failed to forge the necessary compromise formations, which allow for partial gratification while conforming to the limitations imposed by the real other. Nichole explained that Dora never wanted her to lose her childlike liveliness and creativity, both of which the deadness would certainly squash. I could imagine how a woman like Dora, who never had children, might take delight in Nichole's playfulness. I know from my experience with my own daughter how much fun it is to let her take the lead and to see the world as she sees it. But I also know that I have to be constantly vigilant of the dangers my toddler daughter does not perceive. There is always a part of me on alert, constantly ready to redirect her away from danger. It was not so easy to redirect Nichole.

In describing an interaction with a girlfriend, Nichole explained that her girlfriend told her to stop poking her. Though she understood that Nichole meant it to be playful, she found the continued poking to be annoying. As Nichole complained to me about her girlfriend's annoyance, she argued, "Why does she have to call it annoying? Why can't she just see me as a *playful pup?*" She had been expecting me to confirm that there must be something "wrong" with her girlfriend.

Nichole tended to expect others to share the script of her internal reality, and so to match her urges and fit her fantasies. She was imagining herself to be a *playful pup* and wanted to be perceived as such. Taking it a step further, she then resented her girlfriend for not sharing her self-perception. Nichole understood that her girlfriend was informing her that she found the interaction annoying, but to heed this would be to realize that she needed to modify her behavior, to forego what she saw as her whimsy, and to contain the conflict between how she wanted her behavior to be received and the interpersonal reality that was occurring between her and her girlfriend. Unable or unwilling to contain the conflict, she decided that her girlfriend was simply choosing to ruin her fun, as she could just as simply choose to see things Nichole's way. As if pointing out an obvious injustice, Nichole would invoke the power of Dora's authority, explaining that Dora wanted her to be true to her childlike creativity – to be her *true self*. It was almost as if she were saying, "How could anyone possibly challenge Dora's authority?"

The need to control interpersonal realities played out in all of Nichole's friendships and romantic relationships. Any difference with a significant person gave rise to abandonment anxiety, mobilizing her to attempt to change the person's mind. Nichole would attempt to rid herself of the discomfort resulting from a conflict, first by cajoling a friend to see things her way. Eventually, however, she would push her point to the limit just to rid herself of the discomfort, as merely to contain the conflict seemed unbearable. Often, this escalation would eventually lead the relationship to the brink, at which point she engaged in desperate attempts at magical reparations.

Nichole's magical reparation

Unlike true reparation that is motivated by the awareness that we have hurt a person we love, Nichole's magical reparations were motivated by her desire to control the other and to escape her intense abandonment anxiety. Her reparations were not based on what Winnicott (1971) would call a *capacity for concern*, in which one takes responsibility for having hurt another. Rather, they stemmed from a need to escape her own internal emotional distress. Facing the threat of a loss, Nichole quickly took responsibility for the entire conflict, leaving the more scrupulous among her lovers with a sense of being implicated in an injustice; it certainly couldn't be her fault *entirely* (the thought would go) since, after all, it takes two to tango. And yet Nichole would render herself pathetic, reproaching herself to such an extent that her lovers were mobilized to come to her support and to protect her from herself. Incidentally, more than one unscrupulous girlfriend took advantage of this newfound powerful position, exacting significant monetary recompenses for their troubles.

Employing her magical reparation, Nichole would do anything to escape the fear of abandonment and the shame of having brought it upon herself. Although it seemed that she actually had some awareness of her role in the conflict, it was not an awareness that she could hold on to. It wasn't an insight that would help her contain her impulses the next time around, for to contain her impulses deadened her feeling of magical omnipotence and her desire to freely *be herself.* It was an either/or mindset in which either the other had to agree with her, or she had to give in to the other in a fantasized magical merger. Self-sacrifice was the price one paid to sustain a relationship, as she had learned from her mother, who more than once locked her out of the house at a very young age, leaving her banging on the door and pleading to be let back in.[4]

In one instance, after discovering that Nichole had been having an affair, her girlfriend moved out, but Nichole refused to believe that the relationship was over, explaining, "We never had the break-up talk." She hung on for three years making overtures to this woman. In the meantime, she kept insisting that, "I ruined my life. I didn't even really want that other girl." Nichole reasoned that if she could win this woman back, her guilt would be at least partially absolved; what she did couldn't have been *so* bad if it didn't end the relationship for good. Expressing her sense that she had been treated unfairly, she asked, "Why don't I ever get credit for the bad things I don't do?"

As Nichole persisted in talking about the relationship for over three years, I began to realize that as long as she held out the hope of reuniting, she could hold on to the relationship in her mind, even if her calls were not returned. And as long as she could talk about it with me, she could continue to experience the relationship as ongoing, our talks bringing it back to life with each new session. I felt like a sort of medium, offering Nichole a connection to a lost love much as I had done earlier on, in relation to Dora. It was only three years later, when the ex-girlfriend told her that she had started dating other people, that Nichole was able to let go. The specter of having to compete with another for her ex's attention left her feeling finally defeated.

When Nichole did lose a relationship, the loss of the relationship seemed to entail the loss of relational signification itself. It was not only proof that all the good times she had in that relationship had been, in fact, meaningless, but it also meant that what may appear to be significant in any ensuing relationship would be meaningless as well; for the possibility would always exist that it could end in the same way.

My failures become my successes

As I continued to fail adequately to replicate Dora's treatment by recreating the self-experience that Nichole had had with her, Nichole began to vent her anger towards me. Perhaps she was also unconsciously angry with me in Dora's stead, either at the latter's death or because she had never expressed anger to Dora when she was alive.[5] As she expressed her conscious anger toward me for my transgressions, Nichole invoked Dora as a supporting witness, and I increasingly felt like the odd man out. She and Dora were locked in a magical merger, and I was left outside banging on the door. What I did not realize at the time was that when Nichole brought up Dora in moments when she was angry with me, it served to highlight just how different I was from Dora. As she clung to her image of Dora as a type of transitional object under her omnipotent control, I was left free to evolve into a real object, an object she could eventually learn to use in the sense Winnicott (1971) describes in his seminal paper "The Use of the Object." I could become someone she could rely on, available, dependable, but not under her omnipotent control, and thus I could help her to appreciate the limits of her omnipotence. Nicole's demands were also incorporated into a developmentally appropriate request for separation. As Lacan (1977) explains, *demands* of the other are made regarding what cannot be attained from the other, and they thus ultimately lead to the abandonment of the fantasy of the *all giving other* and to the recognition of having to seek in other relationships all the shards of gratification one can find.

The toilet

A situation that typified my emergence as a real object outside of her omnipotent control had to do with the toilet in my office suite. After using the toilet, Nichole walked into the consulting room and in a soft but strained tone that I came to understand as a thinly veiled attempt to mask her anger, she asked, "Shouldn't you be telling your male patients to put the seat back down after using the toilet?" She didn't feel that she should have to touch the toilet seat, insisting that she had felt something wet on the seat when she did. I told her, "No, I don't tell my patients how to use the bathroom." She admonished, "Aren't you supposed to confront them on their behavior?" I said, "I'm not sure what you would have me do." "Well, I noticed that a lot of your male patients don't put the toilet seat back down after they use it. You should tell them to." I found myself feeling as if I had violated her by forcing her to touch another patient's urine. I felt responsible for her discomfort, while at the same time I considered her request intrusive and unreasonable. I would not tell my patients how to comport themselves in the toilet, and I was more than a little annoyed that she was admonishing me. I told her that I could not do as she asked, though I appreciated her discomfort.

Dan

A bigger rupture occurred when Nichole became aware that, unbeknownst to me, I had been working with an acquaintance of hers, a male patient named Dan. At the time Nichole saw Dan entering the office after her session, Dan had been in treatment with me for over six months. Nichole was beside herself. "How could you start working with him without asking me if I was OK with it first? Dora would have never seen him without asking me." As I was unaware of their acquaintance, it would never have occurred to me to mention it to her.

> He must have gotten your number from Mary; I gave your number to Mary. I was OK with *her* seeing you, but not him. He has no boundaries. He is intrusive and makes me feel uncomfortable. You have to tell him that I was here first, and you have to stop seeing him! He only got to you through me.

I tried as well as I could to explain to Nichole that I could not just stop working with Dan. I was sorry that it had caused her such distress. I certainly would have asked her about working with him had I been aware of their acquaintance, but since neither of them ever mentioned the other, there was truly nothing I could do. For a number of weeks, Nichole attempted to get me to terminate with Dan. When this failed, she contacted Dan attempting to get him to stop treatment with me. Dan absolutely refused. Dismissing her, he shared with me, "I knew she was crazy, but she is out of control."

I knew that the situation was causing Nichole real distress; all she had invested in me was now potentially contaminated by the specter of Dan's presence. Unable to tolerate her own competitiveness, Nichole could not tolerate feeling as if she was competing with Dan for my attention. Having failed to exclude Dan, Nichole refused to come to the office for sessions; she couldn't be in the same office as Dan. So I agreed to rent a separate office for an hour a week to see Nichole. I was seeing her four times a week at this point but could not accommodate the travel to that alternative place more than once a week. After a few months of this arrangement, Nichole's girlfriend broke up with her, and Nichole agreed to attend sessions in my office again because she could not cope with seeing me only once a week. I remember noting to myself at the time that it seemed that when necessity called for it, Nichole had the ability to set aside her conflicts to get the care she needed.

Crazy lesbian

When cellphones came into common use, I quickly experienced the trap implicit in the freedom they promised. Nichole took full advantage of what she perceived as my newfound availability. True, I no longer had to worry about what suicidal messages might be waiting for me on my answering machine, but it seemed as if I couldn't attend a social engagement without receiving a desperate phone call. I was feeling increasingly trapped; unable to feel that I could terminate with her without risking a suicide attempt, I contented myself with what seemed like a bit of harmless acting out: I entered her number in my phone under the name, Crazy Lesbian. Not my proudest moment, but it was my way of coping with feeling constantly intruded upon.

At the end of one session, Nichole asked if she could use my phone to call for her messages – her phone had died and she was awaiting an important call. I learned early on that allowing some latitude in boundaries with Nichole was the only way to secure a tranquil exit from my office. Without thinking, I handed Nichole my cell phone instead of the office phone. She dialed her number, retrieved her messages, and then handed the phone back to me with a confused look on her face, saying, "You have me entered in your phone as 'Crazy Lesbian.'" I looked at her and calmly confirmed, "Yes, that's true." "Is that what you think of me? You think I am a lesbian?" I responded, "No, I know that you are also attracted to men."

Fearing the worst after she left, I was surprised to get a phone message later that evening from Nichole calmly explaining that she had figured out why she was labeled in my phone as "Crazy Lesbian." She explained that since she was often calling me, I labeled her that way not just to protect her confidentiality, but also to reassure any boyfriend of mine that there was nothing romantic going on between us. The next session her only expressed concern was that I wasn't calling her a "Drama Queen," or that I was in fact taking her distress to heart and not thinking that she was making a big deal out of insignificant matters. Surprisingly, I never thought of Nichole as a "Drama Queen"; I always believed that her distress was real to her, and that was all that mattered. Now, I began to wonder whether her distress was *in part* a manipulation aimed at entitling her to *care on demand*.

This episode marked a turning point in my understanding of the psychic resources Nichole had at her disposal. Through this inter-action, she demonstrated that she was able to appreciate that she was making extraordinary demands on me. She was able to over-look what would normally be considered a violation of the therap-ist's positive regard for a patient because she understood what her phone calls might be like for me. Her reaction demonstrated that she had the ability to mentalize: to imagine the mental state that motivates the behavior of another person (Bateman & Fonagy, 2013). Her ability to mentalize signaled to me that she was capable of developing the *capacity for concern*. As Winnicott (1971) might explain it, she could appreciate what it was like to be on the receiv-ing end of her intrusions.

This incident was also the beginning of the type of resolution Winnicott (1949) refers to in "Hate in the Countertransference"; this is a surprisingly interpersonal paper from a developmental arrest theorist more known for advocating a holding environment for his patients than for shutting the door of abstinence on them and leaving them outside. It occurred to me that perhaps I could be more present in the treatment, and that my anger could be a valuable resource and not just an impediment to empathy. It also provided the rationale for abandoning a blindly mirroring stance: maybe I could interpret to her in the relative safety of the analytic setting what it was like to be on the receiving end of her intrusive demands. Ultimately, I believe that the name in my phone revealed to Nichole that she was no longer the *daughter* to *the mother in the sky*, but rather the *crazy lesbian* to a challenging, yet caring, ally.

I wish I could say that I arrived at this change through quiet reflection, but the truth is that I was losing hope. What started off as an experiment in following Dora's instructions in *wild analysis* turned into years of what felt like a repetitive failure, even a lesson in futility. Nichole experienced change as inherently threatening, for change always entails a loss. As her analyst, her antipathy toward change gave me a profound sense of dread; after all, a patient who does not want to change is potentially a patient for life. I knew that, if I was going to extricate myself from this enactment and have a positive impact on Nichole's life, I had to be the first to change. As Levenson (1982) explains, the analyst often has to change before the patient does.

I finally garnered the courage to insist that if Nichole were to continue to experience herself as persistently suicidal, I would not continue to work with her unless she started taking medication. This was a battle that had been thwarted at the beginning of our work together, as Nichole had preemptively insisted that she would not take medication, and that if I insisted, she just wouldn't tell me about her suicidal ideation.[6] She explained that she had been on medication in the past and that it made her feel deadened, and, of course, Dora didn't want her to lose her childlike nature. By this point, I was comfortable pointing out that Dora was dead, and I would never be able to be her. I simply would not continue to manage her suicidal phone calls unless she was on medication: it was either take medication or find another therapist. Nichole finally acquiesced and did go on medication for a number of months before weaning herself off it, complaining of side effects. Although she never went back on medication, her suicidal ideation only rarely reappeared.

I attribute this decrease in suicidality, in part, to Nichole's more open expression of anger toward me. Although her anger was distressing for us both, it allowed her the opportunity to experience herself as aggressive, and to own her clingy obsequiousness as masked aggression. I also began to interpret her tendency to obsess about past relationships as the cultivation of anger at being left; that is, her anger fueled her desire to hold on to the relationship in fantasy, as if to say, "I will not let go of you no matter what you may want." Of course, her relationship with Dora was implicated in this interpretation, though this was never explicitly stated.

The triad

As I insisted on being more present in the treatment, I offered Nichole an alternate attachment figure: a real person as opposed to Dora, who was controlled by Nichole's omnipotent fantasy. If Dora was the *mother in the sky*, I was becoming the father on the ground. The traditional father figure is the third to the mother-infant dyad. He provides an alternative attachment figure for the child, and thus facilitates separation and individuation. According to Lacan (1977), the father represents the symbolic order, a necessity for the creation of symbolization and meaning in life. As his presence interferes with the fused mother-infant dyad,[7] he instigates the creation of a transitional space by helping to create the paradoxical experience of simultaneous separateness and togetherness. This is necessary for a triadic form of relating where meaning becomes possible as space opens up between the symbol, the symbolized, and the observing self (Ogden, 1992; Braucher, 2018a).

This triadic form of relating is also necessary for proper mourning. It allows the mourner to relegate past experiences to the past, while still retaining their significance, in symbolic form, in the present. We can learn, grow, and be enriched by our past experiences without attempting to recreate them with substitutes controlled in fantasy. We can experience the paradox of loss, or mourn the absence of a loved one, while retaining our memories and formulating what they will ultimately have meant to us.

Critique of Dora's approach

Having established myself as an object outside of Nichole's omnipotent control afforded me a new perspective, a perspective that allowed me to become more aware of how Nichole actively disowned her abilities. I realized that if Nichole were to own her abilities she would invalidate her claim that she always needed to be taken care of. If left to her own devices, she would have to truly grapple with never having been cared for by a *good enough* mother. Nichole would have to go it alone. Paradoxically, by being encouraged to believe in a replacement mother, Nichole was also encouraged to believe in her inability to care for herself, and she was left alone in a different sense: her actual abilities remained unrecognized. In holding Nichole in this infantilizing manner, Dora was at the very least colluding with Nichole's dysfunctional self-perception. At worst, it may have been a set-up that appealed to Dora as well: she could facilitate the self-experience of being an *all-good mother.*

Though Nichole was frequently angry with me now, she maintained that she never got angry with Dora. I had a hard time believing this; surely Dora had to fail her sometimes. There had to be some conflicts in a ten-year-long intimate relationship. Early on, I felt as if I could not challenge Nichole's claim, or taint the illusion of her all good *mother in the sky*, without suffering serious repercussions. I had to accept Nichole's version of reality much as I imagine she must have felt coerced into disowning her anger to ensure that she would not lose her special connection to Dora; she could thus ensure that Dora would continue mothering her. As Nichole explained it, Dora wanted to replace Nichole's own mother's punitive and shaming voice in Nichole's head with Dora's own soft and sweet one.

Encouraging Nichole to disown her anger, Dora's treatment approach led to the consolidation of Nichole's inability to tolerate conflict and encouraged the belief that conflict came with an implied abandonment. In this way, while Dora was holding Nichole, she was also holding her *back* in a dependent position. Left alone with her aggression, Nichole frequently became suicidal, which invariably led her to become intrusive; psychically she had to reconnect with the good, healthy, and capable parts of herself that were placed in Dora for safekeeping. This was the dynamic behind her feeling entitled to control others, who contained the disowned parts of Nichole which she needed to recover in order to survive.

Hysterical technique

Nichole's entitlement to unfettered access to others was a consequence of her need to disown her capacities and then to use the other as a repository. She employed what Fairbairn (1952) termed the *hysterical technique*: a means of contending with abandonment and engulfment anxieties typical of the developmental period in which a child is beginning to make her initial forays towards separation and individuation.

As the child is developing a burgeoning sense of self and evolving out of a state of complete dependence on his caretaker, he struggles with the tandem fears of being forsaken by the caretaker and yet trapped within their sphere of influence. In an attempt to stay connected while separating, and so to be an individual with attachments, the child employs various techniques that allow him to contend with the conflict inherent in loving the caretaker whom he must also partially reject – the caretaker who is differentiated from and pushed away, and yet still needed.

The adult employing the *hysterical technique* is arrested at this developmental stage. He tends to exaggerate his love of the other as he rejects his own capacities. The exaggeration of his love is a form of overcompensation for his disowned capacities – capacities that are strategically dissociated for fear of losing the connection with the other. By disowning his own capacities by perceiving them as aspects of the other, he internalizes the rejection typically enacted toward the other. In short, he strategically perceives the other as all-desirable and capable, and himself as worthless and depleted.

The more depleted and incapable he experiences himself as being, the more he experiences himself as needing the other. As he attributes his abilities (his goodness) as an aspect of the other, he needs to have a special relationship with this other, for this other contains the desirable and capable aspects of his self. In Kleinian language (Klein, 1975), he imagines that his goodness is kept inside the other for safekeeping, so that it won't be destroyed by the anger he unconsciously feels.

In this sense, Nichole clung to others out of a need for self-preservation. They allowed her access to the good and capable parts of herself that were imagined to be safely sequestered inside the other. Unable to tolerate the conflict inherent in differentiating from those she loved, she was unable to perceive others as whole objects, who were in some ways loved and in others rejected. Containing this conflict is an achievement necessary for true mourning. Unable to mourn Dora, Nichole recreated with me the relationship that she had had with Dora. Doing so gave her an almost immediate psychic claim to me, just as one would reasonably claim money at one branch of a bank even though they deposited their money in another branch of the same bank. Nichole was entitled to on-demand access to me because she employed the same psychic economy she had had with Dora, a relationship in which she embodied all the misery, feebleness, and incompetence within herself. This technique was no doubt significant in helping Nichole survive a childhood with her psychotic mother, who was ill-equipped to deal with her daughter's separation and individuation, not to mention her daughter's aggression. It evolved into her predominant way of relating to her mother and of experiencing herself.

Patient and analyst self-experiences: an interpersonal perspective

Sullivan (1955) conceptualized a sense of self as being formed through interactions with others. According to his pragmatic understanding, there is no self that exists apart from our relationships. We know our self as it is revealed through actual interactions with others. We experience ourselves intimately through our more intimate relationships, and no relationships are more formative than those with our parents.

Working within Sullivan's paradigm, Wolstein (1989) views every patient as unique, every analyst as unique, and every therapeutic dyad as unique. It follows that the loss of an analyst ultimately entails the loss of a unique self-experience for the patient. We can have memories of those past interactions and their concomitant self-experiences. Yet the loss of any relationship necessarily entails not only the absence of the other's continued presence in our lives, but also the loss of the continuing self-experience that we had with that individual (Braucher, 2018b). Of course, we can talk about and share the lost self-experience with other intimates, but the actual self-experience with our analyst remains forever isolated in the consulting room, and witnessed by no one.

Concomitantly, as I believe has been made evident throughout this narrative, the analyst also has unique self-experiences with his patients in isolation. What I assume to have been Dora's self-experience may stand as a testament to analysts becoming attached to the powerful self-experiences that needy patients so often evoke. If I had had a different personality, I may have continued to participate in this prolonged enactment and inhibited Nichole's progress; or, conversely, I may have been able to avoid some of the pitfalls I ran into. Fortunately, my analytic perspective was continuing to expand, and thereby reduced my attachment to the self-experiences I had with Nichole. But we know that the loss of an aggravating attachment is no less of a loss, and as analysts we must contend with the continual loss of self-experiences if we are to allow them to grow, change, and eventually terminate.

Conclusion

Initially, Nichole came to me looking for recognition of, and a replacement for, her relationship with Dora; she wanted not to feel crazy for the extent of the cataclysmic loss she had experienced. In Nichole's mind, through my association with Dora I was the closest thing to a witness of her self-experience with Dora. And maybe my allowing her to attempt to recreate that relationship was important, at least in so far as it served as a form of bearing witness to her loss. My belief in that relationship allowed her eventually to establish an attachment to me. I do feel some embarrassment that it took me so long to question Nichole's professed incapacities, although it was apparently a presentation of which Dora had been convinced, and one in which my initial impotence left me ill equipped to question. Of course, there is no way of knowing whether those struggles could have been addressed in a better way. It is possible that the successes evidenced later in treatment required this early foundation of an internalized holding environment in order to support us through the more contentious times that accompanied my emergence as a real object.

My transformation into a new object allowed Nichole the opportunity to work through her unconscious anger toward Dora that had been crippling her with a persistent melancholia. More importantly, it provided her with a new interpersonal matrix in which she could develop a new self-experience. For years, I felt as if I was failing to be the analyst Nichole needed me to be. In my naivety, I feared my personality would be an intrusion, interfering with Nichole's developing sense of self. I now believe that there is no way to avoid the obstacles a patient has to face in adjusting to the idiosyncrasies of a new analyst, even when that analyst is providing a holding environment. After all, every child adjusts to particular parents. One cannot have a solid sense of self if one doesn't have solid relationships. Ultimately, I believe I was able to provide Nichole with a solid relationship in which I was dependably present, courageous enough to confront her behavior, and creative enough to repair our relationship when needed.

Although I continue to work with Nichole, I now only see her every other week. She resists termination as a vestige of her old self-experience, which I believe will eventually give way to her increasing desire to be an independent actor in the world.

Epilogue

A significant aspect of my transformation during Nichole's treatment was the realization that, to help Nichole, I needed to confront her regarding the capacities she had been disowning. As Nichole continued to start every session with a long face, saying, "I'm having a hard time," I began to read between the lines, discerning how she was hiding her successes – how she was more capable of taking care of herself than she ever let on. Granted, romantic relationships continued to be minefields of temptations, as perceived opportunities to finally achieve a magical merger with another person inevitably exploded into shards of interpersonal estrangement. But relationships with friends and family became more stable as Nichole was able to *hold* the insight that her intrusiveness had a paradoxical effect on others. She learned that interpersonal compromise did not have to result in psychic deadness, and that she could continue to own her desires and childlike creativity without imposing them on others.

With her increased interpersonal stability, Nichole started a business in which she managed several employees. Her growing stability provided an ever-greater and more stable sense of self. And yet Nichole felt a need to present herself as struggling, as needing special attention, as if saying, "Be gentle with me, I'm already contending with so much." I remained relentless, pointing out her presentation and how it did not reflect the positive aspects of her life. In response, Nichole would try to devalue her own achievements. She would explain that she is still a mess and can't get up in the morning and that her business only succeeds because she can work from home from the comfort of her bed. Or she would point out that it was a fluke and all could easily be lost. In turn, I would insist that this business was her accomplishment, and that *even if* it were eventually to fail, no one can take away the original accomplishment: "There is no reason to believe you wouldn't be able to do it again." In a desperate attempt to disown her success, she would argue that her business was not as successful as others'.

The near-constant comparing of herself to others would catapult her into fits of envy, albeit not a productive envy that motivated her to try something different, but one that made her feel bad about herself, causing her to stay in bed all day. Facebook proved an endless resource for discovering how others were succeeding in life where she had failed. Nichole used it as a launch pad for her fantasizing about what others' lives were like. Exploring these fantasies eventually led her to deal with the real losses that she had suffered: the time lost and the possibilities that were sacrificed in her tumultuous earlier years.

Perhaps more importantly, we came to explore her fantasies as just that: *fantasies* as mechanisms of self-expression under her control. Prior to this development, she perceived her fantasies as urgent and undeniable truths that were inseparable from her core sense of self. Now, however, they were increasingly understood as choices. She could choose to compare herself to others based on Facebook posts. She could choose to imagine what it would be like to live the lives of her friends based on an uploaded picture of them with their happy family on a summer day playing in their backyard pool. She could enjoy wallowing in that fantasy, imagining how great it would be, and then use her fantasy to feel bad about herself for not having that life. But, ultimately, she had to accept that these were choices, and that her fantasies were not intrinsic parts of herself that she couldn't question or decide to control.

Keeping in mind her earlier fear of competition as evidenced with my patient, Dan, I wondered if her tendency to compare herself to others, and to become envious, was possibly a rudimentary, fantasy-based form of competing, like a sort of trial competition. It was a compromise formation allowing for the expression of competitive strivings without having to face the interpersonal reality of experiencing the shame of losing in the presence of the other. Moreover, the fantasies allowed her to experience herself as wanting more and achieving it, thus fortifying her desire and eventually leading her to take the risk to achieve her fantasies in reality.

Similarly, Nichole's suicidal ideation came to be understood as a fantasy that allowed her an escape from pain. In the moments when she felt so bad about herself and believed that she would never feel any better, she could imagine taking control and ending the pain. This gave her a sense of agency in moments of utter hopelessness. Previously, her suicidal threats were a confirmation for me and for Nichole that she was truly unable to cope. Every time she felt suicidal she confirmed to herself that she was unable to function in the world. When the suicidal ideation was reframed, however, as an adaptive use of fantasy affording her momentary relief, it was transformed from an indication of her inability to cope into an actual coping mechanism – a form of self-soothing.

After five years, Nichole's business began to fall apart. At about the same time, her stepfather died, leaving her feeling more financially vulnerable than ever. Potentially facing a financial crisis in the future, she had no choice but to find a job, and so to enter into direct competition with others. Although she had a list of reasons why she was unable to go back to school, I asserted that if she needed to do it, she would find her way. After much back and forth, Nichole finally decided to become a social worker and upon graduation she got a job working with children. Although she long insisted that she would never be able to work a nine-to-five job because she couldn't rely on herself to get out of bed in the morning, she has successfully held her job for the past three years and has become a reliable member of the treatment team.

At her job, Nichole initially had difficulties negotiating office politics. She felt a need to convince her supervisor of the rightness of her actions. We explored how she could hold on to her beliefs while still ensuring that her actions complied with her supervisor's instructions. Nichole reflected insightfully, "I know I do that. It's like I always have to get people to agree with me. It's exhausting." Containing the conflict, Nichole has learned how to be dependable vis-à-vis herself; she decided that looking out for herself by keeping her job was more important than getting her supervisor to agree with her.

When Nichole describes her work to me, it seems that her dedication to her young patients is reminiscent of Dora's commitment to her. She clearly takes her responsibility for these young charges to heart. She demonstrates a judicious use of her aggression, which is frequently necessary in order to confront a patient's inappropriate behaviors in the treatment setting. At times, when retelling her interventions, Nichole's voice sometimes takes on some of Dora's soft demeanor, but without being cloying.

Notes

1 Incidentally, the discussion between Nichole and Dora regarding instructions was proof to Nichole that she had been worried about losing Dora. To Nichole this was evidence – a sign of her connectedness to Dora and of her prescience. It was often cited as proof that she and I should take her worries seriously, as omens. In time, I was to learn that Nichole suffered from tremendous abandonment anxiety in all of her relationships and that her anxieties generated many imaginative scenarios.

2 In some ways, I wonder if Nichole and I had formed a macabre and unholy alliance not only to mitigate the fall-out of Dora's death, but also to keep Dora alive, perhaps in denial of death altogether.

3 Incidentally, in a paper I wrote at this point in the treatment, I made the argument that projective identification is a request for a relationship, and that this primitive form of disowning feelings is a rudimentary form of asking for care (Braucher, 2000). Although this paper was about my work with preadolescent boys, it is consistent with the role I often found myself in with Nichole.

4 This was a significant bit of history that I was made privy to only after years of working together. Nichole routinely refused to talk about her abusive childhood, insisting that she had already worked through it with Dora. Attending to the intensity of her persistent conflicts and to the continuous series of crises also served to distract us from this kind of remembering.

5 In "Mourning and Melancholia," Freud (1917) argues that melancholia is a result of taking into the self the lost object who was still too needed to lose or with whom one had unconscious anger. Melancholia was the result of the anger toward this object being enacted against the self.

6 Much later, Nichole informed me that she had been under the impression that an analyst could easily lose everything if they were sued because of a patient's suicide. This drew my attention to the *sue* in *sue-icide: to kill by suing?* – confirmation that suicide is in fact murder, murder of those who will ultimately pay the price even if not the *ultimate price*.

7 Winnicott (1960) explains that there is no such thing as an infant without a mother. Ogden (1992) interprets this to mean that the mother-infant dyad is experienced as a state of oneness.

References

Bateman, A., & Fonagy, P. (2013) 'Mentalization-Based Treatment,' *Psychoanalytic Inquiry* 33(6): 595–613.

Braucher, D. (2000) 'Projective Identification: A Request for Relationship,' *Clinical Social Work Journal* 28(1): 71–83.

Braucher, D. (2018a) 'A Therapeutic Dyad in Search of a Third,' in R. C. Curtis (Ed.), *Psychoanalytic Case Studies from an Interpersonal-Relational Perspective*, pp. 209–212. London: Routledge.

Braucher, D. (2018b) 'Passion of Past-Shunned: The Use of Fantasy to Recreate Past Loving and Sexual Self-Experiences in the Present,' in B. Willock, R. C. Curtis & L. C. Bohm (Eds.), *Psychoanalytic Perspectives on Passion*, pp. 195–202. London: Routledge.

Epstein, L. (1999) 'The Analyst's "Bad-Analyst Feelings,"' *Contemporary Psychoanalysis* 35(2): 311–325.

Fairbairn, W. R. D. (1952) *Psychoanalytic Studies of the Personality.* London: Tavistock Publications Limited.

Freud, S. (1913) 'Totem and Taboo,' *Standard Edition* 13: vii-162.

Freud, S. (1917) 'Mourning and Melancholia,' *Standard Edition* 14: 237–258.

Klein, M. (1975) *Envy and Gratitude and Other Works 1946–1963*. London: The Hogarth Press.

Lacan, J. (1977) *Écrits: A Selection*. New York: Norton.

Levenson, E. A. (1982) 'Follow the Fox – An Inquiry into the Vicissitudes of Psychoanalytic Supervision,' *Contemporary Psychoanalysis* 18: 1–15.

Ogden, T. (1992) *The Matrix of the Mind*. London: Maresfield Library.

Sullivan, H. S. (1955) *The Interpersonal Theory of Psychiatry*. London: Tavistock Publications Limited.

Winnicott, D. W. (1949) 'Hate in the Counter-Transference,' *International Journal of Psychoanalysis* 30: 69–74.

Winnicott, D. W. (1960) 'The Theory of the Parent-Infant Relationship,' *International Journal of Psychoanalysis* 41: 585–595.

Winnicott, D. W. (1971) *Playing and Reality*. New York: Basic Books.

Wolstein, B. (1989) 'Ferenczi, Freud, and the Origins of American Interpersonal Relations,' *Contemporary Psychoanalysis* 25: 672–685.

The ill analyst

Coping with illness and picking up pieces

The analyst's illness from the perspectives of analyst and patient

Therese Rosenblatt

"There's a small tumor on your pancreas," my radiologist said evenly, no sound of alarm in her voice. "It's probably not malignant. It's smooth and oval. But I can't be sure. You'll need to get it biopsied." She delivered this news as she ushered me into a family meeting room, calm yet firm. The room had a box of tissues on display. I was torn between the doctor's tranquil demeanor which suggested that she saw this sort of thing every day and a dissociated mounting panic and disbelief. "Here's the name of an MRI facility where I'd like you to go right now. I'll call your husband to come and pick you up." "My husband?" I thought. "Now? My doctor knows that my husband does not brook interruptions in his work. Is this as serious as it sounds?" Nothing made sense.

It was a hot and sultry July day when I had gone into the doctor's office, just the kind that leaves me feeling free and summery with a sense of promise and of good things to come. The feeling was familiar as a residue from school days – the relief and excitement over summer vacation. I bounced into my radiologist's office. The dress I wore that day is still hanging in my closet, unworn since then. I keep intending to wear it again. I was finally struggling free of my lifelong dread of doctors, medical tests, and the lurking, insidious, and deadly cancer that doctors search out and tests reveal. My paternal grandmother had died at age fifty-one of breast cancer, a grueling seven years after diagnosis. Her nearest female relatives all suffered the same fate at young ages. I was brought up in her shadow, with the sad and hallowed stories of her reaction to her diagnosis, of the course of her illness, and of her demise. The stories about her had the ghostly tinge that Susan Sontag (1990) ascribed to tuberculosis. I am my grandmother's namesake. I wore her wedding gown. My father and grandfather, who had adored her, told me that I was just like her. She was deified in our family and her memory was shrouded in an eerie sadness and adulation.

For once, as I headed to the radiologist, I did not feel certain that the routine, screening tests I was about to undergo would reveal a malignant tumor. My new doctor prescribed several yearly ultra-sounds to screen for ovarian cancer. Chatting one day, he told me that ovarian cancer can begin in the abdomen. "In that case, why don't we include a screening of my abdomen during the ultrasound?" I said. He agreed. Going into the ultrasound, I felt full of energy, brimming with health and optimism. For the first time, I expected a good outcome.

The MRI revealed a threatening looking tumor. There was to be no biopsy before surgery after all because biopsies of the pancreas can be dangerous. My cool and confident surgeon did not want any complications before my Whipple – the very risky, delicate, and arduous (for both surgeon and patient) surgery I needed. Whipple surgery involves the removal of numerous organs and parts of organs, including the part of the pancreas that contains the tumor. The remaining parts are resected and the patient goes home with a reconstructed digestive system – one that is completely different from what nature designed. Taking my cues from doctors again, I noticed that every surgeon I consulted insisted with urgency that surgery was imperative. Yet they allowed me to wait six weeks before having the surgery, leaving me with mixed feelings of panic and optimism.

The Whipple was successful. The tumor was a pre-cancer or a stage 0 cancer, depending on which doctor I spoke to. The tumor was caught just in the nick of time. I was done with treatment. No chemo. No radiation. Not even a chance of a stray or wandering bad cell.

The recovery from a Whipple is brutal. It entailed relearning how to eat and a loss of 10% of my body weight, and it took years until I could adequately absorb nutrition, eat comfortably, and gain weight. I felt so deeply sick at times during recovery that I remember thinking, as a matter of fact, "It's OK if I die now because I really just don't feel well enough to live." No hysterics. Just recognition of my state. It was a deep, systemic pain and sickness that went to the core of me and was utterly incapacitating. As I lay there in the hospital, unable to move,

I remember imagining what would happen if there were an alarm or emergency. I was 100% dependent on others. I felt so fragile.

I was told I would have to take at least six weeks off work. I took four.

I couldn't celebrate. No amount of reassurance from my surgeon about the unlikelihood of recurrence would help. I went into a depression. It was only after about six years post-surgery that I realized how incredibly and unspeakably lucky I am.

As I write this now, eleven years later, I still experience a range of emotions about what happened to me. I have gone from feeling doomed to feeling blessed with a mission to live fully and generatively. How does one make sense of that kind of good fortune? I variously feel a sense of post-traumatic stress disorder, survivor guilt, a pressing sense of reordered priorities in life, and other inchoate emotions. I grapple with why and how I dodged a bullet. Why me? Why did others not have this kind of lucky outcome? What does it mean? I ask myself whether I did really dodge the bullet. Did I imagine this good outcome or will I discover that I actually do have cancer? How and why did the bullet whizz past me, so narrowly missing its target?

The main purpose of this chapter is to reflect upon my experience as an analyst with a serious illness, what I learned from that experience about my work with patients, and how my views were further influenced by the recent, serious illnesses of my own analyst. I will describe my experiences as a patient during my analyst's illnesses, including his handling of them with me. In my discussions I will elucidate ways in which the two experiences interacted with one another to influence my evolving views on the impact of the analyst's illness on psychoanalytic work. Approaches to what is certainly a crisis in the work must be carefully thought out. There is little in analytic training and literature to guide and support the ill analyst facing this dilemma; and yet many analysts will face illness during their long careers. I offer my personal experiences from both sides for the purpose of bringing to light the nuances which are hard to capture in technical accounts. My hope is that some of my experience will resonate with others and spark new thinking.

This chapter will limit discussion to those situations in which the analyst has a limited and curable disease. These issues are different from, though overlap with, those that arise in the case of an analyst who is chronically or terminally ill. In the latter case there is the potential for continued fresh injuries to the work and the analytic dyad.

Fear and informing patients

It was during my August vacation that I met with surgeons and determined that surgery would be scheduled for the day after Labor Day, the very day I was to return to my practice after one month away. Terrified of losing all that I had built and becoming useless, forgotten, and irrelevant, I was determined to take the absolute least amount of time off after surgery. I called my patients and told them that I needed surgery and would be taking off an extra month after the planned month away. I told them that I would not be reachable for two weeks following surgery but that I would be happy to speak after the two weeks if they wished. I did not tell them the nature of the surgery because saying it made it unbearably real. I was still digesting its significance. In a matter of fact tone I tried to convey that all would be OK and that after the month of recovery, the emergency would be over and done with. Wasn't this tone the same as my radiologist's? Had I internalized her attitude? My surgeon extended this optimistic aura with his calm and capable professionalism. I wanted to believe in a happy ending despite monumental and overwhelming fears.

First and foremost, the existential terror – I would have cancer and die. It was mainly this terror that prevented me from telling patients what I had. I was barely able to manage my own fears of death, let alone *their* fears, reactions, needs, wishes, and what I imagined was their potential "ghoulish curiosity," as Lindner (1984) called it. I was not able to set aside my own vulnerability. I felt entitled, given the gravity, to put my own needs for privacy before anyone's wish to know. I had to do what benefitted me in order to be the most effective patient (and, as it turned out, analyst) that I could be. At the time I believed that my patients would be best off not being worried about me, much in the way too much knowledge and exposure to a mother's vulnerabilities and mortality can be detrimental to her child. That was a wishful but logical judgment and a defense against the then unthinkable possibility of "role reversal" (Dewald, 1982, p. 349) with the inevitable shift in power that would occur if the focus were on me as the patient. Years later, once safely out of the press of the intense countertransference reactions to my patients (Abend, 1982) and to my own traumatic response to my illness (Little, 1967), I came to favor an approach to disclosure that would have taken into account individual patients' transferences and histories, as opposed to a uniformly prescribed approach.

A close second to my fear of dying was that of becoming irrelevant and unable to be helpful to my patients. To be strong for others, to help people to manage their emotional and psychological burdens – to be the rock that I wished my own parents had been – is at the core of my motivation and inspiration for being an analyst. The illusion of control that my strength and the role of healer give me has mostly been a healthy defense through which I gain fulfillment and some compensation for not having received the same when I needed it. It serves to contain the sense of helplessness and impotence that we share as humans, when we are faced with our mortality and the vicissitudes of life.

A lurking fear of mine is that a defect within me will be discovered. The revelation of the tumor uncovered in me a sense of inadequacy and injury that manifested itself defensively at the time. For example, I needed to come back to work sooner than was recommended and before I felt ready in order to prove that I was not a lemon of a product. Going back to work helped me to re-establish my self-esteem (Dewald, 1982). The imperfection that was unmasked by my diagnosis proved to me that there was something deeply wrong with me and that what I had to offer to patients (as well as to my children) was inferior. My fantasy of omnipotence was both the expression of a normal human desire for immortality as well as a defense against the passivity, dependence, and regression I longed for yet also feared (Abend, 1982). Suddenly I understood Freud's death instinct in a deeply personal and immediate way (Freud, 1920). I struggled to stay invested in the important people and activities in my life. Although I did manage to stay present, I actively fought off the lure of withdrawal.

In her book *Illness as Metaphor*, Susan Sontag (1990) describes the cancer metaphor as a comment on the character of the person who contracts cancer. She writes that cancer is seen as an invincible predator striking out at its individual victims in punishment for their inability to discharge their passions, specifically rage. She criticizes the humiliating moral and psychological judgments inherent in that attitude. Sontag goes on to conclude that someone who has cancer is "one of life's losers" (Sontag, 1990, p. 49).

People who have long lives are viewed by society as if they have won in the sweepstakes of life. We may feel a patronizing sorrow for people who die young, as if they are pitiful losers, in spite of their best efforts. Oftentimes they are regarded as unable to rise above their unfortunate psychological predilections. I felt that if I had cancer, I would be a double loser. I would die young and I would have succumbed to the legacy of my family and namesake. I would perpetuate the loser line in my family.

This experience led to a sense of humility about who I was in the world. There is a certain inherent arrogance in being healthy. It goes along with the healthy denial of death that is required to get through each day reasonably functional and optimistic. I was reminded of the fine line between existence and non-existence, wellness and sickness, and how quickly my hard earned and highly prized strength could vanish. I was on that line. I was no different from every other human being. I think that most or all people harbor a fantasy somewhere in the dark corners of their unconscious that they might be the exception and live forever. My confrontation with serious illness brought an abrupt end to my apparent unconscious fantasy of immortality and omnipotence. The sense of loss I felt after the tumor was found made me realize that I harbored this fantasy. I mourned the loss of my ability to fantasize about the future and old age. I went from lamenting my ageing to longing for it. I felt humbled in a way that was different from what I had experienced before.

Patients' reactions

My patients' reactions were mostly matter of fact. Nobody complained or voiced concern or anxiety beyond the mild, polite expression of concern one would expect in a business that was less personal than that of therapy and analysis. A few asked if they could be helpful in some way. Others simply accepted what I laid out as the plan. No one asked what the surgery was for or if it was serious. I think their reserve reflected a combination of factors. Judging from my later reaction to my own analyst's major illness and surgery, which I will come to, my patients may have been wary of injuring me further and probably mirrored my only partially unintended cues to please not pry. I imagine that my terse language and crisp tone resulted in what Lasky termed "intimidation into silence" (1990, p. 460) on the part of some patients. But there was something else.

My tone may have reassured patients that this would be a time-limited episode, that I would recover and return to my practice and health. My privacy and need to dose out my own confrontation with illness and mortality were preserved. My sense of omnipotence, my need to avoid my own vulnerability by being the strong one and the giver, and my wish to break from my family history of early cancers were all gratified by my patients. Later, I came to believe that many of them were acting as my therapist. In colluding with my needs, they were taking care of me. In doing so they were also avoiding the confrontation with their own vulnerability and mortality. They may have intuited that I needed them in order to get healthy. By not challenging me, they were soothing and healing me. Several authors have described variations on the idea of the patient protecting the ill analyst, and therefore the treatment, by shielding the analyst from the patient's difficult ideation and affects (Little, 1967), by simply being present (Searles, 1975), and/or by showing care for the work and the analyst (Gurtman, 1990; Silver, 1982). I will return to a discussion of this phenomenon further on in this chapter.

Even more surprisingly, the same neutral reactions continued in the majority of patients after my return to practice, despite my extended absence and gaunt appearance. It is these reactions that I wish to examine in this chapter.

There were five exceptions to these minimal reactions. One patient quit treatment one month following my return. It is unclear whether the cause was my illness, though there were indications that it was at least a trigger. Another patient quit five months following my return and explicitly blamed it on my failure to give her more information about my illness and its circumstances. A third sat in fuming silence peppered with bitter recriminations, three times a week for six months following my return. Her manifest complaints centered on my being out of touch for two weeks and not allowing her to join my family in caring for me. Two other patients expressed anguished reactions following my return. One exclaimed her fear that I had been seriously ill and lamented the phenomenon of healthy people suddenly getting serious illnesses like cancer. The other spewed her rage over the inconvenience of my being out for illness and then quickly thereafter, with barely a pause, expressed her envious fantasy that I "was able to take a vacation with my son." This patient beautifully illustrated Abend's (1982) reminder, which he invoked in support of his exhortation against self-disclosure in the case of the analyst's illness, that transference is stronger than reality. The latter two patients calmed down soon after their outbursts and returned the focus of treatment to themselves.

Perhaps most striking are the relative silence and lack of acting out from the majority of my other patients. They will be the focus here. It's been eleven years since my surgery and virtually no patient has looked back and associated to the time of my illness and return. Most have gone on to productive treatments which have deepened over the years, and in which they have experienced safe and mutative regressions in their work with me, replete with positive and negative transferences. Over the years, as I started to feel less traumatized and more confident of health, I listened and occasionally gently probed for any associations to and derivatives from that time period and have heard little. When I have occasionally heard a derivative and pointed to a possible link to the period of my illness, the patient did not elaborate.

Evolving reflections

If I knew then what I know now, I am not sure that I would have been able to do anything differently. For several years I criticized myself, believing that I should have shared more information and more aggressively elicited transference reactions. In order to follow my own advice, I would have needed to feel less scared of dying and diminishment. I was solidly defended against threats to my physical existence and my sense of self. My psychic energy was invested in protecting my own narcissism and was not available in the ways it usually is. I can only describe an ideal attitude based on what I have learned as I grew healthier and more confident, and as my libido was released and again able to invest in the object world. I saw ways in which I might have done better and now can share what I learned so that analysts can have tools to reach for should they become ill.

> It is universally known, and we take it as a matter of course, that a person who is tormented by organic pain and discomfort gives up his interest in the things of the external world, in so far as they do not concern his suffering ... the sick man withdraws his libidinal cathexes back upon his own ego, and sends them out again when he recovers.
>
> S. Freud (1914, p. 81)

Ideally I would have assessed the needs of each patient and made decisions accordingly. Many of my decisions would have been about how much information to disclose to patients both before the surgery and after my return to practice. Some authors, notably Abend (1982), Lasky (1990), and Rosner (1986), cite the decision about how much information to disclose as being the crucial determinant in handling the analyst's illness with one's patients. Abend (1982) maintains that disclosure serves the analysts' narcissistic needs to confess and should be withheld completely. Lasky (1990) gave a minimal amount of information about his illness, saying only that he was ill and needed surgery. He believed that withholding would leave as much room as possible for "imagination and fantasy to do their work" (1990, p. 459). However, he felt that some "objective information" (1990, p. 459) had to be given in the case of serious illness and a resulting interruption of the work, out of respect to the patient and to behave humanely. Rosner (1986) points out that withholding information could give too much free rein to transference during a time when there is an inadequate holding environment to safely contain the transference. He observes that giving factual information can trigger transference as much as not giving information and that under the circumstances patients may have an ethical right to know. In addition, he argues that patients cannot and should not be insulated from truth and reality. Dewald (1982) believes that decisions about the disclosure of information should vary with each patient. He gives guidelines as to how to make such judgments.

Three relational analysts (Cristy, 2001; Edwards, 2004; Fajardo, 2001) who wrote about the impact of their illnesses on their work advocated a careful, thoughtful, and not automatic form of self-disclosure. In each of these three cases, the analyst had a long term, chronic, or terminal illness which became apparent to patients either through the analyst's disability (Cristy, 2001) or through frequent inter-ruptions to treatment (Edwards, 2004; Fajardo, 2001). Edwards felt compelled to share information about her illness because of her aware-ness that the illness changed the "analytic third" (Ogden, 1994, as cited by Fajardo, 2001) in the treatment. All three felt that the disclosures they did make deepened the treatment. In addition, all three stressed the importance of their own psychotherapies during their illnesses in supporting them and helping to guide their decisions about patients.

Certain of my patients could have potentially benefitted from more information. However, it is not evident from their manifest or latent content that most needed it. I think the most crucial technical decision is not about the matter of self-disclosure. It relates to the analyst's stance of openness, responsiveness, and willingness to entertain and address, occasionally proactively, the patient's curios-ity, fear, wishes, and fantasies regarding the analyst's illness. For example, in hindsight, I imagine I would have questioned certain patients about their failure to comment on my post-surgery gaunt-ness. However, such receptivity to the patient's transference may not be possible for the ill analyst because of her fear, vulnerability, and likely regression to more primitive, brittle defenses.

Receptivity to my patients' primitive transferences, many of which were well defended, could have contributed to a sense of analytic trans-parency, potentially facilitating the therapeutic process. I believe this transparent stance is more important than whether and how much information is disclosed. Being honest about the limits of my ability to discuss my illness further could have facilitated a reassuring sense of transparency, humility, and respect for each patient's subjectivity at a time when I could not authentically offer reassurance about my med-ical situation.

Over the years I've imagined that more openness on my part might have created a safe and therapeutic space in which patients would feel free to express their transference fantasies, fears, wishes, and feelings about the experience. However, the majority thrived in the work in spite of my abstinence. Our work was productive and vital despite patients saying little to nothing about my illness, absence, and gaunt appearance. Their transferences expressed themselves through different kinds of material.

My theory is that through the experience of my illness I became a more attuned and courageous analyst with increased appreciation for patients' vulnerabilities and dependencies, real, imagined, and defended against. Having survived a confrontation with one of my worst fears, I became more transparent and authentic in my work as evidenced through several behaviors starting with a determined unwillingness to shy away from the most difficult affects and content of analytic material. I have adopted a more natural and authentic stance. I am more spontaneous and flexible in my responses to patients and my attitude towards treatment. There is more affect in my vocal inflections. I joke more. I use more metaphor in my interpretations, including references to contemporary culture and news. I have forgiven myself and sometimes accept that occasionally I am wordy in my interpretations, unable, in a passionate moment of analytic work, to adopt the pithy form of expression used by some of my admired mentors and by authors of analytic writing. In short, I now regard my character, my very self, as a technical tool that can be used in my work (Hillman & Rosenblatt, 2018). In this way, difficult content has been able to come into the work even though it may not have been expressed directly or explicitly in response to my illness.

One way to strive for a sense of analytic transparency would be to listen and possibly probe for patients' reactions to the analyst's approach, rather than their reactions to the illness itself. Doing so around the time of illness when the patient's transferences are alive and vivid is critical. This approach respects the analyst's prerogative to give as little or as much information as she desires, while keeping the spirit of analytic inquiry alive and leaving room for patients to express their reactions, fantasies, and anxieties. In retrospect, I could have questioned my patients' silent reactions to my own relative silence in an attempt to understand how they read my behavior.

In her paper "Listening to Listening" (1996), Haydee Faimberg describes such a phenomenon. The paper links analytic listening to Freud's concept of *Nachträglichkeit*, which Faimberg understands as a retroactive assignment of meaning rather than *deferred action*. The two combine to result in Faimberg's idea of listening to listening. Faimberg discovered later in the analytic process that her patient(s) had interpreted her interpretations differently than she had intended them and heard her interpretations through the lenses of their iden-tifications. In missing the catastrophic anxiety that her interpretation caused in one patient, Faimberg realized that a misunderstanding ensued which later gave rise to the analyst's deeper understanding of the patient and her maternal identification. "By listening to how the patient has listened to the interpretation, the analyst is able to retro-actively assign a new meaning to what he (the analyst) said, beyond what he thought he was saying" (Faimberg, 1996, p. 667). Such active attention to the patient's "listening" to what is missing and not said in the work, as in my case, can be just as difficult for the ill ana-lyst as is it is to speak about her illness. What is not represented, a form of Green's idea of the negative (1999), can be impossible to know at the time of occurrence or shortly thereafter. Yet, if the ana-lyst is sensitized to listening to listening, which in this case took the form of something missing, it may still offer a second chance to pro-cess analytic events that occurred around a difficult time for the ana-lytic dyad.

At the time I was trying to get through each day and didn't know what wasn't happening. After time passed I could consider what hap-pened and learn from it. I realized that had I been sensitized to these issues in training or elsewhere, I would have been better equipped to decide on an approach to the entire period surrounding my illness.

Patients' rage reactions were particularly difficult to digest in the aftermath of my return to practice. I had difficulty metabolizing these raw affective experiences into Alpha elements – thoughts that could be thought by the thinker (Bion, 1992/2005a, 1963/2005b, 1970/2004). Analysts' deliberations on patients' rage reactions received little attention in the literature in spite of the fact that such rage is one of the most difficult phenomena for the ill analyst to deal with. I experienced it as unfair retaliation for what I felt to be a punishing act of nature.

In a strikingly courageous admission, the very ill Silver (1982) wrote about her decision upon returning to work from surgery to not treat those patients who viewed her as a "murderous force and engendered too much rage" (1982, p. 323). She resumed working with patients who mostly viewed her as a "constructive force, a good enough mother" (1982, p. 323), and with whom there was mutual pleasure in their work together. Little (1967) wrote about disclosing minimal information about his illness to a certain patient for fear of her rage reactions. He described his patient's collusion with him in diverting her hostility to less evocative material. At a later date, he felt able to reflect therapeutically on his protective "countertransference" (1967, p. 112) and to deal with her raw feelings of abandonment that were elicited by his illness and which activated his own abandonment trauma. These analysts stood out because of their unsparing reflections on the measures they took to protect themselves from patients' rage and retaliation and their clinical decisions that followed.

My admonishments to myself such as "Don't fill patients' heads with information that they may not need and will only scare them" and "Don't impose my own anxieties and wish to share. If it comes to it, I will tell them" were double messages meant for my patients and for me. "Don't tell them anything that would scare, overwhelm, and destabilize me" and "Don't elicit any more anger than I can handle" were warnings meant for me that I couldn't yet articulate even to myself. I wondered whether our mutual silence on the matter was a sign that I missed something in the work and had done my patients a disservice. That is until my own analyst contracted two serious illnesses in a row.

My analyst's illnesses

Approximately two years ago my analyst informed me that he had cancer and would be taking some time off to undergo treatment.

"It's early stage," he said. "I don't need surgery or chemotherapy, just a course of radiation five days a week. The radiation is just insurance. This cancer is not life threatening. There's nothing to worry about."

We would have to miss some sessions but mostly we could continue to meet.

"It's not a big deal. They say I might be just a bit tired but not much else in the way of side effects and I'll feel well enough to continue my normal activities. This shouldn't intrude on our work."

As when my radiologist calmly announced news of my tumor to me, I had a double reaction. What was my analyst saying? He had cancer but it was no biggy?! It was that same nonchalant tone, as if it was all in the course of everyday news.

In fact, there was a little more disruption than he had predicted. When I would inquire about how he was feeling, he respectfully answered me while also brushing off anything drastic. Unlike my own approach, he did indulge my concern and curiosity while gently and firmly limiting my expression of it.

"Oh, just a little tired but nothing much."

Mostly I believed him and launched into my associations. We went on with the work of my now once-a-week analysis. At times I wondered how much he was minimizing his experience. I had flashbacks to the reports of others who had gone through radiation and who spoke of the extreme fatigue and debilitation they experienced. I realized something bigger had to be going on when, in the months following his radiation, I asked how he was feeling and he would report that certain changes in his body due to the radiation were slowly subsiding. I took note of it but felt encouraged by him to get on with my process. Compliantly and self-servingly, at first tentatively but with a measure of relief, I did so and quickly reimmersed myself in my own head, unperturbed by any reduction in strength and wellness that my analyst might have felt (later it turned out that he was so buoyed by his optimistic prognosis that he might well have been energized by this).

Approximately one year later, my analyst announced to me that he needed to have an aortic valve replaced. His presentation was almost exactly the same as it was with the cancer.

> I just need a valve replaced. I have the best surgeon for this procedure. He's done some enormous number of these surgeries and there's pretty much a 100% success rate with them. I should feel great after I recover from the surgery. I only need to take a month off after surgery. The problem was discovered in a random checkup. I have no symptoms. I feel well.

For the third time I had that same reaction of a conscious sense of reassurance, a subliminal sense that there must be more, and – this time – a wait and see attitude. But I wasn't going to rationalize my compliance during his illness. And so I told my analyst that I had some concern about him. But I also had more insight into him and what disease might mean to him. I knew that he not only wanted to reassure me, but also that he needed to reassure himself. He needed to reassure both of us that our work would continue, that he would skip only the bare minimum of beats in our work and in life. This time I could see clearly that he needed our work as much as I did.

This time too, when he returned to our work, there were little signs of ways in which he had suffered and was still suffering more than he acknowledged. He had wound up also needing a bypass because blockages were discovered and fixed.

I found that ultimately I had allowed myself to be reassured by my analyst because I trusted him to care about me and to tell me the truth. That trust and truthfulness are part of the basis of the good and honest analytic process we have. It is the foundation of any effective analytic process. I imagined that he understood me and the nature of the analytic process well enough to know that it was necessary to give me some facts because I would need the respect and solace that some information would provide. I believe that he judged that I could not only tolerate but would actually benefit from the information he gave me. Our mutual trust allowed for some leeway to err in either direction of not enough or too much information without destroying our alliance. It allowed me to hope that if I was angry at him about any mishandling, I could express myself once he was well. If he grew weaker, I told myself, I would not want to show any anger. He would be injured enough.

I was also aware that both of us were more worried about him than either of us wanted to say, but we both needed to keep fear out of our conscious experience together and alone. I still needed him. I had loving feelings for him in addition to the infantile and nurturing transferences that already existed in this analysis. In part, my compliance with this process had to do with my desire to honor his wishes to have his rendition of his own experience respected and not tainted or violated by my prognostications.

After his illnesses it clicked for me that my analyst did a very effective job of lending me his ego. While he communicated some sense of omnipotence that signified denial of the danger, he also projected a sense of faith in the healing environment. His confidence and reassurance allayed much of my anxiety and expanded my belief in my own ability to cope.

While my analyst's approach was helpful in establishing a sense of security in me, it had its disadvantages. His overt message was one of openness and respect for me as well as an invitation to talk about the illness. His covert message, however, placed a firm limit on my discussion of his illness. I could have benefitted from being allowed to question him more and hence to explore more deeply what it meant to me to risk losing him, to see him as frail and vulnerable, and to explore some defended anger at his "inconveniencing me," as my patient put it. I harbored some resentment that he did not acknowledge my worry or leave room for me to express flashes of anger at the audacity he showed in leaving me when I wanted him there.

Despite not having had that experience with him, I do not feel deprived or damaged. I did not have one kind of analytic experience. I did have a different and valuable experience. I felt enhanced in my ability to support him by not making the experience harder than it needed to be. Our mutual stoicism gave me permission to make contact with an adult self-state, one that might otherwise have been eclipsed by the resenting patient/child facing abandonment by the analyst/parent. That was therapeutic for me. It would not have been realistic on either of our parts to handle things differently. He needed to erect a strong narcissistic and medical defense and I was unwilling to threaten that or further damage him. I grew from the experience. In the words of Jessica Benjamin, discussing the importance of the patient's recognition of the analyst's subjectivity,

> Even psychoanalysts are prone to imagining that their patients only need to be given recognition, empathy and understanding, of which they were doubtless deprived, and to miss the strength that comes from giving, being a reciprocally responsive other who can go out into the other's mind and return enriched, able to formulate their own understanding.

(2018, p. 12)

At play was a "hierarchy of needs" (Maslow, 1943) that took place in a kind of concordant (Racker, 1968) transference-countertransference matrix. My and my analyst's instinctive and primary need was to protect both of us from the dangerous idea that his health and our work together might be seriously compromised. I empathized with his need for hope. I drew from his omnipotence even while I keenly imagined the dangers he faced. His optimism and confidence allowed me to defer worrying until I needed to. The analytic third (Ogden, 1994) that we created provided a space that allowed me to continue to focus on myself until it was appropriate that I not do so. I could go on being (Winnicott, 1965/1986).

Recently I had an experience that activated a set of thoughts and feelings I had had towards my analyst during the period of his illnesses and return to practice. When I walked into my session, he looked frail, somewhat bruised, and ill. When I inquired about it, he immediately and energetically reported that he had been hit by a car while crossing the street a few days earlier. With little prompting he told his story in detail. As he narrated it I was aware of feeling a sense of his respect for me which bordered on my feeling privileged that he wanted to tell me so much, that we were sharing a very human moment in which he treated me as a worthy and equal human being who might bring him some solace by listening. I wished to heal him by listening and by acknowledging the trauma. The privileged part seemed to have to do with the oedipal excitement upon gaining entry into the inner circle of the adult, parental world. I saw his humanness. He demonstrated his need as a traumatized person to recount his trauma in the hope of recruiting a witness to help him grasp and integrate the import of the horror (Ghent, 1990) and the dumb luck of survival.

Afterthoughts

My analyst's illnesses enabled me to see more clearly than I could before at least a part of what happened with my silent patients. It allowed me to forgive myself. Was it possible that I had actually convinced them of my viability, that they took their cues from me as to whether and when to worry, that the silent majority had developed a foundation of trust with me and a space that felt safe? After all, in spite of my intense, traumatic anxiety, somewhere tucked away in my mind, I drew from my doctor's optimism and confidence that I would become well. Was it possible that, while my patients might have benefitted from less defensive listening and more pro-active intervention, the lack didn't compromise the work in the way that I had feared for so long? Was it possible that, like me with my analyst, they had one type of mutative analytic experience and not another? The fact is that many have gone on to use our work to great effect – even deepening it, constructively regressing, and exploring fantasies, feelings, and cognitive constructs.

Certainly I colluded with my analyst in his avoidance of his recog-nition of his vulnerability and the seriousness of his illnesses. My patients colluded with me, accepting my silent dismissal of my frail state. In retrospect, I believe that at least some of this collusion is essential for the recuperation and wellness of ill analysts, and that ultimately this preservation of the analyst as a good and resilient object may serve both analysts and patients. My patients went on to explore subjects of loss, anger, mourning, abandonment, and disease over the course of their work with me. In my brush with mortality I experienced intense vulnerability and an internal experience of regression, not to mention a clinical regression as a patient. I longed to indulge wishes for dependence. From this heightened awareness I developed a greater appreciation for my patients' dependencies. I lost much of the fear of regression that I had previously experienced. No fear could eclipse the terror I felt over my illness. A deepened sensi-tivity and loss of fear improved my ability to foster and hold product-ive regressions in my patients.

My patients may have also derived some strengthening benefit from surviving my illness and absence and from witnessing my recovery. As one patient said, "I am proud of how I managed. I was much more adult while you were gone." Having borne witness to my own analyst's evolution from frailty to strength and from listening to him share a little information surrounding his illness, I too felt enhanced and stronger. Had my patients not progressed to constructive regressions I would view their trend towards silence as a defensive flight into health (Fenichel, 1945) rather than as the actual growth that it was.

Searles (1975) and Silver (1982) propose that patients want to be therapists to their analysts. Both believe that patients are "individuals who tried but failed to be therapists to troubled family members" (Silver, 1982, p. 322), and that psychopathology results when these natural, human aims are thwarted. For Searles (1975), the analyst must recognize the patients' strivings in this regard, or face their unconscious resistance to the analytic endeavor. For Silver (1982), when the patient's ill analyst continues to work, there is an implication that the patient is more "constructive than destructive, making explorations of the patient's destructiveness less awesome" (1982, p. 322). My work with my own patients was and is curative for me. So is my analyst's work for him (as he told me). Not only did my patients allow me to feel purposeful, needed, and alive (as I did for my analyst), but also, by going on with business as usual, they allowed me to cure myself by "curing" them. In addition, I was able to experience anxiety vicariously through my appreciation of my patients' anxieties so that mine were temporarily distanced. I felt transformed from a passive victim into an active healer. In a sense, my patients were holding me by not confronting me. In getting cured I was able to provide the holding environment that provided for my patients' safe expressions and working through of difficult and bitter transferences.

At the same time, my patients may have benefitted from a different approach in which there was more explicit discussion of my illness and absence. Ideally, I think several patients, including some who had higher levels of internal structure and a greater ability to contend with my separateness and vulnerability, and others who had poor object permanence and were prone to shame, could have done well with a little more information. Though I may not have given each those opportunities, loss of potential benefit is not the same as sustaining a damaging loss. The silence was an enactment of sorts and may have hindered expression of the transference at that time. However, with no adequate holding environment, the silence may have been containing given the circumstances. Enactments can either destroy the treatment and damage the patient or be mutative if they are understood and worked through between patient and analyst. In the case of my practice, I think the working through may have occurred indirectly and at a later point through the analysis of fantasies and affects around abandonment, illness, and loss stirred up by different events at a time when there was a better holding environment that promoted good analytic work.

The conclusions I draw from my experiences with my own illness taken together with my experiences of my analyst's illnesses represent ideal and potentially unattainable approaches. However, these propositions may still serve as guidelines for analysts who are considering how to handle their illnesses with their patients.

In that spirit I recommend these five methods of engagement which can be taught during training.

1   An attitude of transparency on the part of the analyst, including a stance of openness and availability to even the most difficult affects of the patient, can be constructive and mutative.
2   Listening to the ways in which the patient listens to the analyst's verbal and non-verbal communications can augment a sense of the analyst's transparency as well as strengthen his or her understanding of the patient, and thus deepen the treatment.
3   The amount of information disclosed to the patient depends upon the individual patient, how long they have been in treatment, the frequency of sessions, and the individual history, transference, structural level, narcissistic balance, and makeup of the patient. There should be no automatic or *a priori* decision about how much information to give. Either extreme could be retraumatizing depending upon the individual patient.
4   Analysts cannot divulge more information than they themselves can handle while still setting the conditions they need to narcissistically invest in their own recovery.
5   Given the ubiquity of analysts who are ill at some point over the span of their long careers, a course should be offered during training on the subject of understanding and handling interruptions of and intrusions into treatment due to major life events such as illness, pregnancy, personal crises, and other events of the analyst, and their impact on patients.

References

Abend, S.M. (1982) 'Serious Illness in the Analyst: Countertransference Considerations,' *Journal of the American Psychoanalytic Association* 30: 365–379.

Benjamin, J. (2018) *Beyond Doer and Done to: Recognition Theory, Intersubjectivity and the Third.* New York: Routledge.

Bion, W.R. (2004) *Attention and Interpretation.* Lanham, MD: Rowman & Littefield (original work published 1970).

Bion, W.R. (2005a) *Cogitations.* London: Karnac (original work published 1992).

Bion, W.R. (2005b) *Elements of Psychoanalysis.* London: Karnac (original work published 1963).

Cristy, B.L. (2001) 'Wounded Healer: The Impact of a Therapist's Illness on the Therapeutic Situation,' *Journal of American Academy of Psychoanalysis* 29(1): 33–42.

Dewald, P.A. (1982) 'Serious Illness in the Analyst: Transference, Countertransference and Reality Responses,' *Journal of the American Psychoanalytic Association* 30: 347–363.

Edwards, N. (2004) 'The Ailing Analyst and the Dying Patient: A Relational Perspective,' *Psychoanalytic Dialogues* 14(3): 313–335.

Faimberg, H. (1996) 'Listening to Listening,' *The International Journal of Psychoanalysis* 77: 667–677.

Fajardo, B. (2001) 'Life-Threatening Illness in the Analyst,' *Journal of the American Psychoanalytic Association* 49(2): 569–586.

Fenichel, O. (1945) *The Psychoanalytic Theory of Neurosis.* New York: W.W. Norton Co.

Freud, S. (1914) 'On Narcissism: An Introduction,' *Standard Edition* 14: 67–102.

Freud, S. (1920) 'Beyond the Pleasure Principle,' *Standard Edition* 18: 1–64.

Ghent, E. (1990) 'Masochism, Submission, Surrender—Masochism as a Perversion of Surrender,' *Contemporary Psychoanalysis* 26: 108–136.

Green, A. (1999) *The Work of the Negative.* London: Free Association Books.

Gurtman, J.H. (1990) 'The Impact of the Psychoanalyst's Serious Illness on Psychoanalytic Work,' *Journal of American Academy of Psychoanalysis* 18 (4): 613–625.

Hillman, L. & Rosenblatt, T. (Eds.). (2018) *The Voice of the Analyst: Narratives on Developing a Psychoanalytic Identity.* New York: Routledge.

Lasky, R. (1990) 'Catastrophic Illness in the Analyst and the Analyst's Emotional Reactions to It,' *International Journal of Psychoanalysis* 71: 455–473.

Lindner, H. (1984) 'Therapist and Patient Reactions to Life-threatening Crises in the Therapist's Life,' *International Journal Clinical Experimental Hypnosis* 32: 1–27.

Little, R.B. (1967) 'Transference, Countertransference and Survival Reactions Following an Analyst's Heart Attack,' *The Psychoanalytic Forum* 2 (2): 108–113.

Maslow, A.H. (1943) 'A Theory of Human Motivation,' *Psychological Review* 50(4): 370–396.

Ogden, T. (1994) 'The Analytic Third: Working with Intersubjective Clinical Facts,' *International Journal of Psychoanalysis* 75: 3–19.

Racker, H. (1968) *Transference and Countertransference.* London: Hogarth.

Rosner, S. (1986) 'The Seriously Ill or Dying Analyst and the Limits of Neutrality,' *Psychoanalytic Psychology* 3(4): 357–371.

Searles, H.F. (1975) 'The Patient as Therapist to His Analyst,' in P.L. Giovacchini, A. Flarsheim & L.B. Boyer (Eds.), *Tactics and Techniques in Psychoanalytic Therapy* Vol. ll: *Countertransference* (pp. 95–151). New York: Jason Aronson.

Silver, A. (1982) 'Resuming the Work with a Life-Threatening Illness,' *Contemporary Psychoanalysis* 18: 314–326.

Sontag, S. (1990) *Illness as Metaphor and AIDS and Its Metaphors.* New York: Picador Farrar, Straus and Giroux.

Winnicott, D.W. (1986) *The Maturational Processes and the Facilitating Environment.* New York: International Universities Press (original work published 1965).

Chapter 12

Experiences of a bereaved and suffering second therapist

Replacing a beloved student therapist and a gay psychoanalyst

Hendrika Vande Kemp

Over nearly four decades of clinical work, few cases have touched me as profoundly as the two instances in which I became the "second therapist" after the first therapist had died. In the first case, the deceased therapist was my clinical supervisee who died in a tragic car accident. In the second, the deceased therapist was an impaired psychoanalyst who died of AIDS and failed to provide an adequate termination process. The second case was complicated by my own serious motor vehicle accident and its consequences for me, and by my client's sense of not having enough information about my unexpected absence. They present two very different stories of the loss of the therapist.

Phil's death and Phil's therapy case

Phil's accident and its immediate aftermath

It was Thursday, April 27, 1978, an ordinary academic morning in the remodeled residence on Madison Avenue in Pasadena, CA housing the faculty offices of the Graduate School of Psychology at Fuller Theological Seminary. Several colleagues had left for the 10:00 a.m. chapel service; others remained at their desks, preparing for classes and catching up on research. Then came the life-altering phone call from Rick Merton, the director of emergency services at Pasadena's Huntington Memorial Hospital, who had just returned to his hospital office after his monthly seminar – focused on the interface of psychology and medicine – with interns and student clinicians at the Pasadena Community Counseling Clinic (PCCC), our clinical training center. "Doc" Merton informed us that at 9:52 a.m. a staff physician, Lawrence Green, had pronounced the death of Phil Quixby, one of our fourth-year clinical psychology doctoral students, who was involved in an automobile accident at 8:40 a.m. en route to his clerkship assignment at the University of Southern California.

I recently asked Rick Merton about that morning. He shared his memories, and what he learned from viewing the paramedic and hospital charts. He recalls walking through the unusually quiet emergency department on the way to his office when Dr. Green stopped him so as to recount to him his efforts to resuscitate a young male Fuller student who had been injured in an automobile accident. Merton asked Green for the name: Green wasn't sure, but knew it was a funny name starting with "Qu." Immediately anxious, Merton wondered if it might be Phil, whom he knew well; he was Phil's physician, and Phil had been a regular and formidable opponent on the squash courts at the old Pasadena YMCA. The charts confirmed that the deceased patient was Phil Quixby. Phil, at the wheel of a Volkswagen Beetle, was westbound on a busy one-way Pasadena thoroughfare and at a full stop at a red light when a 1977 Ford northbound on the cross street made an illegal right turn, heading the wrong way on the one-way street. The heavy Ford (apparently an official City of Pasadena pickup truck) crashed into and crushed Phil's tiny stationary car.

Phil was unconscious and unresponsive when paramedics arrived, and was probably dead at the accident scene. He was rushed to the Huntington emergency department, where he was pulseless and unresponsive. Phil died of massive chest and abdominal trauma and may also have had non-fatal blunt head trauma. Merton went to view the body, then to make phone calls. Within a few minutes, two of Phil's good friends, known to Merton from Fuller, came to the office, deeply distraught. He took them to Phil's body, and left them there to grieve.

Back at the School of Psychology, faculty gathered to absorb the devastating news of Phil's death, comforting each other, incapable of comprehending what had happened or of returning to academic routine as we waited (or longed?) for information.

Later, some generated the myth that Phil's body showed no external marks of trauma and that he died of his head injury. Only after my recent inquiry did I learn the truth from Rick Merton and Phil's closest friend, who took possession of Phil's bloody clothes when hospital staff handed them to Phil's stunned wife. News of Phil's death was included in the weekly Fuller Theological Seminary student newsletter, with an invitation to the memorial service at Pasadena Covenant Church, whose pastors and organist were integral parts of the seminary community. The family requested that in lieu of flowers contributions be made to the Phil Quixby Memorial Scholarship Fund. At the time of his death, Phil was the president of the Psychology Graduate Union, a division of the All-Seminary Council (ASC), Fuller's student government organization, and he was an articulate and persistent student advocate and thorn in the flesh of the dean and faculty. The Phil Quixby Memorial Award is now presented "annually to a student in the Clinical Psychology Department who actively promotes a sense of cooperation and unity among the members of the graduate union with fairness and justice" (Fuller Theological Seminary, 2017a, p. 12). Megaphone in hand, Phil was also the self-appointed announcer for an informal softball game between School of Psychology faculty and students. This playful game has morphed into an annual Phil Quixby Memorial Softball Game and Picnic (Fuller Theological Seminary, 2017b).

Phil's death left several communities of mourners, both recognized and disenfranchised: his wife; Phil's family and his wife's; his wife's teacher colleagues; his fellow students, faculty, and staff in the Graduate School of Psychology; seminary students, faculty, staff – especially those involved in the intra-mural softball games where Phil met his wife; other officers in the ASC; his clients; and his high school and college friends.

My own grief was deep and ongoing. I knew Phil through classes, his presence in faculty meetings, and his leadership in the softball games. I was also his clinical supervisor for clients seen at a local church, a satellite location for PCCC. Grieving Phil as a student was a deeply communal experience. In grieving Phil as a therapist and supervisee I was isolated and lonely – I don't recall any colleagues, other than the supervisor for my postdoctoral hours at PCCC, expressing curiosity or concern about Phil's clients, the cases I was supervising. Phil and I had created an intersubjective space characterized by high levels of trust and vulnerability. He trusted me with feelings he had never shared, not even with his wife. He was only a month younger than I, and less challenging than my older male supervisees who resisted a younger female supervisor. Phil fully disclosed in supervision everything he'd written in his nearly illegible case notes, in contrast to the common phenomenon of concealment in supervision (see Yerushalmi, 2002; Yourman, 2003).

My journey with Phil's client: the fear of "rejection by death"

My first rational thought that fatal Thursday morning, in the midst of my own numbing shock, was that Phil's clients must be notified before they heard of his death elsewhere. The PCCC secretary – who had access to records, contact information, and schedules – assumed responsibility for notifying clients and for coordinating case transfers with the clinic's director, my clinical supervisor. I was especially concerned about Ethan, Phil's client since late January, whose mental pain was far more complex than the adjustment disorders common at PCCC. The notification process was challenging. In 1978 it was virtually impossible to reach a client who was not available to answer a corded house phone with a wall connection. PCCC employed an after-hours answering service, as answering machines were still cumbersome and prohibitively expensive. The afternoon edition of the Pasadena *Star News* carried a story headlined "Unidentified Man Dies in Accident," and the local radio news reported the accident, without naming the victim. Unfortunately, Ethan first learned of Phil's death from his own wife (who heard a radio report) and from an announcement in a theology class on Friday morning, hardly an ideal setting for such shattering and very personal news: Ethan could publicly grieve a "fellow student" of the seminary or a classmate, but grieving his therapist was intimate and private, requiring a therapeutic presence. After class he walked over to PCCC, asking what to do: he had an appointment with Phil that afternoon. After the receptionist called me, I arranged to see him. Thus began a twenty-five-month journey, accompanied by Phil's ever-present ghost and my silent grief, a journey in which I gradually comprehended the many layers of Ethan's bewilderment at "what to do."

Ethan was an intelligent, handsome, six-foot-tall, dark blond, mustached, blue-eyed, twenty-five-year-old married student in the second year of Fuller's Master's of Divinity program. He was the second of five children, with three brothers and one sister. He complained of having difficulty in new situations, depression, feelings of worthlessness, fear of his painful feelings, thoughts of self-harm and suicide, an inability to open up to others emotionally, and perfectionism. He expressed concerns about being "schizoid" or "crazy" because of the hidden parts of himself, wondered about "demon possession," and voiced ambivalence about "making evil." He feared his anger, which he associated with both retaliation and an internal, persecutory process. He longed not to feel guilty about crying, and feared other feelings, including those stemming from his intrusive fantasies of bleeding or hurting himself, which would overwhelm him, causing him to withdraw. Because of the intrusive "bloody" fantasies – manifestations of a failure of repression – I had requested psychological testing by an intern, who submitted a report early in April, diagnosing latent schizophrenia. I was skeptical about the diagnosis because of the absence of a thought disorder and my own extensive experience with schizophrenia in my inpatient internship. In the last few sessions with Phil, which had, at Ethan's request, shifted from a Rogerian, person-centered approach to a more psychodynamic mode of treatment, they discussed letting the "wall" down a little bit at a time. Phil's notes indicate that he wanted to help Ethan see the relationship between his anger and hurt on the one hand and, on the other, his images of bleeding and night fears. Ethan also explicitly stated a desire to deal with past hurts from a painful college relationship and from his father's demand for perfectionism. I suspected "schizoid" might apply to Ethan, in the sense that Arieti (1974) described schizoid defenses as a type of character armor:

> The schizoid personality will continue to transform the malevolent Thou into a less disturbing agent, the distressing Thou, or to be more correct, the *distressing other* ... who constitutes the

family and the world. It is a set of defenses built as reaction to chronic danger, not to immediate fear; it provides tepid responses to poorly expressed states of anxiety and anger. By detaching himself emotionally the patient will avoid the pain connected with the attacks on his self-esteem. Furthermore, it will be easier for him to tolerate the inner images.

(p. 103)

In Ethan's first session with me, he picked up where he left off with Phil, not overtly processing Phil's death. Yet he quickly revealed his central concern, that Phil's death might force him again to "put his feelings in a box." He didn't know what he felt about Phil: Phil knew a lot about him but didn't make *himself* known to Ethan, and in response to questions he often confronted Ethan with, "Why are you trying to figure out what I'm thinking?" Despite his intense fear of being flooded emotionally, Ethan expressed empathy for me, apologizing for having to put me through this, by which he meant "talking to all of Phil's clients." He didn't want to attend Phil's funeral or memorial service, acknowledging that his reluctance reflected the problem he'd been addressing: the painful reality that his repressed feelings returned as frightening, bloody fantasies; hence he feared – quite realistically – that an emotional funeral service would trigger the troubling, primitive imagery. Ethan's emotions were in fact so overwhelming that in the later course of therapy we had to schedule hour-and-a-half sessions in order to explore and contain them. Ethan had not yet at this time received feedback on the psychological testing, and was surprised that I was recommending long-term therapy. He definitely wanted to continue, and promised to call within a week, soon confirming the offered appointment slot.

In the second session Ethan quickly launched into the full array of emotional issues, having accessed feelings about Phil and discussed them with his wife. He was embarrassed to admit he felt abandoned. He had felt mad and frustrated about it, and also angry that his father responded to Phil's death with only "Your mother told me about it." In mid-session he suddenly realized he was starting in the middle, behaving as though I knew about him in as much detail as Phil had. He knew he needed to build a new relationship with me, and to trust me as he had learned to trust

Phil in those moments when Phil remained silent. We explored what he would lose if he got rid of, or "exorcized," the internalization of his critical father. In retrospect, this session was representative of the larger course of therapy. At times Ethan lowered his defenses enough to immerse himself in the deep psychic pain of his internal world. At other times we discussed his relationship with his wife, which he genuinely valued and nurtured; the dynamics of his relationships with his father, mother, and siblings; mundane anxieties around term papers, exams, interactions with professors, and requirements for the Presbyterian ordination process; and choices around summer jobs and post-graduation employment. By the third session Ethan trusted me enough to commit to ongoing therapy.

In his fourth session Ethan reported waking up in the morning with high anxiety, then talked about a series of interpersonally challenging events. As we approached the session's end, I asked him if the thing he was afraid of that morning was the therapy session. My comment was the first thing he responded to with any feeling – a wave of shock passed over him. He then returned to his feelings about Phil, worrying that he'd buried all the things he looked at with Phil, wasting all the hard work of those three months. Yet he didn't really know Phil, and didn't quite understand his feelings of abandonment. I commented that Phil had given him a part of himself, and that was gone again. He had also just recognized that he could share with Phil things with which he couldn't burden his wife – an unwitting parallel to Phil's relationship with me. Phil's death made him feel frustration, fear, and depression, the latter a feeling he could not allow himself for long because, if the feeling persisted, he'd start to feel like killing himself. Ethan juggled his summer pastoral internship schedule in order to continue his sessions.

After this session, Phil receded into the background, an implicit reality and ghostly presence which only occasionally became explicit. Early on, Ethan recalled Phil telling him not to expect magic formulas. Later, we discussed his fear of "rejection by death," as he voiced the (ungrounded) fear that his wife might kill herself, and how he suspected his response would be to hide his real feelings by only falling apart inside, cluing me to the psychic pain that underlay his bewilderment at "what to do" when Phil died and left him without a safe container. Eighteen months into therapy he raised these issues again, feeling guilty about not sharing more with his wife, but afraid that if he did and something were to happen to her, he'd be left to deal with the feeling of having opened everything up and "Now what do I do?" He connected this feeling with the images of opening up and bleeding in his dominant fantasies. Ethan felt he could generally control his fantasies but not his depression, and opined that maybe he wouldn't have to suffer at all if he could just "let go" of all that, and let his college girlfriend and Phil's "abandonment by death" become memories rather than his current-day reality. He compared his pain to that of the mythological boy hero of Sparta who died because he allowed his pet fox to eat his stomach rather than let it go from under his robe. Four months later, Ethan started a session with a comment about seeing a dent in my car in the parking lot. He struggled to focus on other therapeutically relevant material after acknowledging my "fender bender," and we stopped to process a now critical therapeutic dynamic, his feeling that after my accident he had to protect me and that I might not be able to help him because of my own (presumed) distress. Unspoken was the likely fear that I would not be able to handle *his* feelings, and that I would consequently leave him alone with them. For a moment, seeing the damaged car in the parking lot, he experienced the actual threat of my abandoning him through death just as Phil had done. Therapy terminated, intentionally, in late May of 1980, after ninety-six sessions. I learned later that Ethan died in 2011 after a brief illness, at the age of fifty-eight. He was a successful pastor with a special interest in diversity, happily married for thirty-five years, and according to his obituary, "raised both of his children in his strong faith and ingrained in them both his values and sense of humor."

Within the next decade I encountered two additional premature deaths of Graduate School of Psychology alumni, a 1979 sudden natural death and a 1988 suicide, so when I offered a seminar on death and dying in 1989, I found it natural, even imperative, to include a session on the death of the therapist (see Vande Kemp, 2017). Shortly after teaching the seminar, I took on another bereaved client.

Bridge therapy after the previous therapist's death by AIDS

I have only sketchy notes on this second case treated after the therapist's death, from June 1989 through August 1992. The client, Ms. A, was a forty-six-year-old, unmarried, highly educated woman referred by the All Saints (Episcopal) Church Regional AIDS Resource Center (2017), where she participated in a group for friends and family members of AIDS patients. The client had been in analytic therapy for eleven years with Dr. Z, starting with treatment for bulimia at the Austin Riggs Center in Massachusetts. She followed him to Los Angeles, where she earned a modest salary as a librarian working to convert the card catalog to digital format. Dr. Z, blaming her parents for her symptoms, insisted they pay for her therapy. His effectiveness apparently ended with the bulimia cure. The client, celibate after a long history of promiscuity, had a strong, uninterpreted sexual transference to Dr. Z, which was very confusing to her after a friend told her that Dr. Z was gay. In contrast to her lengthy psychoanalysis, we engaged in a fairly directive therapy, which focused on her interpersonal issues and a process of differentiation from her parents, and offered a "bridging" consultation process, which is essential before a client can continue analysis after the therapist's death. Clients are "given an opportunity to reminisce, share feelings of loss, talk about the deceased as a real person," and validate "their non-transferential experience of the analyst" (Ziman-Tobin, 1989, p. 433). In these sessions the course of treatment is reversed, in that the transference is dissolved rather than strengthened.

The client had frequently wanted to terminate her analytic therapy, but Dr. Z always talked her out of it. In December 1988 she had again brought up termination, and he again told her she wasn't ready. Then suddenly, when he returned from what he called a six-week sick leave in February 1989, he told her they would be terminating because he had AIDS, and they concluded her treatment in May without addressing either her unresolved transference or her feelings about his illness and termination. He offered no referral, told her she could call him if she needed someone, and did not explicitly say he was dying. It felt very open, as if she could continue to contact him. She remained very confused about being unready to terminate in December, and his sudden change of mind in February. By then there were visible lesions on his face, likely Kaposi's sarcoma. She spoke to him at least once more, discovering he had encephalitis. In January 1990 she heard that he died in August 1989, and she received a copy of the "memorial tribute" which she perceived as "too clinical."

We do not know if Dr. Z took advantage of the available gay psychiatry networks and AIDS resources. In the late 1960s, gay and lesbian psychiatrists began meeting informally at the annual conferences of the American Psychiatric Association (APA). After the APA voted in 1973 to remove homosexuality from the *Diagnostic and Statistical Manual of Mental Disorders*, III (American Psychiatric Association, 1980), lesbian and gay psychiatrists felt more free to meet publicly, no longer fearing for their jobs if they were outed as gay. In the early 1970s they formed the Caucus of Gay, Lesbian and Bisexual Members of the American Psychiatric Association (CGLBMAPA), which started publishing newsletters in the mid-1970s,[1] and continued even after the APA recognized the Caucus of Homosexual Identified Psychiatrists (CHIP) in 1982. In 1985 CGLBMAPA changed its name to the Association of Gay and Lesbian Psychiatrists (AGLP), allied with but independent from the APA (Drescher & Merlino, 2007). In the Fall 1983 CGLBMAPA newsletter, President Stuart S. Nichols wrote a column on AIDS, urging colleagues to make themselves available to work with AIDS patients and their caretakers. Dr. Z had access to the resources of the AIDS Project Los Angeles, an AIDS hotline established in late 1983 on the premises of the Los Angeles Gay and Lesbian Community Services Center (Founding, 2017).

There was, of course, an extensive AIDS-related stigma in society, intensified by homophobia. Herek and Glunt (1988) identified the sources of a dual stigma: "first, from identification of AIDS as a serious illness; second, from the identification of AIDS with persons and groups already stigmatized prior to the epidemic" (p. 887). Gay men were also exceedingly prone to bereavement overload. Martin (1988) noted that "anecdotal and journalistic reports of entire gay social networks decimated by AIDS are common" (p. 856). In New York City, one-quarter of gay men "had experienced the death of one or more close friends or lovers by 1985," with an average of six losses (Kemeny et al., 1994, p. 15). The Gay Men's Chorus of Los Angeles lost twenty-nine singers to AIDS, out of 150, between 1984 and 1989 (Mitchell, 1990). Later writers noted that these multiple losses were accompanied by hidden, or disenfranchised, grief (Dane & Miller, 1992; Murphy & Perry, 1988; Vande Kemp, 1999). Consequently, losing a therapist to AIDS creates another layer to the disenfranchised grief that already accompanies the death of the therapist (Doka, 1987). The issue of gay therapists disclosing their HIV diagnosis was rarely discussed openly before 1994 (see Cadwell, Burnham, & Forstein, 1994), and Dr. Z apparently handled the termination process without professional consultation.

By November 1989 it was obvious that Ms. A was completely unable to take Dr. Z's perspective: to grasp that in the face of terminal illness he might have become self-focused. I believed that her therapy must focus in part on my helping her to attain such empathy for Dr. Z so that she would eventually be able to forgive him. Step by step, in a process similar to that later described by Hargrave (1994), I gently helped her to take his perspective. It took a long time, but in February 1991 she was finally able to conceptualize Dr. Z's inconsistency in terms of the relationship between denial and lying: could he tell *her* of his impending death if he was not acknowledging it himself? In her words, we put him "on trial" for the crimes committed against her. We spoke in explicitly religious language of guilt and forgiveness, which turned the process in a productive direction that ultimately led to her forgiving Dr. Z.

The client initially feared that with Dr. Z's death she would lose all the health she had gained with him. In what appeared to be a guilt reaction to her growing attachment to me, her new therapist, she attempted to terminate her treatment with me in December of 1989. She was feeling increasingly uncomfortable with how enmeshed she was with her parents, who continued to pay for her therapy. Unlike Dr. Z, I considered her discomfort to be a healthy instinct. Because Ms. A couldn't afford my standard hourly fee on her small salary, I suggested we negotiate the fee to an amount she could afford. She was truly stunned that I would even consider this, but we arrived at a fee that was possible for her and acceptable to me. This was a crucial therapeutic moment, as she realized that

I supported her healthy efforts to differentiate from her parents and to separate from Dr. Z. This step towards financial independence strengthened her growing trust in me.

In March and April of 1990, Ms. A often spoke about her stuffed toy, "Snuffleopagus," a lovable character from *Sesame Street*, which she brought to sessions and eventually left with me. For Ms. A, Snuffleopagus was a symbol of comfort against coldness and logic, and I kept him clearly visible in my office. Leaving Snuffleopagus with me set the stage for a successful differentiation from both her parents and Dr. Z, and for greater autonomy in her other relationships; it also ensured that *I* did not forget *her*. This case was far more challenging than the simple grief work of a family member, lover, or friend that I anticipated when signing up to take referrals from the Regional AIDS Resource Center. Nothing had prepared me to help a client mourn the death of a therapist to AIDS, and I could only rely on what I already knew about grief and mourning through personal experience and academic study.

Lurking in the background: the therapist's journey of pain and suffering and questions of self-disclosure

On July 12, 1989, one month after this client started therapy, I was involved in a serious car accident and was forced to cancel her afternoon session. The client told me the next week that when my faculty secretary notified her of the cancellation, she felt that "she would never be the emergency for which a session was canceled." It did not seem appropriate at that point to tell her that I myself had the emergency; this was, on my part, a clinical judgment based primarily on therapeutic intuition and the nature of her transference at that time, which clinical experience led me to contrast with two very different types of clients in my case load. First, I had encountered clients who appeared to have no inner fantasy life, and therefore no transference distortions. With one of these women I had shared openly in 1987 after my brother was diagnosed with leukemia: her responses were socially appropriate and empathic, and she did not try to take care of me or become distracted from the hard work of therapy. Second, there were those who were attuned to my mental states, necessitating the processing of the intersubjective space. For example, I later had a client who manifested a variety of primitive defenses and developed a strong positive transference to me. She started a session by reporting a dream in which I appeared much distressed. In the dream she was with me in a session, and unable to do anything to comfort me. She sensed that I needed to be alone, and so she left the session. When recounting this dream, she also spoke of her old friends who were totally insensitive to feelings. I considered this dream to be evidence of her interpersonal sensitivity and attunement to me, and confirmed her feeling that I was in fact sad about circumstances in my life (which by then included my brother's death). I told her that she might have picked up on my feelings and perhaps even felt abandoned by me. This sharing offered considerable relief for my client, who feared that the dream might mean she was going crazy, and it helped her to explore her sensitivity as a strength and our connection as significant. That client was still in therapy when I had my accident, which never came up in the sessions, likely because I took great care to be in a relaxed state beforehand. My injuries were invisible – which made my recovery all the more difficult – and all my clients remained unaware of how much I was actually struggling with the serious after-effects of this accident. Throughout the course of therapy with Ms. A, and far beyond, I faced a long series of medical and legal challenges. I was, in fact, learning to live with an invisible disability that lingers to this day (see Vande Kemp, Chen, Nagel Erickson, & Friesen, 2003). I was also dealing with chronic pain, primarily from post-traumatic headaches that included features of migraine, cluster, and tension headaches, as well as a stabbing neuropathic pain that was so severe that I later resorted to creating a headache sculpture to depict the pain for my neurologist at UCLA's Neuropsychiatric Institute (see Vande Kemp, 1993). I had, in fact, entered an entirely new phenomenal world, which I later described in a book chapter addressing therapists:

> The roles of patient and plaintiff propelled me from a world centered on work, family, friends, church, and professional activities into an entirely new phenomenal world in which protracted periods were spent receiving medical treatment, exercising, sleeping, commuting to UCLA/NPI, and coping with extensive

paperwork. I was forced to interact with my attorneys, defense attorneys, judge, jury, accident witnesses, police, diverse expert witnesses, and health and auto insurance company representatives. Old networks of professional colleagues and church leaders drifted to the periphery as I reduced my teaching load and eliminated virtually all extra-curricular activities in order to concentrate on rehabilitation, teaching, and writing. I became increasingly detached from siblings and others who were unable to enter my phenomenal world.

(Vande Kemp, 2001, p. 179)

I managed my schedule carefully, so that I could be refreshed and totally present for the few clients I saw, centering myself and setting aside my external concerns, one hour at a time.

The accident involved a multiple-impact collision between my 1986 Honda Accord and a Freightliner hauling a 42-foot trailer: the truck hit the driver's (my) door, pulling my car counter-clockwise around the truck, with three additional points of impact. My car was destroyed. During the accident, I experienced multiple whiplash forces. At first impact, my head moved right and left in a coup-contrecoup motion, while at second impact, my head and neck rotated counterclockwise and, likely, forward and backward, which resulted in a left-frontal lobe injury. My door was forced into my seat, and I had to be removed through the passenger door by the emergency technicians. Despite being carried into the hospital on a stretcher with my head and neck secured, I was released from the emergency room with nothing more than a warning that by the next day I'd start hurting. I had no inkling of what was to come: I began experiencing excruciating headaches, extreme sensitivity to noise, and flashbacks to the accident that included a long series of post-traumatic dreams with intrusive scenes that Hartmann (1996) might describe as "encapsulated memories," as well as repeated traditional nightmares with pseudo-memories (Bryant, 1996) that apparently assisted the process of assimilating the accident and its aftermath into my personal experience (Vande Kemp, 1993, 2001).

In September 1989 I started five years of psychotherapy and other treatments to deal with post-traumatic headaches, fatigue, increasingly obvious cognitive symptoms, and the trauma of the accident. The emergency room physicians failed to diagnose a mild traumatic brain injury (MBTI), with post-concussive syndrome, and my recovery involved attending support groups sponsored by the Brain Injury Association of America. For two years I also regularly made a two-hour round-trip commute to engage in neuro-feedback that included computer-aided arousal regulation training (focused on bringing the brain waves into the "rest" state) and neuro-cognitive pacing skills. Daily naps to prevent fatigue states have been part of my routine ever since, a cumbersome but necessary life-style adaptation. With some coaching at the Neuropsychiatric Institute (NPI), I also learned and devised a variety of strategies to compensate for cognitive losses.

In May and June of 1990 – before the MBTI was diagnosed – I was forced to take a six-week leave from my clinical practice due to an unfortunate sequence of events triggered by a series of medical mis-steps. The neurologist treating my post-traumatic headaches prescribed Nardil, a monoamine oxidase inhibitor, unaware that psychotropic drugs are contraindicated after a head injury. After two weeks on Nardil I experienced a full-blown manic reaction with an inability to sleep, ataxia, and parathesia, as well as more severe headaches, double vision, and elevated blood pressure. When I reported these symptoms to my psychotherapist, I was admitted for a six-day inpatient hospitalization which ended only because my insurance wouldn't cover the cost, inaccurately classifying my hospitalization as "substance abuse treatment" – adding insult to injury. Hospital doctors prescribed Restoril, Mellaril, and Trilafon, medications that left me increasingly disoriented and distressed. With my psychotherapist's support, I discontinued these medications and soon recovered my sanity. I had adjusted my teaching workload with the assistance of my dean, and, with my psychotherapist's assistance, set other boundaries, including a limited schedule in which I spent only five to six hours a day at the office. Both the dean and my therapist felt it was critical to protect my practice from any possible repercussions of my manic episode, and so I canceled sessions with my few remaining clients, but maintained regular telephone contact with them. In reflecting back on my work at that time, I'm amazed that the clients didn't notice anything, even when I was literally "seeing two-headed clients." Despite my mental state before the hospitalization, I appear to have displayed few symptoms to clients, as no one asked questions, commented, or expressed worry about my absence. The telephone contact seemed to secure my therapeutic bond with clients, and reassure them of my welfare, and I experienced no client attrition. The only memorable response was that of Ms. A, who felt there wasn't enough information about my absence, thus appropriately keeping the focus on her experience.

When Ms. A's therapy resumed after my absence (a session which fell, coincidentally, on the first anniversary of my accident), we returned to a discussion of the session I had canceled a year before, when she voiced that there was not enough information. Ms. A continued to wonder if she was as important as "some emergency." Because this was a significant issue in her life, we discussed it in relationship to her other interpersonal issues. Ms. A's therapy continued for another year with a focus both on this issue and on the ongoing dissolution of her transference to Dr. Z. In the Fall of 1990 I had finally been referred to the UCLA Neuropsychiatric for diagnosis and treatment of my head injury, and was in ongoing legal negotiations with the trucking company, which culminated in a demeaning personal injury trial in the fall of 1992, after I had terminated with Ms. A.

Whether I would have shared more about my personal journey with a different client remains an unanswered question. At that time we did not have Jamison's (1995) memoir, *An Unquiet Mind*, or later memoirs that detail experiences of mental illness. I was familiar with Anton Boisen's autobiographical account of his mental illness (1960), and with the early work of Clifford Beers (1908), but neither these authors nor Jamison argued for self-disclosure of the therapist's personal experience with mental illness (even a temporary one) in the therapy process. I did share much of my experience openly with students, self-disclosure that included showing photos of EEG recordings from neuro-feedback and SPECT scans to my history of psychology students, making clear to them all that the post-concussive syndrome might result in glaring errors on their course syllabi, and that they should not be afraid to point out these errors. I also talked about the drug-induced mania in an intern seminar. And I eventually published several very personal accounts (Vande Kemp, 1990, 1993, 2001).

When my attorney prepared a request to have the records of my personal injury trial sealed, I was forced to think about questions related to my right to privacy: who has the right to know about my neuropsychological testing reports, past and present psychotherapy summaries, psychiatric hospital records, and, even, demeaning comments in reports by defense experts, such as a neurologist's dismissal of me as a "spinster." In a letter to my attorney, I also discussed concerns about interns, clinical trainees, and practicum students having access to records at the courthouse only a few blocks from our Graduate School of Psychology offices. My letter indicates that in this case far more was involved than disclosure to a particular client:

> In both my private practice as a licensed psychologist and my supervision of students, I encounter persons who are seriously disturbed (borderline personality disorders, etc.), who engage in various forms of harassment of their therapists (they are able to discover unlisted home telephone numbers and use them to invade the privacy of their therapists; they use every other means possible to try to discover information about the personal lives of their therapists, calling friends or other therapists in efforts to obtain such information; when angry at their therapist, they try to find ways to hurt the therapist; they make threats of bodily harm). I do not wish to be more vulnerable to clients who have such difficult boundary and self-control problems, and I feel that the psychiatric hospitalization which was a direct result of this accident makes me particularly vulnerable to (false) charges that I am an "impaired psychotherapist" and should not be seeing clients. I do not wish to have any questions about my competence raised in the professional community.

In addition, I did not wish to have clients feeling concern for me, and the limits I had set on my practice allowed me to conduct therapy sessions before pain and fatigue set in. Yet clinically informed self-disclosure had been part of my training and experience from my earliest years at the University of Massachusetts, when I was supervised by Norman Simonson and his graduate assistant Kenneth Bundza. Their (1973) article on therapist self-disclosure is a frequently cited classic in the field. Sheldon Cashdan (1973), who first taught me interpersonal psychotherapy, describes the emotional coupling essential to the early "hooking" stage of therapy: the therapist must convince the client that she can accurately and sympathetically perceive the feelings of the client, and judicious self-disclosure can be a part of that process. I was further trained in Sullivan's interpersonal model (1953, 1954), which emphasizes "participant observation" and the very real engagement of therapist and client, which often involves judicious self-disclosure. Orange, Atwood, and Stolorow (1997) discuss the role of carefully considered therapist self-disclosure in empathic-introspective inquiry, basing their decisions to self-disclose in part on collaborative input from the client. The importance of a "real" psychotherapist is also central in Friedman's (1985) classic, *The Healing Dialogue in Psychotherapy*, and in the current relational psychoanalysis movement. I tried to follow the advice of Benjamin (2003), who observes that "a therapist can give simple, factual answers to personal questions, while remaining alert to the possible meanings of the questions and impacts of the response" (p. 177). My limited answers to Ms. A were in that spirit, with an awareness that her boundary issues made sharing risky.

Benefits and risks of therapist self-disclosure

In later years, I frequently disclosed to clients my issues related to chronic pain, fatigue, head injury, and post-traumatic stress. This became an issue in 2011 in a case of a middle-aged man who injured his pelvis in a fall on a gym floor. He suffered from severe pain, and underwent a series of unsuccessful surgeries. In therapy we had frank discussions about his suicidal feelings and his physical and psychic pain because it was critical that he recognize that his suicidal feelings, like other feelings, could be explored and contained, and are separate from any action that might be taken on them. During the summer of 2010 he was no longer seeing me because the drive was too painful and he did not have the financial resources for therapy. He was relying on an informal support network that included pastoral and lay counselors and the suicide hotlines. In one such call to a suicide hotline he spoke about our therapy, and I received a phone call in which the very young hot-line worker, who was involved in evaluating the client for a Mobile Crisis Unit, interrogated me about my approach to therapeutic self-disclosure and to suicidality. I explained that I normalized the client's psychic pain in response to his intense physical pain, and that my approach to suicidality entailed talking about the *feelings* openly, regarding that as an effective anti-suicide strategy. I also often encouraged clients to read Hillman's (1997) *Suicide and the Soul*, which reveals exquisite attunement to psychic pain. A complaint to the state licensing board was lodged against me by this young man, who interpreted these therapeutic discussions as "encouraging suicide." In its inquiry, the licensing board asked if I disclosed my chronic pain to this client or other clients. My answer was "yes," and I offered the following rationale:

> Many clients are referred to me specifically *because* I have extensive experience working with persons with physical disabilities. Generally my "disclosure" is limited to describing my professional experience and answering briefly with the information that I survived a very serious car accident that entailed several years of severe chronic pain. I do not discuss specifics with clients except to establish that some of my experience comes from "having been there" when they desire a therapist with personal experience of pain and/or disability. I follow advice of Nouwen (1972), that healers who have been wounded themselves can be particularly effective, but not if they bring open wounds to the encounter.

Ultimately the licensing board did not sustain the complaint (which was made without the client's knowledge, and without his consent to release records). The stress of receiving a letter from the licensing board, hiring an attorney, and preparing a defense was detrimental to my physical and emotional health, and contributed to my decision to retire in my late sixties. The client, whose suicidal urges never went beyond expressing his feelings, found the therapy helpful – my file contains a handwritten thank you note written at least a year after this incident, after I wrote several reports to doctors who were treating his pain, and saw him again with family members. My approach worked well with him and with other suicidal clients. But all therapists are vulnerable to the judgments of outsiders who evaluate our work on the basis of limited, out-of-context client reports. Yet the outcome of this case proves the old adage that keeping accurate and extensive records, and the ability to write a thoughtful report, are the best defense against a licensing board complaint.

Final comments

I have presented two "second therapist" cases, each a pivotal growth experience for me and my clients. In the first, I mourned a beloved student and supervisee, and in the process of working with his abandoned client I shared in a redemptive process of mutual growth and increasing awareness of primitive mental states and of my own clinical skills, a learning process that influenced my teaching and writing. In the second, I was plunged into the world of AIDS and of HIV-infected therapists, and I engaged in a difficult bridge therapy and a painful differentiation process. While immersed in this bridge therapy, I was also coping with a serious personal injury, a medication-induced manic episode, and a stressful legal process which highlighted questions of therapist self-disclosure about illness and injury, and later exposed the potential legal risks of appropriate therapeutic self-disclosure.

Note

1 The earliest newsletter in the archives is Vol. 3, # 2 June 1978. Volume 1 apparently appeared in 1976 (Drescher & Merlino, 2007, p. xxxi). The archive is available on the AGLP website at www.aglp.org/pages/AGLP NewsletterArchive.php.

References

All Saints Church. (2017) *Affiliated Organizations: AIDS Service Center*. Retrieved April 26, 2017 from www.allsaints-pas.org/community/affiliated-organizations/aids-service-center/.

American Psychiatric Association. (1980) *DSM-III. Diagnostic and Statistical Manual of Mental Disorders* (3rd ed.). Arlington, VA: American Psychiatric Association.

Arieti, S. (1974) *Interpretation of Schizophrenia* (2nd ed.). New York: Basic Books.

Beers, C. W. (1908) *A Mind that Found Itself: An Autobiography.* New York: Longmans, Green.

Benjamin, L. S. (2003) *Interpersonal Reconstructive Therapy.* New York: Guilford Press.

Boisen, A. T. (1960) *Out of the Depths: An Autobiographical Study of Mental Disorder and Religious Experience.* New York: Harper & Brothers.

Bryant, R. A. (1996) 'Posttraumatic Stress Disorder, Flashbacks, and Pseudomemories in Closed Head Injury,' *Journal of Traumatic Stress* 9: 621–630.

Cadwell, S. A., Burnham, R. A., & Forstein, M. (Eds.). (1994) *Therapists on the Front Line: Psychotherapy with Gay Men in the Age of AIDS.* Washington, DC: American Psychiatric Press.

Cashdan, S. (1973) *Interactional Psychotherapy: Stages and Strategies in Behavioral Change.* New York: Grune & Stratton.

Dane, B. O., & Miller, S. O. (1992) *AIDS: Intervening with Hidden Grievers.* Westport, CT: Greenwood Press.

Doka, K. J. (1987) *Disenfranchised Grief: Recognizing Hidden Sorrow.* Lexington, MA: Lexington Books.

Drescher, J., & Merlino, J. P. (Eds.). (2007) *American Psychiatry and Homosexuality: An Oral History.* New York: Harrington Park Press.

Founding. (2017) *Aids Project Los Angeles Health.* Retrieved April 26, 2017 from https://aplahealth.org/about/history/.

Friedman, M. (1985) *The Healing Dialogue in Psychotherapy.* New York: Jason Aronson.

Fuller Theological Seminary. (2017a) *2014–2015 School of Psychology Scholarship Application.* Retrieved April 26, 2017 from http://fuller.edu /uploadedFiles/Siteroot/Offices/Student_Financial_Services/ 1415_sop_scholarships.pdf.

Fuller Theological Seminary. (2017b) *School of Psychology. Psychology Graduate Union.* Retrieved June 6, 2019 from https://digitalcommons. fuller.edu/cgi/viewcontent.cgi?article=1000&context=academic_catalogs.

Hargrave, T. D. (1994) *Families and Forgiveness: Healing Wounds in the Intergenerational Family.* New York: Brunner/Mazel.

Hartmann, E. (1996) 'Who Develops PTSD Nightmares and Who Doesn't?' In D. Barrett (Ed.), *Trauma and Dreams* (pp. 100–113). Cambridge, MA: Harvard University Press.

Herek, G. M., & Glunt, E. K. (1988) 'An Epidemic of Stigma: Public Reactions to AIDS,' *American Psychologist* 43: 886–891.

Hillman, J. (1997) *Suicide and the Soul* (2nd ed.). Woodstock, CT: Spring Publications.

Jamison, K. R. (1995) *An Unquiet Mind.* New York: A. A. Knopf.

Kemeny, M. E., Weiner, H., Taylor, S. E., Schneider, S., Vissher, B., & Fahey, J. L. (1994) 'Repeated Bereavement, Depressed Mood, and Immune Parameters in HIV Serpositive and Seronegative Gay Men,' *Health Psychology* 13: 14–24.

Martin, J. L. (1988) 'Psychological Consequences of AIDS-Related Bereavement among Gay Men,' *Journal of Consulting and Clinical Psychology* 56: 856–862.

Mitchell, S. (1990, 26 December) 'AIDS and the Arts: Behind the Scenes of a Tragedy.' *Los Angeles Times.* Retrieved April 28, 2017 from http://articles.latimes.com/1990-12-26/entertainment/ca-1044_1_aids-activist/2.

Murphy, P., & Perry, K. (1988) 'Hidden Grievers,' *Death Studies* 12: 451–462.

Nouwen, H. (1972) *The Wounded Healer.* New York: Doubleday.

Orange, D., Atwood, G., & Stolorow, R. (1997) *Working Intersubjectively.* Hillsdale, NJ: The Analytic Press.

Simonson, N. R., & Bundza, K. A. (1973) 'Therapist Self-Disclosure: Its Effect on Impressions of Therapist and Willingness to Disclose,' *Psychotherapy: Theory, Research, and Practice* 10: 215–217.

Sullivan, H. S. (1953) *The Interpersonal Theory of Psychiatry* (H. S. Perry & M. L. Gawell, Eds.). New York: W. W. Norton.

Sullivan, H. S. (1954) *The Psychiatric Interview* (H. Swick Perry & M. Ladd Gawell, Eds.). New York: W. W. Norton.

Vande Kemp, H. (1990) 'Character Armor or the Armor of Faith? Reflections on Psychologies of Suffering,' *Journal of Psychology and Christianity* 9: 5–17.

Vande Kemp, H. (1993) 'Adrift in Pain, Anchored by Grace.' In J. Lee (Ed.), *Storying Ourselves: A Narrative Perspective on Christians in Psychology* (pp. 261–291). Grand Rapids, MI: Baker Book House.

Vande Kemp, H. (1999) 'Grieving the Death of a Sibling or the Death of a Friend,' *Journal of Psychology and Christianity* 18: 354–366.

Vande Kemp, H. (2001) 'The Patient-Philosopher Evaluates the Scientist-Practitioner: A Case Study.' In B. D. Slife, R. N. Williams, & S. H. Barlow (Eds.), *Critical Issues in Psychotherapy: Translating New Ideas into Practice* (pp. 171–185). Thousand Oaks, CA: Sage.

Vande Kemp, H. (2017) 'The Death of the Therapist and the Bereaved Client and Colleague: An Introduction to the Literature,' *Journal of Psychology and Christianity* 36: 334–348.

Vande Kemp, H., Chen, J. C., Nagel Erickson, G., & Friesen, N. (2003) 'ADA Accommodation of Therapists with Disabilities in Clinical Training.' In M. E. Banks (Ed.), *Women with Visible and Invisible Disabilities:*

Multiple Intersections, Multiple Issues, Multiple Therapies (pp. 155–168). New York: Haworth Press.

Yerushalmi, H. (2002) 'On the Concealment of the Interpersonal Therapeutic Reality in the Course of Supervision,' *Psychotherapy* 29: 438–446.

Yourman, D. B. (2003) 'Trainee Disclosure in Psychotherapy Supervision: The Impact of Shame,' *Journal of Clinical Psychology* 59: 601–609.

Ziman-Tobin, P. (1989) 'Consultation as a Bridging Function,' *Contemporary Psychoanalysis* 25: 432–438.

Psychoanalytic institutes and training

Chapter 13

Death begets growth

Catherine Lowry

Training

The subject of this chapter is my long-time mentor, trainer, and advisor, whom I will refer to as Peter. I met Peter in 2004, when I attended a two-day training session he offered in Ego State Therapy. Peter was a psychiatrist who had had traditional analytic training. Through his work with clients he came to see what he viewed as the limitations of a more classical analytic approach and began to explore alternatives. Eventually he adopted Ego State Therapy. Like many therapy clients, I followed the path of my mentor. At that time, I had been in private practice since 1998 and had been exposed to a variety of theoretical approaches. I officially described myself as "eclectic," meaning I hadn't yet found a theoretical home. I found Ego State Therapy fascinating, and it very much resonated with me. The theoretical construct of individuals having multiple ego states made sense to me, and I found compelling the use of imagery to access the psyche beneath the intellectual level. I continued to attend his periodic two-day trainings, and I eventually joined one of Peter's ongoing clinical consultation groups.

In these group sessions we discussed the theory and technique of Ego State Therapy as it could apply to our cases, which we often presented. Of course, group members frequently did personal work, too. A lot of the training was experiential: Peter often read imagery exercises, which were designed to have the listener meet one or some of their "parts." We each did the exercise silently, in our "mind's eye," and then shared with the group about our experience. We would also practice with each other – one person acting as the therapist, the other as the client, while the other group members observed. The person acting as the client used a real issue or ego state on which they wanted to work. If one of us was presenting a case in which there was a countertransference issue, Peter would offer the presenter the opportunity to do a piece of work with the ego state involved with the countertransference. We all felt that Peter's workshop was a safe space in which we could be – and work – together.

Over the years, as the consultation group continued, a core group of us came to know each other very well, and the group became a haven for us all. Following the lead of our mentor, we began integrating and becoming more proficient in Ego State Therapy principles and techniques. More than any of the other group members, I adopted it as my primary mode of working with clients. Peter was kind, patient, thoughtful, humorous, and often brilliant in his understanding and use of this approach. He was always able to articulate his reasoning for each intervention, and he understood fully the ego state development and conflicts within the client. He was truly a master clinician, and – needless to say – I found his mastery more than a bit intimidating. But my feelings of intimidation stemmed more from my own insecurities than from any personality trait of Peter. As a child, I tried to win the approval of my controlling and critical mother, yet I also rebelled against her control. That rebelliousness never showed up with any other authority figures in my life. I was typically deferential to teachers, bosses, and other authority figures. I carried that tendency into my relationship with Peter, and it certainly contributed to my idealization of him.

Peter was deeply supportive in so many ways: he encouraged me to believe in myself, to trust myself, to go to the depths of our client's psyche with them, to tackle the tough clients, and to continue with them even when we felt defeated. It seemed possible to take on those challenges with his support and guidance. It was not uncommon for someone to present a new client, to feel completely overwhelmed at the thought of being that person's therapist, and to feel more able when Peter would say something to the effect of, "Well, it won't be quick, but you can handle this!" These types of comments were so common that I was left with the sense that sticking with a client, no matter how challenging the patient, was essential. I never stopped to examine this belief fully. I incorporated it into me without realizing it: it was how Peter seemed to view it, and so it was how I viewed it too.

Over time my competency in the use of Ego State Therapy enabled me to identify it as my definitive theoretical orientation, and it became my primary mode of working with clients. I was able to use the Ego State model with everyone I saw in my practice, even if I didn't always explicitly use the imagery technique. I worked mainly with trauma and dissociative disorders, and I found that the more dissociative the client, the more pronounced were the different ego states. Although present in everyone, varying ego states are not always as distinct in a healthy person as they are in patients who are dissociative; in a healthy person, each ego state is part of an integrated whole.

Susan

I had one extremely challenging client, Susan. In more traditional terms she would most likely have been diagnosed as having Borderline Personality Disorder. She was extremely sensitive to perceived abandonment and would frequently threaten to hurt herself when she was angry at me; at times she engaged in self-harming behavior, such as cutting. After she had cut herself, she would come in to my office, show me her cut, and say, "See what you made me do." Through the lens of traumatology, the appropriate diagnosis would have been Dissociative Disorder NOS, and by the time I ended my work with her, I concluded she suffered from Dissociative Identity Disorder (DID). Extremely dissociative clients commonly have their most severe symptoms hidden at the beginning of treatment, and the more severe pathology only becomes apparent with time. Susan came to me with a history of experiencing intense emotional attachments to a series of women, most of whom had been older than she, although at least one was her peer. Susan's attachment, at times, became so intense that her whole life revolved around the woman, and spending time with that person became the most important thing in her world. Predictably, Susan developed in the transference the same very intense attachment to me. I believed that in the therapeutic process we would be able to resolve this pattern.

The goal would be to uncover the ego state that held this attachment pattern (almost certainly a child ego state, possibly an infant ego state), and heal it so that Susan could relate to others from her adult self. Instead, Susan became increasingly fixated on me over a period of years, as she had with previous women, and the treatment became stuck. Susan's attachment manifested itself in the great difficulty she had with ending sessions. Eventually, her difficulty was so extreme that the main focus of any given session was on how she would be able to cope with its ending. If Susan did not cope well, she often became very regressed by the session's end. She also stalked me several times; for example, she sometimes drove by my house (not my office) looking for me. I discussed her case with Peter and the group with regularity, and Peter offered me his guidance and, more specifically, his encouragement: it seemed to me that he felt I should keep working with her. His faith in me allowed me to believe I could successfully work with this client, helping her to resolve her issues. I had faith in both Ego State Therapy and in the therapy process. But there was an undercurrent of doubt within me, and I sometimes questioned whether I was really helping her. On the days when she had difficulty with ending the session, Susan would remain in the waiting room in a regressed state for a significant duration after the session. Some of my suitemates were concerned with this arrangement, wondering if she really was appropriate for outpatient psychotherapy. I was aware of how unusual it was, and to some extent I shared their concerns, but I didn't think it was reason enough to end my work with her. I mostly felt that the therapy was progressing: this was the kind of support a very dissociative client needed. Despite the difficulties and the stress, I found working with Susan fascinating, and I learned a tremendous amount from her.

After working together for a number of years, Susan arrived one day in what for me was a new ego state, and she made verbal threats to physically harm me. I was quite surprised. I really didn't have any idea that this ego state was within her. She had at times been angry at perceived slights or at perceived abandonment, but she had never become threatening towards me. I typically encountered her needy infant state, but this was quite different. After repeatedly asking her to leave the session, only to have her refuse,

I called the police. It was the first and only time I have ever taken that action in my practice. However, Susan ran out of the office just before the police arrived. I did not press charges, but – unsure of her whereabouts, and concerned that she might be in the parking lot near my car – I did have the police escort me to my car. I wasn't scared, believing that she would not really physically attack me; but I certainly couldn't count on her to respect my boundaries, and I didn't want any further interactions with her that night.

Later that night I decided to terminate Susan's treatment. This was a momentous decision for me, after having worked so hard and for so long to help her heal. Physical threats and the need to call the police are, of course, unacceptable occurrences within a therapeutic treatment. But I also remember thinking: "Here's my chance!" It was as if I needed to seize on a justifiable reason to end the treatment. I feared that if I didn't do it immediately, I would have her forever. If I continued treating Susan, I would also have communicated to her that her behavior was acceptable, which I did not want to do. Susan was very challenging because she had many issues with anger, a desire to harm herself, and a propensity to push designated boundaries. I thought about her case often, I discussed it a great deal, and in many respects I found it to be very burdensome.

Sitting in my office that night, I didn't call Peter to discuss what had happened with Susan. I felt sure he would have encouraged me to keep working with her despite my gut feeling that I should not, and I knew that I didn't want to continue. My perception about Peter may have been wrong, but I doubt it. Given how much I respected him, I wasn't sure I would have been able to follow my instinct and end Susan's treatment if he were encouraging me to continue. Once I actually transferred Susan to another therapist, I told Peter what had happened and discussed it with my group. Peter and the group provided valuable guidance that helped me with the protracted termination process with Susan, one that took place over the phone, and had one final goodbye – supervised by her mother – in a public place. I never explained to Peter why I didn't call him that night, and he never asked. In retrospect, I think my inability to speak to him about it illuminates how intellectually subservient I felt in relation to him. I'll never know why he didn't ask me about my reasons for not telling him about Susan. Peter's style was generally warm and welcoming, a "you can tell me anything" attitude, but he tended not to press people to reveal things they weren't ready to divulge. I think a second reason I didn't call him that night was because I couldn't quite handle the dissonance between what I wanted to do – end with the client – and what I imagined he would have encouraged me to do – remain working with her. I couldn't process the decision with him because I didn't feel he was a neutral party who would help me to make a decision that was best for me: he would have had a bias, which would have been expressed very subtly, but communicated nonetheless.

But why could I only talk to him if he was neutral? I don't think I was able to tolerate the prospect of disagreeing with my honored mentor. Disagreeing with authority figures was something I still struggled with in those days because I tended to be deferential, a propensity that had been part of my psychological make-up since childhood; although I'd worked through it to some extent, my propensity to defer was clearly present and active in my relationship with Peter. I would never have been able outwardly to defy him; instead (and without conscious recognition), I would have simply moved away – distanced myself – if only internally: that was not something I wanted to do. In some ways, the fact that he was so kind and understanding made it harder for me. He was in no way authoritarian, which might have stirred up some rebelliousness on my part, as it had with my mother. As it was, he remained firmly on his pedestal.

Loss

Then, in July of 2012, the unimaginable happened: Peter was murdered – shot by one of his clients during a session at his home office. The client then immediately killed herself. The news was shocking, to say the least. Since the perpetrator was also dead, there was no investigation, and few details were made public. Even though I was close to Peter, I wasn't part of his inner circle, and so I was not privy to details that others possibly knew.

Of course, there was a lot of talking among all the therapists who knew Peter or knew of him. Some things I heard made me uneasy, especially that he had had a "dual" relationship with the client who had murdered him. At one point in time, when she wasn't his client, he had sublet office space to her. There was an article in the local paper with an interview of a colleague of Peter's, who said that Peter had told him the day before the murder-suicide that Peter had been thinking that he needed to end the treatment with the patient; no reason for his desire to end the treatment was given in the article.

So much was going through my mind. I was stunned by the loss. I counted on Peter so much, and even though I hadn't wanted to rely on him when I made the decision about ending Susan's treatment, I still viewed him as my primary mentor in Ego State work. I also still idealized him. I did not understand how something had gone so terribly wrong: How did he not see the danger this client presented? As part of my ongoing training and consultation with him, he would frequently make reference to Gavin de Becker's *The Gift of Fear*, a book about recognizing and trusting one's gut instinct when it comes to danger. Yet Peter seems not to have sensed the danger from this client.

Or had he? Maybe that was why he was considering ending the treatment with the client. The irony was clear: he was thinking of ending with the client, yet up until his murder I'd believed that he would never end with a client, no matter how difficult or worrisome. Clearly I had been wrong in that belief. Looking back, I suspect that he encouraged us with his "you can do it" message to help us become better clinicians, who had faith in ourselves; he didn't mean to convey that there weren't good reasons to end treatments.

I wonder now if my own tendency towards persistence influenced my perceptions of his beliefs. I never thought to ask him explicitly about when it might make sense to end a treatment, and because I never heard discussion of this issue in other realms, it remained unexamined. Not only did I idealize Peter, but there was also no one else who even came close to influencing me to the same degree. Of course I took other training programs, and even participated in an ongoing study group with one of his colleagues, but, for me, no one was comparable to him. I do think the very personal nature of the experiential training I did with him contributed to my feelings: he was the authority, the supervisor, the trainer who knew me the best.

I was very disturbed about the dual relationship that Peter had with his client; it felt as if the nature of their relationship was the key to understanding what had happened. In our small group we couldn't help but speculate about what had been going on. What could have caused the client to act out like that? I wondered if the client had a romantic transference to him. If she did, it seemed likely that the dual relationship could have encouraged that attraction. Allowing a dual relationship seemed like such a basic error to make, and yet he was so clinically sophisticated.

The parallels between Peter and his client and me and my client, Susan, were rather striking. My client had had an intense attachment-transference to me, and it seemed likely that Peter's had one to him. And both had become aggressive. When my client started to act toward me in threatening ways, I ended the treatment immediately. Most of my colleagues supported my decision, but some had thought I should keep going, and that Susan wasn't really dangerous. Peter's murder made it clear to me that I had possibly been in a dangerous situation, or it could have become one; his death in some ways confirmed for me that I had made the right decision. Although danger to myself was not my primary motivation for ending Susan's treatment, in retrospect it's probably something I should have been considering more seriously.

Growth

I idealized Peter – as a person, and as a therapist. He was my kind, wise, nurturing therapy Father, and I didn't think he could make a mistake. Yet he had been murdered during a session by a client. I felt guilty even thinking about it, but I couldn't get away from the likelihood that somewhere in this case he had made a terrible mistake. The boundary violation, his not sensing the danger – something had been very wrong. I shared these thoughts with only a couple of very close colleagues, who I knew would keep my confidence. I also knew I'd never find out the nature of the mistake because there was no way to learn about the details. I wanted to know what had happened, what error he had made, because I sought to know if the things he had taught me were in some way faulty.

Despite my feeling that he had made a grave error, I was intent on protecting his reputation. I wondered if his closest friends and colleagues felt in a similar way, and if their desire to protect him led to the dearth of details relating to the case. The impulse to protect him continues to this day: even while writing this chapter, I wouldn't want anyone to be able to figure out Peter's true identity. It would feel like a betrayal of him.

My need to protect Peter, and my feeling that he had made a terrible error that ultimately led to his death, spurred in me a process of reckoning. I began to realize how much I idolized him, how much I "swallowed whole" what he had offered. Of course, what he taught me was very good and enormously helpful, but I had never made his teachings my own – I never fully allowed my own perspectives, sensibilities, and judgments to inform my clinical work and growth as a therapist. I also realized that no matter how much information, advice, or guidance I received from Peter, I was fully responsible for all my own clinical choices. I think that, in the beginning, I had unconsciously adopted the role and attitude of an apprentice to a Master. The Master had all the answers, and the apprentice's goal was to learn from and emulate him. In the next few years, after his murder, I made a significant shift and no longer felt like I was trying to be a version of Peter. I became committed to integrating what he had taught me, and yet I focused primarily on becoming my best version of myself. The loss of Peter brought to my awareness that, although I needed mentors to develop myself, my idealization of him ultimately limited my own power and potential.

About a year after Peter's murder, I had another very challenging client, Barbara. She had an extensive history of trauma, and she was dissociative, chaotic, and without a clear narrative of her history and recent experiences. She felt extremely depressed and wasn't getting relief from medications. Barbara spoke with her psychiatrist and agreed to try transcranial magnetic stimulation (TMS). However, the TMS wasn't helpful, and it negatively impacted her memory, which was already impaired, most likely because she was so dissociated. In a particular session after the end of the TMS treatments, Barbara became very angry at me, accusing me of "sending a lamb to the slaughter" by recommending TMS. I reminded her that, although we had discussed her plan, the recommendation and referral to TMS had come from her psychiatrist. Yet she remained angry and blamed me. I began to feel scared by the extreme degree of her anger, and – as she reached for her purse and began to look inside for something – I had a sudden and fearful fantasy that she was reaching for a gun, just as Peter's client had. She wasn't, but my heart was pounding. I got through the rest of the session, and after she left, I thought about what had occurred. How could I possibly continue with a client of whom I felt that afraid? But I'd actually been afraid of nothing: there was no gun. I spoke with a number of colleagues, and got a variety of reactions. One suggested that my fear was a PTSD reaction to Peter's murder. While that might have been true, the fact remained that I was now scared of this client. And what if it were the opposite: what if Peter's murder was the object lesson in how to respond to a case like this, namely never underestimate the capacity of a client to act out and endanger – even kill – a therapist? I didn't know this client well, and so I really had no idea about what she was capable of. All I knew was that, even in this early stage of treatment, she was already quite angry at me and blaming me for something I did not do.

Within a few days I decided to end with the client. I made sure that my suitemates would be in the office during the session in which I informed Barbara that I was terminating her treatment. She did not take the news well, telling me that I was acting unprofessionally by abandoning her; she threatened to sue me or to file a complaint with the social work board. Her threats strengthened my resolve to end her treatment, but now she scared me in a different way.

After the treatment with Barbara was over, I felt haunted by an image of Peter, shocked and alarmed by his client when she pulled out a gun. Did he think he could handle it? Talk her out of it? Did she shoot him when he briefly turned his back to her to get something? Was he facing her and knew what was coming? I loved Peter, and it made me sick to imagine the scene; whatever mistakes he made, he was fundamentally kind, good-hearted, and doing his best. He obviously didn't deserve to be murdered. After experiencing the surge of fear with Barbara during her session, I hoped that Peter didn't see it coming, and that he didn't have to experience the terror of facing a gun. After imagining that Barbara had a gun, I was very frightened to have her final session. In addition to my general lack of skills and knowledge relating to when and how to end with clients, my fear of her made the prospect of the session all the more daunting; but I did it, and I was glad that I had done so.

After Peter's death, our group has continued, with members leaving and new ones joining over time. Since we no longer had our teacher, we decided to make it a study group and began reading other authors who write about Ego State and Parts Psychology. I found reading other theoreticians quite helpful; I hadn't really read other practitioners when I was studying with Peter. Not only were there different ideas and approaches, but I could also critically evaluate the information I read more fully. I was now able to determine for myself what I actually thought about the merits and flaws of particular theories precisely because there was no master present. This process helped me to develop further my clinical self; I could incorporate other Ego State theoretician's ideas about theory and technique. I haven't had a mentor since losing Peter. I'm open to new ideas and approaches, and I don't feel the need to follow one person anymore. I'm very comfortable with my work, and I no longer feel like an apprentice.

Now that Peter is gone, there is no one in our area who offers trainings in Ego State Therapy. I have thought about offering trainings using, more or less, Peter's model: small groups, periodic trainings, and ongoing consultation groups. And yet right now my practice is full, and so my idea remains on the back burner. I also suspect that the idea of stepping into Peter's shoes, especially without his explicit blessing, is a stumbling block.

I still miss Peter dearly, and I continue to feel the loss of him. Yet I can't help but notice that his death, especially because of the particular manner in which it happened, spurred both my personal and professional growth.

Chapter 14

Hidden illness

Nancy Einbinder

There have been many papers written about how clinicians cope with terminal illness in their individual practices. But there is a paucity of literature on how analytic institutions deal with these situations, and how and whether they help candidate-analysands with the illness or death of their analyst. Hence the title of this chapter, "Hidden illness," which refers to the secrecy that training analysts often maintain around terminal illness and how institutes often collude with that secrecy.

It is true that in our private offices we may be "traveling affectively alone" (Schwaber, 1998), but I believe it should be possible for our institutes to do better in providing guidance and comfort when training analysts are faced with their own death, and when candidates need assistance in navigating these uncharted waters. Knowing that there is a "holding" structure within the institute if needed, both for the ones leaving and the ones left behind, could be an important source of relief.

The Institute for Psychoanalytic Training and Research (IPTAR), the institute which I currently head and where I have been a member since 1993, like many others, has put in place a committee to address this very issue. Our committee is called the Disabled Analyst Committee (other institutes refer to theirs as the Psychoanalyst Assistance Committee). There has been little written about how these committees function and get utilized. In this chapter, I hope to communicate how ours came into being, and to share some of my thoughts about its importance for members and candidates.

I will begin by telling you about my own experience within my institute, as a young candidate and as a member, as well as by providing a survey of some of the literature. In my current capacity as president and training analyst, my primary concern in this area remains the same as it was years ago: how the death of the analyst impacts candidates who are in treatment at the time.

Societal culture has shifted in terms of how we think about death, and institute culture has also changed over the years. Increased participation by candidates in almost all aspects of the institute's activities and a general trend toward democratization in my institute have certainly contributed to an increased overall transparency. However, the impaired functioning of a training analyst due to illness remains an under-discussed topic and contributes to the under-utilization of the Disabled Analyst Committee's capacities. We seem to be clear about our professional responsibility toward our patients, but I believe that, as training analysts and as representatives of our institutes, we have just as great, if not a greater, responsibility in our work with candidate-analysands.

The traditional hierarchy within institutes operated for years with an unquestioned acceptance of the anonymity of the training analysts. The question to ask, therefore, is, if a dying training analyst who is treating a candidate-analysand is not making "appropriate" plans, and if members become aware of the situation, does the institute have a responsibility, and, if it does, just what is the nature of that responsibility?

I first started to think about this in the 1990s, and it felt almost like a boundary violation to talk about this issue because of the potential intrusion into the private life of the analyst, as well as the disregard for the highly held importance of anonymity. Trying to work through this tension has much to do with the ethical culture of any institute. The very understandable wish to preserve anonymity for the sake of the training analysis of candidates within the social structure of the institute shifted "technical neutrality into social anonymity" (Kernberg, 2000).

My interest in this topic began when my control supervisor died in 1990. At the time, I was a candidate, working with her on my first control case. Though I suspected she was ill and often asked after her health, she always replied that she was fine, "just having back problems." I was not aware of any impairment in her functioning as a supervisor, but I kept on feeling that something was very off. The experience of knowing and not knowing was troubling. During a vacation, I received a message from a member of the institute who was a close friend of my supervisor – a message asking me to call him. I did so, and the conversation went something like this: "Nancy, you will no longer be in supervision with S." He gave me no further explanation about why. I asked him if I could call her, to which he replied, "No, you should not call her as she will not be returning." I asked if she was dying, and he replied, "I can't say anything more. Give yourself some time and find another supervisor."

After the call, I very much wanted to say goodbye and convey my appreciation for all she had given me, and so I wrote her a letter. Even though I was not sure that I would receive a reply, it helped me feel less helpless. It also felt healing to me. At her memorial service, I was told that she had received my letter and had been touched by it. Technology not being what it is today, when I might immediately find a group of other candidates struggling with what seemed like an impending death knell, I felt very alone with this information. Word did spread, however, and supervisees and analysands of S ultimately found each other. Most of us had not been forewarned or given the opportunity to say goodbye. Those who had been in analysis with S were in deep grief. Some of the conversations centered on feelings of betrayal, abandonment, and anger. The anger contaminated the ability to grieve.

This experience helped me years later when a patient came to see me after her therapist had left the workplace with no notice. This patient had arrived for her scheduled appointment, and the receptionist at the clinic told her that her therapist was ill and closing her practice. This patient came to me for a consultation to help with this situation, and she specifically wanted help with writing her therapist a letter. The receptionist had provided an address. We worked on the letter together for a few meetings and, at the same time, we talked about how this news, delivered in this way, had impacted her. After a few meetings, she decided to take a respite from therapy. She eventually returned for a full resumption of treatment after about three months. The death of her previous therapist, and the way in which it had been handled, reverberated through our work for years.

Prior to my supervisor's death, no one from the institute had reached out to me. I continued with my control case, imagining my supervisor reassuringly hovering over my shoulder, while at the same time feeling very abandoned. I wondered what would happen to my case. Would this affect my progression at the institute? And I didn't know whom to go to for continued supervision. What if someone didn't "get" how I was working? How would I be able to catch someone up on years of work with my patient? I also felt guilty because I was only a supervisee and couldn't imagine what her analysands were feeling. It was a very strange time. I felt quite alone. In addition, no one reached out to me after her death, either to check in with me in a personal way, or even to see if I needed help resuming supervision. The first person who expressed empathy toward me was the supervisor I next worked with. In our first meeting, he attended to my experience and spoke about S's denial and how she had kept many of us in the dark, while at the same time we had known that something else was occurring.

In 1998, another training analyst at our institute died. Again, the death felt abrupt to her analysands and supervisees because no one had been forewarned. Again, the silence was deafening. Some of us heard later on that she had been ill and knew she was dying, and that she was nevertheless still talking about wanting referrals. In response to her death and what was again an absence of transparency, I formed a working group which was made up of six members. We called ourselves "The Disabled Analyst Committee." We read and discussed papers, shared our thoughts and experiences of loss within the institute, and began to formulate ideas as to how we could have an impact institutionally on the ways in which life-threatening illness and death are handled.

It was clear to us that there had been an absence of a committee that could have been helpful. No committee had thus far been structured and designated to serve the needs and special needs of the membership in such situations. If we were solely in private practice, there would be no unmet expectations. But as members of an institute, we felt part of a psychoanalytic, professional family, and the feelings of aloneness did not feel appropriate. Psychoanalytic institutes were not designed to address the personal needs of their members. They were designed to train candidates in the practice of psychoanalysis and to serve the professional needs of their members.

The idea of an institute serving as a substitute, albeit professional, family feels important to me. Blum (1986) wrote about the impairment of the analyst in an article on countertransference. He asserted that this type of situation becomes very difficult when it has to do with a senior analyst who is held in high esteem, and that there is shared denial of the impairment by the analytic group. He went on to say that a candidate in analysis is "better protected" than the patient in an "ordinary personal analysis" because the latter "is not privy to the parental protection of the institute." It strikes me as interesting that he was thinking about this twenty years ago; yet I think it would not be presumptuous to say that at that time the majority of candidates did not feel protected by their institutes.

Many of the articles our working group read focused on the concepts of neutrality, abstinence, and disclosure, and how they impact what we do in our offices. If we expand these ideas beyond our individual practices, then it is understandable that they have bled into our institutional functioning as well. Schwaber (1998) and others (Morrison, 1997; Pizer, 1997) remind us that the paradigm shift from a one-person to a two-person psychology allowed for a greater flexibility in treatment and for a beginning allowance for intentional self-disclosure. Morrison had cancer and continued working for many years. She describes her thinking and choice about disclosure based on each patient's diagnosis, state of the transference, past losses, and other factors. She was one of the earlier authors who recommended discussion of these issues during training, and who believed that professional organizations needed to establish standards for closing practices. Clark (1995) also felt that provisions in the case of catastrophe in the life of the analyst need to be articulated for the profession. She recommended the use of an analytic consultant who can help the dying analyst to figure out just how to proceed. Feinsilver (1998) also spoke of how few guidelines exist for the profession. He speculated that Freud, who lived with oral cancer for sixteen years and worked until his last few weeks yet never wrote about how this impacted his work, has been our model. In this way, Freud contributed to an analytic ideal. Feinsilver makes reference to the workshops that were run by the American Psychoanalytic Association. These discussions generated much interest; after meeting annually for several years, however, there was no agreement on the topic of intentional self-disclosure. The best guideline that our group found for a procedural model on how to write a professional will was offered by Firestein (2007). This model gives excellent step-by-step instructions for an individual practitioner, but not for an institute. Firestein was not addressing the issue of disclosure but rather the practical aspects of closing a practice. His recommendations make it easier to begin to think about our responsibility as training analysts to our patients not only when we know that death is imminent, but also well before that point. He sets out a procedure that is very sensible.

Emboldened by the literature, our Disabled Analyst Committee wanted to be acknowledged by IPTAR, and we wanted an official vehicle by which we could disseminate some of these ideas. At the time, I met with two colleagues who were working on the Ethics Code for IPTAR. One of them suggested that I contact the institute president to find out what procedures were needed for our group to become a bona fide committee, rather than merely an investigative body or a study group. We wanted "official" committee status that would serve the institute. Our group wrote a formal proposal requesting committee status with both member and Fellow participation. Consequently, I was invited to speak to the board. The board members were interested in what we were doing, and agreed that a committee designated by the board was needed. They understood that, up to that point, in the history of the institute, there had been no such committee designed to serve the special needs of members and candidates in crisis. There was agreement that this new entity would be a committee separate from the Ethics Committee.

What followed at the board meeting was a brief discussion about who would constitute such a committee. One Fellow proposed that it be made up only of Fellows because it is "such an important committee." I lobbied for shared participation by members. At that point in time, our group had not even considered the participation of candidates. That possibility had never crossed our minds even though it was the candidates whom we wanted most to help. Our working group had been established mostly by members with a genuine concern regarding analysands who had been left in the lurch not only by their analysts, but also by the institute. We too, in a reflection of the institute culture at the time, had not invited candidates to join our working group. And the board was considering that the committee be constituted only by Fellows. The focus was on maintaining the prevailing hierarchy. Nevertheless, an "official" committee was born. The board voted that the chair needed to be a Fellow. Two Fellows took the helm, and they invited me to be part of the governance structure. I was the token "member" member, but in effect had to bring them up to speed about our group's prior work and findings.

At this point in writing this chapter, I had a dream:

> I am in the hospital having been diagnosed with blood cancer. I am lying in bed, very weak, having not had any food. I tell my mother to go get my appointment book so that I can call my patients and tell them I cannot come back to work. My father is weeping. Then some doctors come in, and I tell them my plan to stop working and ask them how much time I have. The "head" doctor tells me I am having an anxiety attack and am not actively dying, and that I feel like I am because I haven't eaten. They start bringing me plates and plates of meat, mostly steaks, and tell me that I will ultimately die from this disease but it can be treated in the meantime.

These were my associations to the dream: I have a patient with blood cancer – lots of thoughts about her after this dream. I am trying to work on this chapter in my sleep. I will die, but don't know when. There is no need yet to tell patients or the institute. But my close colleagues know I have cancer. Will they be discreet? Will I still get referrals? Dare I take on an analysand? In a way, it would be simpler just to stop working and get these problems over with; maybe I wouldn't be so anxious. I don't want to burden patients unnecessarily. I am not a big meat eater.

The dream seemed to be a screen for the larger issue, which is how to get the institute more aware of, and more protective toward, their analysand-candidates. Manifestly, I am focused on my own practice and how I will help myself and my patients handle my death. The dream is also an expression of guilt related to disparaging my "professional family," to many of whom I was (and still am) very close. Well, many of them are dead now. Can I be this critical of a group I am so attached to and that has given me so much nourishment without my developing a fatal illness?

In addition, I think this dream reflected a universal phenomenon wherein we all have some ethical qualms about a major issue: those of us of a certain age who are taking on young candidate-analysands are exposing them to the analyst-death scenario.

Firestein (2007) wrote that "the death of the analyst ... is an unmitigated catastrophe" (pp. 30–31). He views it as unethical to practice without having precautionary measures in place. Fajardo (2001) believes that continuing to work under the duress of a life-threatening illness without the support of a professional, more object-ive, person is unethical. In the abstract, this stance sounds reasonable; in practice, however, it is impossible to ascertain just how many of us actually have a back-up plan.

Our official committee, The Disabled Analyst Committee, distrib-uted Firestein's article with his template of an analytic will to the entire membership of IPTAR. Following his recommendations, our committee proposed to the board that all members have two people (preferably younger) who have a list of our patients (initials or first names only and phone numbers) to be contacted in the event of an analyst's death. In addition, our administrator would have the names of these two individuals. This proposal was unanimously agreed on, but we also agreed that it was non-enforceable. We distributed Fire-stein's article in any Ethics course given, and also suggested introdu-cing the idea of an analytic will to candidates at their matriculation interview, which occurs at the end of their first year in training. The intended message was that a major responsibility came with seeing patients. The committee also hoped that a younger generation would take to these ideas (analytic will and Disabled Analyst Committee) more easily than had their elders. From my readings, it seems it has been especially difficult for the older generation to accept the idea of an analytic will (objections to a presumed lack of confidentiality), let alone of intervention by a committee.

Candidates at IPTAR see patients from our clinic, under the insti-tute's auspices, with supervision by members. We need to make spe-cial efforts to instill in these young analysts-to-be their professional responsibilities. It takes years to develop analytic integrity and a professional self. From the very beginning of training, institute members need to understand that we carry some responsibility for our candidates' and members' behavior.

An analytic will serves to keep one focused on the continuity of care for one's patients. Each year (or still more frequently, depending on the nature of one's practice), the pertinent information should be updated, with a recent list of patients given to the designated colleague(s). Any new instructions should also be given at this time. In doing so, we might also help direct our attention to our responsibility to those candidates who are in treatment with us, and to how our death would impact their training. This blueprint implies, in addition, a responsibility to the institute that we conduct ourselves in ways that make continuity of training less disruptive and traumatic. The death of any analyst would impact any patient. Patients who are also candidates in our institutes should have the opportunity, and I believe also the right, to be taken under the protective wing of the institute, and given a place collectively to mourn, and to seek consultation and support as they begin to stabilize in the face of the death of their analyst.

Many years ago, in one of my classes, we were faced with an instructor who was either very sick or on heavy medication, or both. She nodded off in class, was very non-interactive, and left us pretty much on our own for case presentations. Our group became chaotic and acted out in terms of hyper-criticalness toward each other. Even as a group, we didn't know what to do or whom to tell, and so we opted for silence. It was after evaluations were written that the situation was addressed and resolved. It seems inconceivable that this situation could occur today. The candidates today feel much more able to speak up about an intolerable situation. This instructor was not seriously ill, but on very heavy pain medication and her functioning was impaired. Our passivity clearly contributed to the situation, but the existence of a Disabled Analyst Committee would have helped. There would have been concern about this analyst's health and how she was functioning, and we would have had a clear path to follow.

Years ago, I was supervising a beginner student at a psychotherapy institute. One of the first cases assigned to her was a patient whose analyst had died. The patient had not been informed of the death in a timely fashion. He had arrived for his session and had found a note on the door. I soon recognized the players and knew that the deceased analyst had been a seasoned clinician, someone who had died abruptly and whose spouse had managed to contact most of her patients. This patient had fallen through the cracks. I was appalled that he was now seeking treatment through a clinic, and had been assigned to this student (and at a high fee, to boot!). To my relief, within a few weeks, this patient chose someone else with whom he had been consulting. Had there been an analytic will naming a professional colleague (besides her husband) who would have taken care to contact each patient and help guide them, perhaps this distraught man would not have been randomly searching for a new therapist.

I heard a troubling anecdote that occurred at another institute. When a candidate's analyst abruptly died, that candidate sought consultation with the deceased analyst's spouse, who took on the patient for analysis. There seemed to be no procedure in place to advise the candidate. Or, if there was someone or a training committee involved, they clearly had the analyst's needs in mind, and not those of the candidate-analysand whose treatment was inevitably compromised.

Only a few authors have written about institutional responsibility. Judith Rendely (1999), in writing about her experience of her own analyst's death, says "the trauma may be softened if the analytic community actively acknowledges the difficulty of the analysand's position." She recommends some interventions at specific junctures. Rendely addresses the importance of (1) the initial phone call; (2) the period of consultation; and (3) the resumption of analysis. She favors a member of the institute or another colleague making the initial call, and recommends that information should be provided and questions should be directly and honestly answered, and that this is no time for anonymity. Some analysands might want to meet and talk with the caller, while others might want occasional contact or a referral at some point. Traesdal (2005) refers to this person as the "bridging analyst." During the period of consultation, if there is such a period, the consultant needs to soften the analytic stance of non-disclosure and validate the analysand's experience of grief. Feelings of abandonment will be "complicated if the analyst avoided, denied, or withheld information about her state of health" (Rendely, 1999).

Galatzer-Levy (2004), in "The Death of the Analyst," wrote that "there is an enormous unmet need for analysts and the analytic community to think through our attitudes to life-threatening and terminal illness in the analyst." He continues, "many of them (analysands) felt that the analytic community and, in particular, the administration of their institute should have done something to protect them" (p. 1003). He recommends the establishment of a committee so that institutes can have systematic procedures to deal with these situations.

How does the idea of utilizing such a committee become part of any institute's culture? I think there is, in general, some group resistance to thinking about this question. How can we preserve some training analysts' wishes for privacy and yet also protect our candidates who are in analysis? Can an institute internalize some sense of responsibility without becoming too superego-ish? It seems that most training analysts who are dying do not make it public within the institute, and that reticence seems appropriate. One hopes that they are dealing privately with their candidate-analysands in a humane way, and making arrangements that are sensible, perhaps under the guidance of wise, objective colleagues who can help them. But what if they are not? We need to recognize that the decision about how to handle such situations rests with each individual training analyst. A committee dedicated to these issues is there to assist these analysts if they call on us. Some authors have written about the myriad inhibitions that prevent training analysts from consulting such a committee. Some institutes report instances of analysts making use of this kind of committee. Our committee at IPTAR has not been called on even once in all these years.

I suspect that at the individual level many people have made their own preparations. Whether that includes contact instructions given to our administrative person, I don't know. I know that some elderly analysts closed their practices while they were still in (relatively) good health. And I know of no situation in which any candidate felt that his or her analyst was too impaired to function. So, I think the institute and its members have to some extent internalized these ideas as important values. On the other hand, every once in a while, I hear that someone has no idea that this committee exists, or that there is an occasional request for a copy of Firestein's analytic will. Usually, these conversations and requests get revisited after there has been a death. Clearly, our committee has not been proactive enough – a situation possibly pointing to some form of collusion with the larger group's wish not to deal with such a distressing topic.

Much less has been written about candidates raising concerns about a training analyst's or control supervisor's suspected impairment. I believe that, in order to have any effect, the committee has to function for both ends of the membership spectrum – for the training analyst as well as for the candidate-analysand. Candidates would have to feel very forthright, brave, and trusting that this committee would confidentially hear their concerns, take them seriously, and deal with the information. Key procedures would include taking the concern to the analyst in question, finding out if there is a condition that is affecting their work, and, if so, beginning the process of helping the analyst adjust to his or her new circumstances. It would feel excruciatingly painful for all parties involved, but I think it more bearable than the unplanned-for death of the analyst who has not utilized an analytic will or, if actively dying, has only just begun talking about his or her circumstances to his or her candidate-analysands.

Our committee exists to suggest, review, and disseminate current ideal standards for how training analysts can handle serious illness or terminal situations. It exists to serve as a confidential consultant body to help any training analyst prepare for the closing – be it temporary or permanent – of their practice. I am also proposing that any candidate can use the committee as a safe place to voice concern about a training analyst's perceived impairment, whether as an instructor, analyst, or supervisor. It seems to me that dyadic intentional disclosure by the analyst is much more desirable than hearing from a committee that there has been an anonymous complaint. Perhaps the mere existence of our committee will spur the analyst to write down in the form of an analytic will the specifics of closing his practice. In addition, in the case of terminal illness, the analyst can begin to plan for how he or she will reduce his or her duties at the institute. The committee serves as a backup for analysts who have not prepared an analytic will, and/or are not proactively handling their situation with their analysands. If all members were aware that candidates can also avail themselves of the committee's assistance, that awareness in and of itself would hopefully raise the standard of how training analysts conduct themselves in these situations.

I recognize that what I am suggesting may border on a "big brother is watching" mentality. But given the non-transparency of the not-so-distant past, I believe that what is being offered here is a more reasonable plan than others that have been suggested. Some institutes have tried and then abandoned the idea of a mandatory retirement age. The idea of a committee evaluating competency beyond a certain age has also not taken hold; nor do these ideas tackle the issue of the onset of impairment in the non-elderly. Whenever there is an inability or inhibition to self-report (either to the institute or to the candidate-analysand), it is up to the candidates and analysands or colleagues to weigh in and for the committee to evaluate the matter. This model shifts the responsibility and blame for dysfunctional practice due to impairment, from the analyst to a shared responsibility, thus helping to turn around the "culture of silence." Sometimes, it is the "children" in the family who need to protect the "parent" from his or her own dysfunction. In this way, the candidates in analysis/supervision/classes are also protecting the institute and its reputation as a place of integrity and transparency, and even the analysts, supervisors, and teachers themselves. In all of this, there is no implication or assumption that anyone would be forced to stop working. The goal is to assist them.

There is no recognized ritual for the grieving analysand-candidate, and no organized mourning process that might provide a holding or sustaining function. The institute itself needs to find "space" for this to occur, and also a design for how most productively to fill that "space." It seems to me that, in the face of trauma, more and more members turn towards the institute, as their community, to find comfort. This occurred after 9/11, and recently after the 2016 election, when so many felt in shock and wanted to convene and share their thoughts and feelings. It may be that not everyone will want or need this resource, but it is important that it be available and easily accessible. The trauma caused by the abrupt death of an analyst can be so personal and so "familial" in the transference, and, as in the case of a real-life loss, there is no better place to grieve than within the institute, whose members are able to share in the profound experience of grief for one of our own.

References

Blum, H.P. (1986) 'Countertransference and the Theory of Technique: Discussion,' *Journal of the American Psychoanalytic Association* 34: 309–328.

Clark, R.W. (1995) 'The Pope's Confessor: A Metaphor Relating to Illness in the Analyst,' *Journal of the American Psychoanalytic Association* 43: 137–149.

Fajardo, B. (2001) 'Life-Threatening Illness in the Analyst,' *Journal of the American Psychoanalytic Association* 49(2): 569–586.

Feinsilver, D.B. (1998) 'The Therapist as a Person Facing Death: The Hardest of External Realities and Therapeutic Action,' *International Journal of Psychoanalysis* 79: 1131–1150.

Firestein, S.K. (2007) 'The Patient or the Analyst Dies: Ethical Considerations,' *The American Psychoanalyst* 41(3): 30–31.

Galatzer-Levy, R.M. (2004) 'The Death of the Analyst: Patients Whose Previous Analyst Died While They Were in Treatment,' *Journal of the American Psychoanalytic Association* 52(4): 999–1024.

Kernberg, O.F. (2000) 'A Concerned Critique of Psychoanalytic Education,' *International Journal of Psychoanalysis* 81(1): 97–120.

Morrison, A.L. (1997) 'Ten Years of Doing Psychotherapy While Living with a Life-Threatening Illness: Self-Disclosure and Other Ramifications,' *Psychoanalytic Dialogues* 7(2): 225–241.

Pizer, B. (1997) 'When the Analyst is Ill: Dimensions of Self-Disclosure,' *Psychoanalytic Quarterly* 66: 450–469.

Rendely, J. (1999) 'The Death of an Analyst: The Loss of a Real Relationship,' *Contemporary Psychoanalysis* 35(1): 131–152.

Schwaber, E.A. (1998) 'Traveling Affectively Alone: A Personal Derailment in Analytic Listening,' *Journal of the American Psychoanalytic Association* 46(4): 1045–1065.

Traesdal, T. (2005) 'When the Analyst Dies: Dealing with the Aftermath,' *Journal of the American Psychoanalytic Association* 53(4): 1235–1255.

Epilogue

Claudia Heilbrunn

As the chapters in this volume amply demonstrate, the ways in which patients may feel and react when an analyst dies are as varied as are the patients themselves. Having lost three analysts, I can say with conviction that how an analyst broaches his or her illness and death within the analytic treatment itself greatly impacts a patient's ability to cope with his or her loss: it can mean the difference between a sense of utter desolation and desperation on the one hand, and, on the other, a condition of intensely painful yet ultimately manageable grief and mourning.

Yet while an analyst's ability to deal with his or her own death is inseparable from, and even crucial to, the patient's ability to handle it, I cannot stress enough just how greatly the psychic state of patients also impacts their ability to cope with the loss of an analyst. This seems an obvious point, but I think that it bears repeating because so many of our patients are acutely vulnerable at this most sensitive transition point in their treatment. Our deaths can be catastrophic for them. And they are the people for whom we are responsible. We actively take them on, committing ourselves to helping them to overcome whatever ails them psychically. Part of our commitment must surely extend to our fully recognizing and comprehending how important we become to our patients. I think about the shock I felt as a brand new analyst in training when I treated my first clinic patient, a "recovered" heroin addict who hadn't used the drug in two years. I went away for a week during the Christmas/ New Year holiday, and she relapsed. I had no idea that such a relapse could happen as a result of my week-long break. It never dawned on me (nor, I guess, on my supervisor); but now I know differently.

This book is my attempt to awaken the analytic community to a need that has gone unheeded for too long. I hope that, equipped with the concrete knowledge of what patients experience after their analysts die, and with the awareness of just how excruciating that experience can be, analysts will recognize the seriousness of the issue and take action. Just as I could never again be ignorant of what my week-long break could do to a patient, and never again fail to take measures to ensure to the best of my ability that a fragile patient will feel held during any break I take, so I want as many analysts as possible to acknowledge just how large they loom in the lives of their patients. They can then proceed, I hope, with their eyes open, choosing ahead of time how they will deal with their terminal illnesses and deaths. I hope that analysts will recognize that there is a large chance that they will fall prey to their own denial, a condition that is admittedly sometimes appropriate and even necessary. But I hope that with recognition comes action: a plan that is put into place ahead of time, whether for the ill analyst to seek consultation with another analyst, who will keep an eye on how the dyad is faring, seeing what the ill analyst cannot see for him or herself; or for the analyst to seek support from an institute's Psychoanalyst Assistance Committee, which could help the ailing practitioner navigate both the logistics and the psychic realities of the analyst–patient relationship. Creating an analytic will is, of course, essential, but it is only a beginning.

Junkers (2013b) has already set forth in the "Epilogue" to *The Empty Couch: The Taboo of Ageing and Retirement in Psychoanalysis* a thorough list of recommendations that are aimed at protecting patients, candidates, ageing analysts, and psychoanalysis as a whole; for convenience, I offer below a prescriptive list that details the steps our communities and their members could take or, at least, should consider taking in order to protect both their patients and themselves. Many of the points listed below have already been registered by Junkers, and the following compilation has no pretension to being an original contribution; it simply offers a sequence of recommendations that might fittingly follow on from the experiences, yearnings, and affects of the chapters assembled in this volume.

- All practitioners who treat patients should have a "professional will" (O'Neil, 2013; Chapter 3 in this volume), which is updated whenever new patients are taken on. The will might specify (1) who should call patients when the analyst can no longer work or has died; (2) referrals for patients in need of immediate support and/or ongoing treatment; (3) how to handle confidential patient records (those that exist on paper, in personal computers, and on the web); and (4) wishes pertaining to patients' attendance at memorial/funeral services. Professional wills should become required for all members of institutes, for candidates working in clinics, and for clinicians in all types of therapeutic practices (e.g., psychiatry, social work, art and dance therapy).
- Analysts who face terminal illness or who are in physical difficulty should be able to access help within their institute, through a "Psychoanalyst Assistance Committee" or an equivalent committee that goes by a different name (see Chapter 14). Analysts could seek assistance with decisions about particular patients, reducing institutional responsibilities, closing down their practice if required, etc.
- Ill analysts might enter into supervision with a trusted colleague so that someone other than the analyst can ascertain any dynamics and enactments that the ill analyst might not see because of his or her own denial or hampered state. A colleague who is so entrusted could help an ill analyst with clinical matters, including whether or how to broach his or her own illness with particular patients, given that patient's particular transference issues, vulnerabilities, history of trauma, etc.
- A course focusing on the issues pertaining to analysts' ageing, illness, and death should be added to curriculums, as should course work relating to the issues that arise when working with patients who have lost their analysts prematurely to death (see Rosenblatt's "five methods of engagement" in Chapter 11; see also Chapters 10 and 11). The patient typologies in this volume's accounts of losing an analyst (Chapters 1–8) at times correspond in significant ways: (1) many patients felt as if they were "invisible mourners," who lacked mourning rituals and were set apart from those who knew the deceased; hence their grief was unshared and lonely; (2) some mourned the loss of a relationship that had no witness, and they

struggled to hold on to aspects of themselves of which only their now-dead analyst knew; (3) some struggled in their second ana-lyses, desiring their new analyst to be a replica of the deceased; (4) some patients felt toxic and guilty after their analyst died, as if the extremity of their need and "negative" feelings overwhelmed their analyst and killed him or her; and (5) many patients were aware of their analyst's illness and desired to take care of them des-pite, and in an effort to maintain and protect, their analyst's own denial.

• Active discussion and debates in conferences and workshops are to be pursued. Topics of discussion might include but are not limited to (1) decisions about transparency within the treatment session when an analyst falls ill or faces terminal illness (see Chapter 11); (2) analysts' denial of mortality and their patients' belief in their analysts' ever-lasting presence and support (Junkers, 2013b; Denis, 2013; see also Chapter 8 in this volume); (3) different ways to sup-port bereaved patients, both those who are and those who are not in the field; and (4) further research into the impact of an analyst's death on his or her patient.

References

Denis, P. (2013) 'Psychoanalyst: A Profession for an Immortal?' in Junkers, G. (ed.), *The Empty Couch: The Taboo of Ageing and Retiring in Psychoanalysis.* New York: Routledge, pp. 32–45.

Junkers, G. (2013a) 'The Ageing Psychoanalyst: Thoughts on Preparing for a Life Without the Couch,' in Junkers, G. (ed.), *The Empty Couch: The Taboo of Ageing and Retiring in Psychoanalysis.* New York: Routledge, pp. 3–6.

Junkers, G. (2013b) 'Epilogue,' in *The Empty Couch: The Taboo of Ageing and Retiring in Psychoanalysis.* New York: Routledge, pp. 176–179.

O'Neil, M.K. (2013) 'Now Is the Time for Action: The Professional Will: An Ethical Responsibility of the Analyst and the Profession,' in Junkers, G. (ed.), *The Empty Couch: The Taboo of Ageing and Retiring in Psychoanaly-sis.* New York: Routledge, pp. 150–160.

Index

acknowledgement of grieving patients 150–51; *see also* grief/grieving

adjustment to new analyst/therapist 38–40, 55, 67–69, 73–74, 86–88, 90–98, 94; Chapter 6 *passim* 148, 165–66, 167–74, 182–83, 185–90; Chapter 12 *passim* ; *see also* "bridge" analysis/ interim analyst

aggression 40, 44, 174, 176, 178, 183, 200, 201–02, 203, 208, 268

"aggressive breakdown products" 164

AIDS 14, 20, 111, 115, 235, 243, 244–45, 246, 254

"anaclitic depression" 162

analyst cancelling sessions due to illness 29, 65, 68, 127, 130, 246, 249, 250

"analyst-death scenario" 279

analyst dying repeatedly 115

analyst as "episodically attuned" 103

analyst as god-like 13, 15, 17

analyst keeping promises 15, 17, 21

analyst mandatory retirement age 284

analyst murdered 266–68, 270

analyst as proxy for another analyst 189–90

analyst saying goodbye to patient 27, 30, 35–36, 42, 133, 141–44, 274

analyst as second-choice therapist 87–88, 102, 105–06, 109–10; *see also* adjustment to new analyst/therapist

analyst stalked by patient 264

analyst telling "falsehoods" 20

analyst as useable object 183

analyst using work as diversion from illness 23, 139

analyst's anger *see* anger

analyst's appearance-change in illness 16, 25, 34, 64, 140, 219, 223

analyst's availability 152, 188, 197

analyst's counterdependency on patient 187

analyst's death *see* death

analyst's disclosure to patients about illness *see* analyst's illness

analyst's fear of patient 270

analyst's fear of patient's suicide 189

analyst's frankness in speaking of impending death 137–41, 231; limits to 222–23

analyst's illness: as beneficial for patient 230–31; denial of 4, 25, 34, 40–43, 85, 91, 100, 103, 228, 245, 275, 276, 287, 288, 289; diagnosis of 213, 217; disclosure of 220–23, 225–27, 232; failure to discuss 35; fear of 216–17; feelings about 215; growth from 228–31; as "hidden" 272; patient's reactions to 218–20, 224–25, 226–27; recovery from 214–15; reflections about 220–25; in sessions with patients 83–85, 127–30, 137–41, 225–29, 232, 246–52; telling patients about 216

analyst's loss of fear 230

analyst's memorial service *see* funeral/ memorial service

analyst's rivalry with another analyst 165–66, 175

analytic alliance 76, 162–63, 227

"analytic consultant" 276; *see also* supervision

"analytic toilet" 162

"analytic transparency" 252

anger 14, 15, 230, 239, 265; at analyst 28, 32, 38, 41–42, 43, 45, 85, 97, 131, 148, 172, 184, 189, 195–96, 200, 201, 205, 227, 228, 251, 263, 264, 269, 270, 274;

analyst's 199; as destructive force 44,
   225; disowning anger 201; in dream
   111; at father 170, 173, 175, 240; fear
   of 239; hampering ability to grieve
   274; at husband 169, 176; at illness
   139; lack of 24, 128; at mother 172,
   173; projected 203; in response to loss
   164; in schizoid personalities 239–40
anorexia/bulimia 13, 17, 19, 20, 27,
   64, 243
anti-depressants 19
anxiety due to lack of information 137
art, seeking comfort through 56–59, 65,
   126–27, 129

Beers, Clifford 250
bereavement *see* mourning
Boisen, Anton 250
borderline personality disorder 251, 263
"bridge" analysis/interim analyst 94–98,
   243–46, 254, 281
Bundza, Kenneth 251

cancer 1, 22, 23, 24, 25, 27, 28, 29, 30,
   32, 34, 43, 44, 68, 69, 81, 83, 86,
   88–89, 107, 111, 120, 125, 128, 136,
   137, 138–40, 141, 213–15, 216, 217–18,
   219, 220, 225–26, 276, 278
capacity for concern 193
caretaker: child as 22; patient as xviii,
   22, 23, 27, 28, 148, 219, 289; *see also*
   hysterical technique
Cashdan, Sheldon 252
chemotherapy 25, 34, 68, 88, 136, 138,
   140, 214, 225
community responsibility 55–56; *see also*
   institutional responsibility when
   analyst dies
compromise formation 170, 171, 175,
   179, 192–93, 207
concrete remembrances 153; lack of 145
corrective emotional experience 188
couch: use of 24, 38, 93, 106, 140, 168,
   173, 176, 178–79, 191; as form of
   comfort 104, 105; in patient's
   dream 44
countertransference 6, 40, 73, 162, 166,
   174, 177, 217, 225, 229, 262, 276

de Becker, Gavin 267
death: as abandonment 162; as catalyst
   to become a psychoanalyst 31, 66,

71–72; of father 125, 126, 129, 131,
   134, 161, 162, 167, 168, 169, 171–72,
   178, 179; therapist's handling of
   25–27, 29, 34–35, 65, 68, 85, 130–32,
   141–44, 172, 243–44, 286–87; *see also*
   patient's fear of analyst dying
developmental arrest approach 186, 187,
   188, 199
Disabled Analyst Committee 272, 273,
   275, 277, 279, 280; *see also*
   Psychoanalyst Assistance Committee
dissociative identity disorder 263
dreams 44, 70, 99, 103, 107–08, 110–11,
   112, 115, 117–18, 119–20, 127, 130,
   133, 134, 161, 168, 173, 174, 176,
   178–79, 247, 248, 278–79

Ego State Therapy 261–63, 264, 267, 271
"encapsulated memories" 248
ethics of working while facing life-
   threatening illness 279
expanding knowledge base about the
   death of an analyst 153–54, 232

Faimberg, Haydee 224
father 16, 22, 70, 125, 130, 132; absent
   182; in dream 278; mentor as 268;
   patient's aggression towards 170, 173,
   174, 175, 178; patient's relationship to
   125, 168, 170–72, 173, 240, 241;
   "primal" 190; as related to analyst's
   countertransference 175; in the
   transference 172, 175, 176; *see also*
   death
"fetal self" 103
frequency of sessions 17, 39, 63, 64, 81,
   126, 133, 136, 168, 232
funeral/memorial service: attending
   analyst's 2, 36–37, 54, 93, 133, 142–43,
   144–45, 151, 240, 288; decisions about
   151–52

grief/grieving 53–54, 66, 69, 73, 75, 83,
   108, 126, 130, 162, 246; aloneness in 1,
   2, 27, 32, 35, 36–37, 42, 54, 132, 133,
   275, 288; dead therapist 5, 7, 19,
   35–37, 42, 69, 94, 96, 133–34, 137,
   143, 144, 147, 148, 152, 237, 238, 274,
   281, 284, 286; defense against 162;
   dissipating 114, 120, 134, 148; impact
   on analyst's work 146; invisible 145,
   245, 288; as living presence 42;

masking 42; as natural 147; patient
and analyst's shared grief 75; in
"second" analyses 38, 55, 68, 70, 71,
74, 90–91, 94–96, 98, 99, 100–02, 104,
105, 114, 116, 117–18, 168; of
"second" analyst 74, 75–76, 88, 237;
support for in supervision 37, 145–46;
unspoken 129; use of art to heal
56–59; *see also* mourning: feeling
invisible while; mourning rituals;
supporting bereaved patients
grief rituals *see* mourning rituals
grieving as communal experience 144,
237
guilt 45, 77, 82, 91, 99, 100, 112, 131,
162, 163, 169–70, 171, 173–78, 194,
239, 242, 245, 268, 275, 278; in the
countertransference 166; about feeling
anger at dead analyst 97, 172; about
leaving analyst 176; about needing ill
analyst 65, 85; oedipal 172; of second
analyst 166; survivor 215; triggered by
moving forward after analyst's death
38, 42, 45, 117; *see also* patient as
toxic to analyst

"hierarchy of needs" 229
hysterical technique 202–03

illness as metaphor 217–18
immortality: analyst's 36; desire for 217,
218; fostering of 152
Institute for Expressive Analysis 72
institutional responsibility when analyst
dies Chapter 3 *passim* 54–55, 272–77,
279–84, 288–89
"intimidation into silence" 219
IPTAR (Institute for Psychoanalytic
Training and Research) 1, 7, 31,
Chapter 14 *passim*

Lacan, Jacques 195, 200
last session with analyst 17, 25–26, 132,
142–44
leukemia 75, 246
loneliness in reaction to therapist's death
see grief/grieving, aloneness in
loss, multiple meanings 164

magical reparation 193–95
mandala 57–58

medication 19, 199–200, 249, 254, 269,
280
Mellaril 249; *see also* medication
misinformation about analyst *see* patient
misled about analyst's illness
mortality: awareness of 56, 58, 129,
138–41, 152, 217, 219, 230; denial of
43, 289; of mother 216, transcending
36; *see also* immortality
mother 13, 15, 17, 27, 52–53, 61, 143,
262, 266; in analytic sessions 108, 109,
114, 164, 241; patient's relationship to
22, 39, 40, 41, 43, 45, 63, 70, 85, 113,
169–70, 171, 172–73, 178, 182, 184,
194, 203; in dreams 107–08, 112, 278;
therapist as 36, 61, 69, 87, 95, 117,
175–76, 178, 188, 189–90, 199, 200,
201, 225
Mount St. Helens 19, 107
mourning 6, 7, 20, 53, 56–59, 73–74, 75,
98, 118, 133, 134, 137, 148, 200, 203,
286; during the AIDS epidemic
244–46; feeling invisible while 2, 54,
145, 151, 152, 288; patient's challenges
with 147, 182, 190; supervisor 165;
see also funeral/memorial service;
mourning rituals
mourning rituals 19, 53–54, 57, 143, 144,
153; lack of 27, 55, 145, 284, 288;
see also grief rituals

Nachträglichkeit 224
Nardil 249; *see also* medication
notifying patients of therapist's death 52,
54–55, 238, 279–80, 281, 288; *see also*
patient: hearing news of analyst's
death

patient as analyst's supervisor 183
patient as caregiver to therapist *see*
caretaker
patient hearing news of analyst's death
18, 35, 50–51, 66, 81, 133, 144, 238,
244
patient misled about analyst's illness 89,
96–97, 109
patient as Pygmalion figure for analyst
20
patient as toxic to analyst 23, 31, 39–40,
64, 82, 84, 96, 109, 112, 113, 115, 162,
225, 219, 289

patient reactions to analyst's death 1–3,
18–21, 27–28, 30–31, 32, 33, 35–36,
42–43, 50–53, 61, 66–67, 93–96, 99,
133–35, 144–48, 162–64, 167–68,
182–83, 238–39, 240–41, 244–45,
288–89; *see also* art, seeking comfort
through; mourning rituals
patient taking care of analyst *see*
caretaker
patient visiting dead analyst's office
93–94
patient as werewolf 106
patient's adjustment to new analyst
37–40, 55, 67–72, 73–78, 86–96;
Chapter 6 *passim* 148–50, 162, 165–68,
182–83, 185–89, 238–42
patient's dependency on analyst 14, 30,
31, 61, 63, 96, 100, 162, 175, 186, 201,
206, 230; fear of 110, 130; as harmful
to analyst 77; *see also* patient as toxic
to analyst
patient's devotion to analyst 14–15,
21, 31
patient's fear 36, 39–41, 62, 64, 71,
76, 77, 82, 87, 90–91, 95, 99,
100–02, 105, 116, 127, 131, 133,
177, 270; of abandonment 194; of
airplanes 166, 169, 171; of analyst
dying 23, 30, 40–41, 66, 88, 129,
139, 140, 148, 163; of analyst's
illness 65, 83; of competition 207;
denial of 85; of dependency 110; of
father's death 131; of feelings 239,
240; of filling analyst's shoes 72; of
horses 166; of increased sessions 39;
of letting go 189; of loss 41, 45,
129, 171; others' denial of 85; of
powerlessness 45; of rupture 43; in
schizoid personality 239–40; *see also*
hysterical technique; patient as toxic
to analyst
patient's idealization of analyst 7, 40–42,
63, 104, 166, 267, 268–69; *see also*
analyst as god-like
patient's interest in analyst's life 51–52
patient's longing for analyst after death
38
patient's sense of betrayal by analyst 36,
38, 97, 111, 112, 274
phone sessions 22, 63, 65, 68, 126, 130,
134, 187
photography 58

planning for arrangements after the
analyst's death 142–43, 282; *see also*
funeral/memorial service
play therapy 187
post-analyst-death treatments *see*
patient's adjustment to new analyst
Pound, Ezra 19
primary maternal preoccupation 188
professional/analytic will 52, 55–56, 151,
279–80, 282–83, 287, 288
Psychoanalyst Assistance Committee
272, 287, 288; *see also* Disabled
Analyst Committee
psychoanalytic institute as "substitute"
family 275–76

Restoril 249; *see also* medication
"ribbon person" 101–02
role-reversal 217; *see also* caretaker:
child as; patient as

scale of loss when therapist dies 36;
see also patient reactions to analyst's
death
schizoid personality 239
"second" analyst as symbolic equivalent
to first 189–90; *see also* adjustment to
new analyst/therapist; analyst
as second-choice therapist
self-disclosure 6, 44, 216–17, 220, 222,
250, 251–54, 276; *see also* analyst's
illness: telling patients about
self-experience 183, 185, 186, 188, 195,
201, 203–05
Simonson, Norman 251
Sontag, Susan 213, 217–18
suicidal ideation 167, 187, 188–89,
199–200, 207
suicide/suicidal 164, 182, 185, 197, 202,
239, 242, 252–54, 267
suicide hotline 252
supervision 62, 184, 238, 273–75; at the
IPTAR Clinical Center 179; as
support for patient after analyst's
death 37, 145–56; as support for ill
analysts 288; *see also* grief/grieving:
support for in supervision
supporting bereaved patients 152,
288–89
supporting ill and dying analysts 151,
276, 288; *see also* Disabled Analyst
Committee

teenage therapy 13–14, 125
termination 13, 176, 178–79, 205, 243,
    245, 265; death as 3, 29, 30; in dream
    119; in face of terminal illness 132–33,
    141–44; failure to discuss 15, 16, 243;
    lack of 30, 33, 130–31, 235
therapeutic alliance *see* analytic alliance
transcranial magnetic stimulation 269
transference 28, 38, 40, 41, 63, 71, 73, 88,
    144, 153, 163, 169, 172, 187, 217, 220,
    221, 222–23, 227, 229, 231, 243,
    246–47, 263, 268, 276, 284, 288;
    analyst capacity to tolerate 220, 222;

dissolution of 250; "good patient" in
    4; to "second" analyst 109, 161, 163,
    175, 246; *see also* mother
Trilafon 249; *see also* medication
"trust fall" 39

Valium 167, 171, 173; *see also*
    medication

Whipple procedure 214
"wild analysis" 183, 199
Winnicott, D.W. 187, 193, 195, 198, 199
working alliance *see* analytic alliance